Knowing Language

Robin Scarcella

Director - Program in Academic English

University of California Irvine

UCI Program in Academic English

FOUNTAINHEAD
PRESS

Our green initiatives include:

Electronic Products

We deliver products in non-paper form whenever possible. This includes pdf downloadables, flash drives, and CDs.

Electronic Samples

We use Xample, a new electronic sampling system. Instructor samples are sent via a personalized web page that links to pdf downloads.

FSC Certified Printers

All of our printers are certified by the Forest Service Council, which promotes environmentally and so-cially responsible management of the world's forests. This program allows consumer groups, individual consumers, and businesses to work together hand-in-hand to promote responsible use of the world's forests as a renewable and sustainable resource.

Recycled Paper

Most of our products are printed on a minimum of 30% post-consumer waste recycled paper.

Support of Green Causes

When we do print, we donate a portion of our revenue to green causes. Listed below are a few of the organizations that have received donations from Fountainhead Press. We welcome your feedback and suggestions for contributions, as we are always searching for worthy initiatives.

Rainforest 2 Reef

Environmental Working Group

Some photos/images by Regents of the University of California

Cover and text design by Carol Hill

Books may be purchased for educational purposes. For information, please call or write:
1-800-586-0330
Fountainhead Press
Southlake, TX 76092
Web site: www.fountainheadpress.com
E-mail: customerservice@fountainheadpress.com

ISBN: 978-1-68036-365-4

Printed in the United States of America

Table of Contents

Acknowledgments iv

INTRODUCTION

1 Knowing Language: Writing in Diverse Academic Contexts. 1

SECTION I: Types of University Writing

2 Informational Writing: Definitions, Extended Definitions, and Summary Writing . 17
3 Argumentive Writing: The Writing Process and Finding Your Way 31
4 Being Aware of Your Readers and Considering Stance 55
5 Reflective Writing. 63
6 Business Letters, Cover Letters, and Resumes 83
7 Communicating with Email Messages. 93
8 Narratives 101
9 Rhetorical Analyses 115
10 Writing in the Sciences: Data Commentary and Reports 127

SECTION II: Using Sources

11 Using Sources in Academic Writing:. 139

SECTION III: Cohesion

12 Writing Cohesively 165

SECTION IV: Revision and Editing

13 Revising, Editing, and Polishing Your Writing 187

SECTION V: Language Concerns

14 Using Grammar Effectively. 203
15 Punctuation, Capitalization, and Spelling. 235
16 Different Kinds of English: British and US-American English 245

SECTION VI: Reading

17 Reading in University Contexts 251

SECTION VII: Oral Language

18 Oral Interaction and Presentations 271

Index. 289

Acknowledgments

Knowing Language is the product of the hard work of administrators, faculty, and staff in the Program of Academic English of the School of Humanities, University of California at Irvine. In addition to authoring this book, various individuals gathered information, revised and edited it, and organized submissions. The feedback from instructors and students and student contributions were instrumental in creating this edition of *Knowing Language*.

Editors

General Editors
Rose Jones
Robin Scarcella
Anna Striedter

Managing and Contributing Previous Editors
Rebecca Beck
Joyce Cain
Susan Earle-Carlin
Kathie Levin
Robin Scarcella
Anna Striedter

Editorial Board
Cassandra Cruz
Benjamin Duncan
Percival Guevarra
Rose Jones
Rica Kaufel
Larisa Karkafi
Sei Lee
Sunny Lee
Karen Lenz
Tina Matuchniak
Kerri McCanna
Carey Minnis
Victorya Nam

Aziz Qureshi
Gina Ruggiero
Christie Sosa
Heather Stern
Robin Stewart
Anna Striedter
Debra Thiercof

Major Contributors
Catherine Colman
Benjamin Duncan
Anita Fischer
Percival Guevarra
Rose Jones
Hansol Lee
Jerry Lee
Sei Lee
Karen Lenz
Kathie Levin
Jacob Ludwig
Gina Ruggiero
Arnie Seong
Christie Sosa
Brenna Shepherd
Paul Spencer
Heather Stern
Robin Stewart
Anna Striedter

Debra Thiercof
Cindy Ting Lin
Cathy Vimuttinan
Mary Ellen Wynn
Omaima Zayed

Art Contributor, Cover Design
Eunice Choi (front cover, Academic English flowchart)

Special Thanks
In addition to the individuals listed, special thanks are due to
Kimberly Ayala
Eunice Choi
Erica Green
Daniel Gross
Holly Hare
Michelle Hu
Jerry Lee
Tina Matuchniak
Carol B. Olson
Bradley Queen
Anna Wimberly

And all the instructors and students whose assistance and insights over the years have contributed so much to this book, enlivening the process of writing it and leading to the completion of this edition.

Knowing Language:
Writing in Diverse Academic Contexts

As the cover of the book suggests, knowing language can be compared to tide pools. If you haven't seen them, you'll find them in nearby Corona del Mar. They consist of rocky pools on the ocean shore. They're often filled with seawater and many are only found at low tide. Adaptable species of animals and plants, like shell lichens, barnacles and seaweed, live in tide pools. Like the water connects them, language connects human beings.

John Steinbeck wrote in *The Log from the Sea of Cortez*, "It is advisable to look from the tide pool to the stars and then back to the tide pool again." Similarly, in language learning, it is best to look towards the stars, but at the same time, to be aware of the broader context of what you are using language for, what your intentions and goals are, what you are trying to communicate, and how you are being perceived. You'll also look back at the tide pool you stand in, the narrower context of time and place in which you are communicating.

When you walk into a tide pool and don't understand what is going on, for example, whether the tides are high or low, you take into account the changing dynamics of the ocean and your surroundings. You want to know what to look for in the tide pool. You don't usually just jump into it, though that is one possible strategy. Keeping in mind the stars and the tide pool, communicating well involves being aware of the *context* in which you are communicating and understanding that all contexts change. Consider the tide pool. One moment the rocks are seen, and the next moment they are completely covered by water.

The Rhetorical Situation

If you want to communicate well, you want to have a deep awareness of how context changes. The terms *rhetoric* and *rhetorical situation* provide fundamental insight. The word *rhetoric* comes from ancient Greek, referring to formal public speaking, in other words, oration. Nowadays it is often used to mean a set of strategies, techniques, or methods used to communicate effectively in both speech and writing.

Rhetorical situation refers to a specific way of looking at communication by breaking it up into parts or components. Among the most commonly discussed components in a rhetorical situation are text, rhetor (speaker/writer), and audience (reader/listener). These three components can be illustrated in the shape of a triangle, as shown in the left-hand margin. The components are situated in a context.

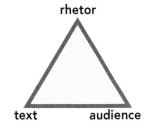

The **rhetor** is the technical word for a communicator, a speaker or a writer. Writing specialists use this term. But this specialized term does not simply refer to a person who communicates. The term has additional meanings. A rhetor is often considered a person who is good at the art of rhetoric. Think of a historical person like Abraham Lincoln. That person can be considered a rhetor and very skilled in rhetoric. Whether consciously or sub-consciously, your audience often wants to know what your motives are for your communication. Has anyone ever talked to you, and you have asked yourself: What exactly is it that this person wants from me? Are they providing information? Are they trying to persuade me or change my beliefs? Is this person asking me to do something or behave in a particular way? Your readers may ask themselves similar questions. Your readers may ask themselves: *Are you providing information? Are you asking me to do something or think something? Are you attempting to persuade me to change a perspective or firmly held belief? Are you presenting ideas for problem solving or analysis?* The way in which the identity of the writer (or speaker) affects the argument is known as *ethos—your character and persona.* Ethos is the way you establish who you are in your communication. You let the audience know who it is dealing with. You might want to show that you are competent to discuss a particular issue or are even an authority on that topic. You might want to reveal what your motives are, what your attitude is, or what you believe, value, and assume. You might want to establish credibility, the quality of being trusted. You might want to show your sincerity, or friendliness. On the other hand, perhaps you want to portray* yourself as an intellectual. Effective writers modify the way they depict themselves in their writing. Rather than portraying themselves in a single way, they vary their persona* to fit each situation depending on the purpose of their text, their audience, and the situation in which they are communicating.

*****portray**

(verb): to describe or show yourself (or someone) in a particular way; to depict

*****persona**

(noun): the way writers are in a particular situation, which gives people a particular idea about their character

The **audience** refers to your readers, listeners, or viewers. Whenever you communicate, you must consider them carefully. Imagine describing your hometown to someone from the same country and someone who has never even visited your home country. Surely your descriptions would be very different. When you communicate, in writing or in speech, you need to understand your audience. Knowing who you're addressing helps you avoid using technical terms when speaking to lay people or "dumbing down" the content if your message is intended for professionals. Questions you might consider include: *What are the audience's expectations? How will they use the information? What is the audience hoping to take away after reading/ listening and what would you like them to take away from it? What do you need to do to make them receptive to understanding your points and views? What is your purpose? Why are you communicating with this audience in the first place?*

You might want to appeal to the emotions of the audience, which is known as **pathos**. The audience needs to be engaged by what you are saying. Are you trying to evoke a feeling of fear, trust, or loyalty? Do you want to refer to shared values you want to draw on? How do your audience's beliefs fit with your message? Connecting with your audience through pathos can be a strong means of gaining their support. Knowing who your audience is can help you do this more effectively.

Text refers to any piece of communication, written, spoken or viewed. Texts can be divided into two broad categories, nonfiction and fiction. Examples of nonfiction texts are articles, science textbooks, and essays. Examples of fiction texts are novels, short stories, and plays. Texts can also be divided by text type or *genre*, which have distinct language and rhetorical characteristics and conventions. Examples include *informational texts* that inform—like summaries, definitions, technical books about history and economics, and biographies; *argumentative texts* that present an argument, for instance, stating a point or claim—like newspaper opinion pieces, literary analyses, and persuasive essays; and *narrative writing* that tells a story.

Context refers to the surrounding political, historical/cultural and social context, the time and place of the communicative act. All communication takes place in a context, although communicators are rarely aware fully of all the contextual features. Effective communicators take into account the key features that affect what they are communicating and the way their communication is perceived. Time and place are important. If you do not take into account the time and the place of the tide pools you want to investigate, you might end up miserable and perhaps drown. On the other hand, you might end up lucky and end up having a wonderful experience exploring nature – finding just the right tide pools at the right time of day.

When you are in the process of language development (and everyone is), you don't want to leave many types of communication up to luck. This is especially the case at the university, where you are often evaluated on the basis of the language you use. Some types of communicative acts are so important that you will want to be aware of the context and all the variables that affect your communication and gain power over them. How you do this is by gaining rhetorical know-how, increasing your knowledge of language to use that rhetorical know-how effectively. Language use and language development occur in context. At the university, you'll mostly be writing academic kinds of writing.

In your university life, you will experience new contexts that require different types of insights for language learning. First, you are the rhetor, a college student, who is expected to be knowledgeable, to handle university assignments and to participate in and benefit from a premier university education. How you communicate and convey your needs, wishes, goals, viewpoints, attitude, values, and identity can fundamentally affect your later success. You will find that you do not have one single "identity."* Your "identity" will vary depending on your audience, text and purpose One moment you may be using writing to learn informally and the next moment, you may be using writing to formally communicate your view to others. Second, audiences are varied and not limited to your peers. Your professors, classmates, and other public audiences will read your writing pieces and evaluate your capability. Third, the texts you read and write will increase in number and in characteristics, and you will be called upon to compose diverse types of writing for diverse audiences and purposes.

identity

(noun): your identity is who you are

Language Considerations for Academic Writing

To communicate well, you'll need to develop the academic language that the situation requires. At the simplest level, you'll need to develop the body of knowledge, strategies, behaviors, skills, and resources necessary to accomplish specific communicative acts in particular contexts. The language you use is dynamic and must be considered anew each time you communicate.

Vocabulary is just one essential component of this knowledge. Every time you study a new topic in your classroom and need to use this word in your communication, you must learn the words associated with the topic and their associated grammatical features. Even though you may know the basic subject-verb agreement rules governing most commonly occurring English nouns, you will still have to learn new agreement rules when you encounter new noun forms. For instance, you must learn that that the plural of gene is genes but the plural of bacterium is bacteria if writing about genes and bacteria. Knowing a word is complex. To understand the term *stability* in an ecosystem, for example, you'll need to understand other important concepts like biodiversity, relative rates of birth, and decomposers. Some of the specific ways words are used in science are outlined in Table 1.1.

Table 1.1: Types of Words Used in Science Textbooks

Type of Words	Examples
1. Technical words pertaining to science	lithosphere, convection, seismic
2. Everyday vocabulary that has special meanings in science	fault, reflection, power, force, active, plate
3. Academic words that are used across discipline areas and are often used to define technical words in science	component, constitute, stimulate, generate
4. Synonyms	shows, represents, signifies
5. Homophones	break/brake, whole/hole
6. Words that are spelled similarly and are easily confused	affect/effect, breathe/breath
7. Difficult fixed and semi-fixed expressions (also called collocations)	If…then,…, If and only if…, and Given that…, the effects of + Noun, the speed of + Noun
8. Word families (also called word derivations)	volcano/volcanic, flexible/flexibility, collide/collision/colliding

Vocabulary in the university setting is more than just vocabulary, however; it also involves grammar and discourse. Grammar refers to the rules by which words change their forms and are combined into sentences to convey meaning and discourse refers to ways that language is used in speech and writing to communicate appropriately. To write well at the university you'll also need a disposition (a particular character that makes someone likely to behave or react in a specific way) that enables you to construct your own knowledge in a reflective way and to communicate effectively in academic situations in both speaking and writing. You'll need the inseparable skills of critical reading, writing, listening, and speaking as well as digital literacy. Digital literacy entails the ability to understand information and evaluate it in multiple formats from a wide array of sources that are obtained on the computer. Writing at the university also involves cognitive components, including higher-order thinking (critical literacy), cognitive strategies, and metalinguistic knowledge. At the university, you will use writing in a number of ways – to hypothesize, generalize, compare, contrast, explain, describe, define, justify, give examples, sequence, and evaluate.

Cognitive Constraints

*overloaded

(adjective): having too much work or information to pay attention, concentrate, or function appropriately

You may at times become cognitively overloaded*, especially when given challenging assignments. You face the dual challenge of learning how to write while at the same time you are still developing proficiency in the English language. In addition to that, you may have to bridge the gap from your home culture to American culture, keeping the differences in mind both when reading and when writing. These combined challenges exert considerable and sometimes competing demands on the cognitive system. In order to write effectively, you must not only have obtained much knowledge about what to write (appropriate content and prior knowledge), but also know ways to access and use this knowledge during the composing process. You should also have an awareness of why you are writing and for what audience (rhetorical knowledge). You furthermore must acquire a good deal of language-specific knowledge—knowledge that spans the breadth from selecting appropriate vocabulary (lexical knowledge) to putting words together into sentences (syntactic knowledge) in order to effectively convey meaning (semantic knowledge). Moreover, in order to engage in the knowledge changing processes of composing, you first must develop a complex mental representation of the writing assignment. In other words, you need to know what is being asked of you. Then you have to engage in problem analysis, that is, deciding what to say and how to say it, and finally plan how you will go about doing so.

*to juggle

(verb): to change things or arrange them in a way you want or in a way that makes it possible for you to do something

Each of these demands places a burden on your working memory system, sometimes resulting in your being "overloaded" as a result of having to juggle* these multiple processes.

*trade-off

(countable noun): a balance between two opposing things that you are willing to accept in order to achieve something

Working memory is thought to be a limited-capacity cognitive system wherein trade-offs* may occur between knowledge storage and knowledge-processing demands. As more resources are devoted to processing functions, fewer resources are available for storage of information. Furthermore, every increase in the cognitive load associated with one process results in a decrease in the remaining resources available for other processes. Therefore, due to the limited processing capacity of working memory, at any given time only a limited number of cognitive operations can be completed. The other operations must be performed automatically in order to lessen the amount of cognitive work that must be done. This idea of a limited-capacity, information-processing system is especially significant for students who have to simultaneously get used to dealing with many competing demands when writing.

You may experience increased demands on your working memory due to your developing language proficiency. As a result, you may resort* to a knowledge-telling approach to writing, wherein you simply retell what you know about a given topic instead of analyzing a topic. Knowledge telling usually requires simple retrieval* of information from long-term memory, unlike knowledge changing or transforming, which additionally engages planning and revising processes that require considerably more mental effort. You may also resort to using inappropriate formulaic writing or essay templates that you may have learned earlier to take SAT tests or other writing tests. When you produce formulaic writing, you use ideas, language, or even essay structures that have been used many times and are not very interesting. This type of writing is not acceptable. Since the working memory has a limited capacity, you may have to make decisions about which writing processes to prioritize when under pressure to produce text rapidly. Often, formulation (planning, writing down words) concerns take precedence,* as they are more critical and needing to be taken care of first, rather than execution (handwriting/typing) and monitoring (revising, editing) processes. You may find that writing down your words is problematic if you still have limited language resources and/or difficulty accessing these resources. Writing thus involves not only the language system but also the cognitive system for memory and thinking. In order to write effectively, you must not only have a good deal of knowledge about language and writing, but also be able to rapidly retrieve such information and actively maintain it in working memory. This is possible only when there is sufficient working memory capacity available to plan and write (in other words, to consider *What am I going to say next?*), while at the same time reviewing content and text that have already been generated (*How does this fit in with what I said before?*). Because working memory is limited in capacity, control depends on reducing the cognitive work of these acts of composing through making some writing processes automatic, done without thinking.

*to resort to

(verb): do something wrong because you can't think of another way to do it

*retrieval

(noun): the act of getting back something you have lost

*to take precedence

(verb phrase): to consider something more important than something else and therefore have to deal with it

Linguistic Constraints

Adding to cognitive constraints is the constraint of mastering the constellation of language knowledge necessary to successfully participate in school. When you write, you draw upon the sum of your language experiences. For instance, when you have to decide how to spell a word, where to place a period or an adjective, how to introduce a character, or how to organize supporting details, you utilize your linguistic resources as well as your metalinguistic awareness or conscious attention to the ways in which language is used and expresses meaning.

Your linguistic resources include your knowledge of:

- The sound system
- Vocabulary
- Morphology (the ways small parts of language make words)
- Syntactic rules for forming sentences
- s (the study of the meanings of words and phrases) of the English language
- Pragmatics, which determines when and why a specific language feature is used

Whereas some of you may have good oral language proficiency, many may lack the academic language proficiency necessary for success at college. Consider Van Nguyen who arrived in the United States at the age of 5 and never received English language development instruction in elementary school or secondary school. By the time she reached the University of California, Irvine, she was convinced she had acquired high proficiency in English. She had received high grades in her honors English and A.P. English courses and spoke English at home. When she was placed in a low-level ESL course at the University of California, Irvine, she wrote the following letter to her instructor:

Dear Mrs. Robbin,

I really not need humanity 20 writing class because since time I come to United State all my friend speak language. Until now everyone understand me and I dont' need study language. I don't know Vietnam language. I speak only English. I have no communication problem with my friend in dorm. My English teacher in high school key person to teach me.

My teacher explained to me that how important the book was for the student and persuaded me read many book. I get A in English throughout high school and I never take ESL. I agree that some student need class but you has not made a correct decision put me in English class. Please do not makes me lose the face. I have confident in English. (Scarcella, 2003, p. 161)

Van, like some international students, has acquired informal or social English and uses this English even in academic settings. When using this type of English in daily conversation, it is possible for Van to communicate her thoughts without using English in a grammatically correct way. Van could be understood well without using sophisticated vocabulary, articles, prepositions, or even adding -s endings to words. She had not learned academic language, the language of school and assessments as well as the language of power. Academic language is associated with academic contexts. It is precisely the type of specialized knowledge that many UCI writers are still developing. It encompasses many different types of academic writing, ranging from very formal to informal.

Scarcella, Robin (2003). Academic English: A conceptual framework (Tech Report No 2003-1). Irvine: University of California, Irvine. University of California Linguistic Minority Research Institute.

Sometimes, writing in an academic context while still struggling with the language can be frustrating. You know you have great ideas in your head, but once you put them into English and on the paper, they read like someone much younger wrote them. Your great ideas suddenly seem simplistic and far less great. Frustrating as this is, it is also a natural part of language learning. Keep at it, work on learning more complex sentence structures and widen your vocabulary, and soon you will be able to communicate your ideas in all their greatness.

We use the term *register* here to refer to specific features of language that vary according to the context, content, and purpose of communication. Many academic registers are characterized by precision and economy of expression, logical progression of ideas, controlled sentence structure, variety in sentence structure, support for claims, conceptual/abstract treatment of topics, and adherence to the expectations of specific types of writing such as arguments. These same features are often aligned with university and work expectations. They enable you to use language in increasingly sophisticated and accurate ways to accomplish a range of functions, for example, formulating claims and hypotheses, synthesizing information, and developing explanations.

Understanding academic registers, which can be difficult and confusing even for monolingual English-speaking students, can also be challenging for international students and others. You may receive wide exposure to everyday, informal registers of English outside of class but only restricted exposure to academic registers in class. However, research shows that control of academic language is one of the key determiners of success in developing academic writing proficiency.

Additionally, the acquisition of specific aspects of academic writing proficiency is constrained by factors affecting language development and the entire language acquisition process. For example, rate of language acquisition varies as a function of the degree to which you have been exposed to literacy and academic language; your access to continuous formal education, including writing instruction and feedback; and your ability to use your home language to read and write for academic purposes. Rate also is affected by the extent to which you pay attention to words and word parts, and your previous development of linguistic features.

Communicative Constraints

In addition to the constraints imposed by language and cognition, you are also affected by communicative constraints, or the constraints caused by the need to write for a specified audience. Just as when we talk to others in face-to-face situations and we adapt our language to their communicative needs, so, too, do good writers modify their language to meet the needs of different audiences. They think about why they are writing to specific readers and what goals they want to accomplish. Effective writers, then, are able to construct rich and detailed representations of the audience, which, in turn, informs their composing processes in equally rich and elaborate ways. As a language learner, you may have limited ability to "assume the point of view" of the reader. Your reader and you may not have a "shared language" and "shared experiences." Developing this language and experiences involves acquiring new language and having new experiences.

Some instructors have had students who have sent the following type of email messages to them:

> Subject: Plz Rite me ASAP!!!
> From: SKATA4LIFE@xxxx.com
> Date: Fri, January 27, 2012 4:26 pm
>
> To: xxxx@xxusd.edu
>
> Hey my teacher,
>
> It's me. Sorry I did not turn in my wting in class today. Bad luck 4 me. I forgot to bring my binder. I now that's not so gr8t, but everything was in the binder. I was busy this morning and yesterday study for chemisty test and ya know what? I went to bed at almost 3:00 in the morning. I waked up at 6:30 and tried to leave at 7:30. Although I know that I must be responsble for my class but student sometiems can make mistake right? So you take my essay now!!! I attach it!!! Ple::::z respond right away!!!!
>
> Thank you and have a nice day.

Most instructors don't like to receive such messages. They consider them poorly edited and question the competence of the writer.

Like your monolingual English-speaking peers, you are in the process of learning the linguistic features of a large number of registers, the varieties of language used for particular purposes and in specific social settings. Those who have learned only informal, everyday language may not know that they need to shift to a more formal variety of English when writing email messages to instructors. Those students who have arrived in the United States recently may not understand the communicative needs of diverse American audiences and may still be learning to vary their language appropriately to meet those needs.

Contextual Constraints

Contextual constraints involve the circumstances in which writing takes place. The context or situation in which you write, including the writing assignment, the topic, the intended audience, the writer's motivation, as well as any and all relevant information, can have a strong influence on your composing processes. For example, are you in a timed on-demand writing situation responding to an unfamiliar prompt with high-stakes consequences? Or are you writing on a topic of your choice in a succession of drafts that will evolve over time with supportive feedback from your instructor and peers? Is the instruction you are receiving instructor-centered or student-centered? Do you have opportunities to collaborate with one another or are you expected to work in isolation? Is your audience themselves, a peer, a trusted adult, the instructor, or unknown audiences? The particular context can influence how writers decide what information is relevant, how they construct meaning, and the voice or register they adopt. You'll need to understand the writing circumstances to produce high-quality, first-draft writing under timed conditions as well as the capacity to revise and improve multiple-draft writing over extended time frames.

Textual Constraints

When you are composing, you'll bring to the writing task knowledge of the content and the form of all prior texts you have previously written. Not only do expert writers have a great deal of such knowledge, but their knowledge is highly organized and conceptually integrated so that they are able to rapidly recognize familiar patterns of information. It is important for you to learn to write varied types of writing or texts. Writing in one genre (or type of writing) often calls on expertise from other types of writing. Writing a persuasive essay, for example, can involve providing a narrative example, drawing a comparison, or explaining a scientific concept in order to support a point.

Textual constraints can be challenging to learn, especially if the discourse features of a genre in English are different from those in the students' first language. To overcome these constraints and enhance your textual repertoire, it is important to read and write texts in a variety of text types (narrative, informative/explanatory, argument) and sub-genres (i.e., friendly letter, diary entry, recipe, newspaper article, controversial issue essay, and so forth).

Affective Constraints

Some constraints relate to moods, feelings and attitudes. To write well, you'll find you must gain both confidence and competence. You may disengage when you are not interested in your writing and this can negatively affect your writing development. If you feel uncomfortable in your classroom or feel you are not a valued member of the classroom community, you may come not to like writing and stop paying attention to your instructor. You will need both the "skill and the will" in order to succeed in writing.

You may need to juggle affective constraints, as they can contribute to cognitive overload. Your anxiety can cloud your thinking. Developing perseverance and a "can do" attitude can help you develop your confidence, motivation, and self-esteem.

Understand that your classroom is a safe space where it is okay to participate, even with less-than-perfect English and where your instructors will provide clear expectations and supportive feedback and instruction.

Cultural Concerns

Students bring rich and varied cultural knowledge to the task of writing. Your cultural background is an asset. Regardless of your culture, your instructors will be building on your background knowledge to the greatest extent possible. In some instances, you'll need more information about U.S./American culture in order to achieve success as writers. In your classes you're expected to already have learned a great deal of cultural information. Styles of narration and expository writing can vary across cultures. You'll sometimes use rhetorical features from your first languages to communicate in writing. For instance, students from some Asian first language backgrounds might transfer an indirect approach that they have learned in their home countries into their English compositions by writing around a topic instead of getting directly to the point. As a student, you'll want to adhere to the conventions expected at an American university. They might embrace an indirect style of writing in which thesis statements are avoided, implied, or stated indirectly. Because the use of evidence varies across cultures, you might not know what evidence to cite to support specific claims, where to put this evidence, or how to cite it. What you have learned about evidence in your home countries might affect your use of evidence in your English writing.

Juggling Constraints

Let us return to the tidepool and consider the constraints you must was juggle when you visit it. First and foremost, you must juggle constraints when wading in the ocean, looking at the tide and considering the time a day. Otherwise the beautiful tide pool may become washed away, and you may have to swim quickly away.

Just like tide pools, writing can present you with constraints. As a writer, you must juggle the contextual constraint of producing complex texts at the university under timed and untimed writing conditions. You'll face a textual constraint because you have had limited prior exposure to university writing and may be unfamiliar with the conventions of academic writing. You may also struggle with linguistic and communicative constraints because you are writing for instructors and even more public audiences who evaluate your writing and you do not have command of the register of academic English required for the essential "university-types" of writing that you may be asked to compose. Add to these three kinds of cognitive constraints others. You may have only developing knowledge of discipline specific and academic topics and strategies to take apart writing prompts and understand them, brainstorm ideas, plan compositions, revise under timed and untimed conditions, and edit your paper. Your limited knowledge can place a cognitive strain on your working memory. As a result, you may resort to a knowledge-telling approach to your writing, essentially summarizing what happened rather than adopting a knowledge-transforming stance. You may also resort to the practice of writing a formulaic essay using a template approach to writing. You may feel anxious and your anxiety may undermine your success.

"Constraints on Language Development" section adapted from: Olson, Carol Booth, Robin Scarcella, and Tina Matuchniak. *Helping English Learners to Write*. New York: Teachers College Press, 2015.1-21. With permission.

Knowing Language

Knowledge of tide pools can teach you how to behave around them. Once you obtain this knowledge, you can explore them easily and discover their beauty. Similarly, knowledge of language can help you greatly. This book lays a foundation for analyzing and responding to rhetorical situations and rhetoric in ways that help you develop academic language.

Your instructor will introduce you to a variety of reading, writing, and oral language activities designed to reach different audiences, accomplish different purposes, and, at times, use different media. You will analyze texts, reflect on them, and deepen your knowledge of them to credibly develop unique and complex thesis statements and support them with analysis (text). You will read, write, and converse about ideas, discover new ideas, and use linguistic resources to create, interpret, and evaluate a variety of types of writing. You will communicate to learn, develop, evaluate, and explore ideas, and convey your thoughts to readers. When you write, you will become aware of the importance of writing multiple drafts in many types of academic writing and of the development of flexible strategies for the completion of assignments. It is through your actions that much of your language development will occur. However, your instructors will provide you with explicit instruction of language, feedback, and opportunities to practice using English to help you gain control of specific language features required to communicate in different types of writing in different contexts.

Knowing Language provides you with an introduction to rhetoric, academic language, and language development. It will explain the rationale for the instructional approaches used. You'll discover that writing is both individual and social, and is best acquired through your active involvement in a range of activities, involving collaborative and social processes. You'll learn the value of turning to others for support but also the value of doing your own work and gaining self-reliance. You'll also learn the value of considering different audiences and adopting an appropriate level of formality. You'll discover that despite your best effort, it's not possible for you to master vocabulary or sentence structure or gain language features in an orderly fashion. Nonetheless, you can expect to improve your control over language features gradually over time, experiencing more than a few difficulties along the way and discovering practices and strategies that work for you and that help you to overcome the obstacles you encounter.

The first chapters (1 through 10) provide useful strategies for writing many different types of texts. The information in these chapters will prepare you for composition and other courses with heavy language demands. In Chapter 2, you'll learn useful tips for writing definitions and summaries as well as other types of informational texts. The next two chapters will help you write the different types of arguments your professors assign, including responses to questions that call for well-reasoned, evidence-based answers and formal, argumentative essays. Chapter 5: Reflective Writing will give you tips for ways to think deeply about your experiences and learn from them. The following two chapters (6 and 7) will help you to write professional, polished business letters, resume cover letters, resumes, and email messages.

The next chapters (8, 9, and 10) will teach you how to write narratives, rhetorical analyses, as well as science reports and data commentary. In Chapter 11, you'll study ways to cite information and paraphrase to avoid academic misconduct. The next chapters (12 through 16) are important ones, focusing on the development of revising

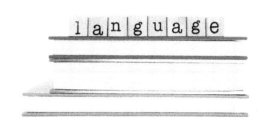

and editing skills as well as specific aspects of language—cohesive devices that provide connections between sentences, phrases, and words; grammar; and punctuation. The final chapters (Chapter 17 and 18) will help you develop your reading and oral language abilities.

Approach and Methodology

Underlying this book is a particular approach and methodology that are characterized by the following:

- Regular classroom instruction using a variety of modes for learning, including participating in class discussions, conducting Internet research, collaborating in small groups, and providing feedback to classmates during reviews of their writing

- Ample exposure to the types of reading that is required in order to build your language proficiency

- Multiple opportunities to attend to the language features of your reading

- Multiple opportunities to use language from your reading in your speech and writing in a variety of genres (types of text)

- Completion of various writing-related oral language assignments in a variety of genres

- Frequent periodic review of and commentary on successive drafts of writing assignments by your classmates and instructor

- Regular reflection on writing, reading, and language development

- Instruction shaped to meet the unique and specific needs and interests of students of diverse cultural and linguistic backgrounds

Regardless of your academic interests, needs, professional goals, or major, the ability to communicate, using language effectively to meet your own purposes, will be key to your success at college. We hope you enjoy your time as writers. *Knowing Language* is designed to make your experience in English language and writing classes a pleasurable one and serve a a valuable resource.

Tide pools at sunset, at Little Corona Beach, in Corona del Mar, California.

> 66 Communicating well involves being aware of the context in which you are communicating and understanding that all contexts change. Consider the tide pool. One moment the rocks are seen, and the next moment they are completely covered by water. 99

Informational Writing:
Definitions, Extended Definitions, and Summary Writing

nformational writing provides facts and information about a nonfiction topic. This type of writing does not express opinions about the topic. It tends to use impersonal, objective language. In informational writing, your goal is to explain complex ideas and information with clarity and accuracy. When you **compose** informational texts, you'll carefully select information that you discuss, organize it logically, and analyze it thoughtfully. Separate nouns with commas and change all nouns forms to noun plurals.

Examples include:

- Research reports

- Newspaper articles

- Summaries

- Definitions

- Brochures

- Pamphlets

Expository and informational writing are often linked because they share a common purpose—to share information or to inform others of an aspect of the social or natural world. Informational writing often requires you to combine information from multiple sources. These sources may provide conflicting information, so you will need to be a critical reader and analyze the sources carefully. Characteristic text structures of informational text include descriptions and sequencing.

In your college classes, you will write informational text that you'll incorporate into your argumentative writing. For instance, when you introduce new concepts in your argumentative writing, you'll initially explain these concepts, defining them and then further elaborating on them. Your factual explanation is a type of informational writing. When you incorporate explanations and definitions, you may need to use transition words like *for example, for instance, in fact, in other words*, and *hence*. You'll often use the timeless present tense

Key Point:

You'll need to come up with original definitions. Using a learner's dictionary like *Longman's Dictionary of Contemporary English* will help you, but you should not use dictionary definitions in your academic writing. Your instructors expect you to write your own original definitions.

Insider Tip

A primary reason to include definitions in your writing is to prevent your readers from misunderstanding you. You may use them to clarify the particular way you are using a word, examine differences of opinion regarding the use of a word, or explain a word that has many different interpretations. Definitions are often used in academic writing to ensure that your reader is thinking about the same concept that you are.

to convey general truths. The timeless present tense refers to using simple present when discussing general truths or facts. You'll use many academic words, like *concept*, which are used across subject areas, and use fewer everyday, commonly occurring words, like *idea*.

Short, Formal Definitions and Extended Definitions

In some of your assignments, you'll need to define key words. A *definition* explains a word and answers the question, "What does the word mean?" You'll write two kinds of original definitions in some of your writing assignments papers: short, formal definitions that state the meaning of a word in one or two sentences and *extended definitions*, long definitions that can add coherence to your papers and help you present your arguments.

The Importance of Definitions

Definitions are important because they create a shared understanding of technical terms or key concepts. They help you express yourself clearly.

Using and Writing Short, Formal Definitions

Short, formal definitions are often required in these circumstances:

- When the term is obscure or not likely to be known by the reader
- When a precise, shared understanding of the term is necessary
- When the term can have multiple meanings and you want to focus on one of them

Following are a sentence frame and two simple steps for writing a formal definition. These general steps are almost always used when writers develop formal definitions.

Sentence Frame: A [term] is a [classification] that [*distinguishing features].

Steps:

1. Put the word into the group of things to which it belongs (classification).

2. Identify the qualities that make the word different from other things of its class (distinguishing features) (See Table 2.1).

*distinguishing

(adjective): distinctive, different or unique

Table 2.1: Examples of Definitions

Term	Classification	Distinguishing Feature
a grasshopper	is an insect	that makes a loud chirping noise
misogyny	is a feeling of hatred	against women
a syllabus	is an outline of topics	that is covered in a course

Additional Tips for Writing Short, Formal Definitions

- Unless you have an excellent reason for doing so, avoid writing a short definition with the words "X is when" and "X is where."

- Define a noun with a noun and a verb with a verb, etc.

- Do not define a word by just restating the word.
  "To rhyme means to turn into a rhyme."
  Better: "To rhyme is to use an art form consisting of lines whose final words consistently contain identical, final stressed vowel sounds."

- Define a word with language that your readers can understand. Your readers should not have to look up the words in your definition.

Jia Wong, a writing student, argues:

*"Use short definitions to explain important terms and technical words that your readers may not know. Use extended definitions to explore abstract concepts like **'love'** that can mean different things to different people. When I first started college, I didn't always know what terms would be unfamiliar to my readers. Sometimes, I asked my instructor for advice. But when I didn't get a chance to do that, I just came up with my own definition. I deleted it later if my instructor told me the definition wasn't needed. That strategy seemed to work."*

Insider Tip

In writing an extended definition, you explain the concept—not just the word.

Using Extended Definitions

Sometimes it's necessary to go beyond a basic standard definition and write a paragraph or whole paper explaining a term. Discipline-specific terms often require extended definitions. When you write, you may discover that you need to explain certain basic terms before you can discuss the main topic. For example, if you were writing a paper about greed, you'd need a section defining greed. In a paper on the benefits of altruism, you'd need to write an **extended definition** of "altruism," giving examples of what it is and maybe even what it isn't.

When you write for your other courses, you'll need to come up with extended definitions as well. For example, if you need to write a paper showing how small businesses can weather economic recessions, you'll first need to define the term **economic recession**.

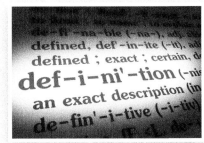

An extended definition can be a paragraph or two or an entire paper that explains a complex term. One of the first things to do when you write an extended definition is to compose the short, formal definition of the word you are defining. Place it toward the beginning of the extended definition. It'll establish the focus for the rest of your discussion of the word.

Most university professors will want you to come up with your own original definitions of words and not rely on dictionary definitions.

You can elaborate on your short, formal definition by various means. It's up to you to determine which ones you use, and in what order, taking into account what it is you are defining, what you think your readers know already, and whether you think they are unfamiliar with the concept, or have it confused with other, somewhat similar concepts. Some of the **primary methods** of writing an extended definition are listed below.

"In writing an extended definition, you explain the **concept**—*not just the* **word**.*"*

- **Description:** Giving details
- **Narration:** Telling stories
- **Illustration:** Giving examples
- **Comparisons and Contrasts:** Discussing the word's similarities to and differences from a different word
- **Causal Analysis:** Discussing the word's causes and/or effects
- **Process Analysis:** Explaining how the concepts to which the word refers works or functions

Other Methods You Might Use

- **Using Examples with Explanations.** Sometimes you'll need many examples, but often you can use just one or two well-chosen examples and accompany them with explanations. If you are defining *domestic cat*, for instance, you could show why a Maine Coon Cat is a *domestic cat*, while a Cerval Cat is not, though they are both small members of the *cat family*.

- **Using Tests.** You can use a test to figure out if something is what you are defining, discovering its operational definition. For instance, a pen can be considered a ballpoint pen if on a specific test, it performs in a particular way.

- **Describing Concepts in Terms of Other Concepts.** You could also describe the concept in relation to other concepts. Often cause-and-effect reasoning is useful here. Where does the domestic cat come from? Did the domestic cat become what it is because of the way people have treated cats over the centuries? How does your concept of domestic cat relate to the concept of pet? How is the concept of lying related to the concept of honesty—would you say people are honest only if they never, ever lie?

Key Point:

There is no one right way to write an extended definition. Usually using a combination of methods is best.

Insider Tips

Whenever you need to define a term with no agreed-upon meaning (for instance, abusive language), you might note some differing definitions or views of the term and then state your own definition or view. If the term has resulted from recent advances (such as social media apps), you might mention these advances.

A short extended definition of a colloquial or slang term can be an interesting way to start some kinds of introductions. Introductions can include a short definition. The definition helps to establish the focus of the paper and clarify the author's interpretation of an important concept. Writers can challenge existing definitions and write their own new ones.

Summary Writing

Another type of informational text is summary writing. This type of writing can have different goals. Summary writing can help writers remember key points of their reading, learn from their reading, and use important concepts and points from their reading in their writing. It can also give readers an *accurate, objective, complete, concise* view of a piece of writing that they may not have read. Students might write short, informal, and, often, impromptu summaries, mostly for their own benefit, to help them learn. For instance, they might write summaries of lecture notes and assigned readings that they use as study guides, summaries of information that they are trying to learn, or summaries of reports that they plan to refer to later in their own writing. Students might also write different kinds of more formal summaries of documents or research reports for their instructors. One common type of summary you'll encounter at the beginning of journal articles is the **abstract**, a short written statement containing the most important ideas in the article. In college, you'll write informative summaries of a specific nature in which you summarize, in your own words, the main ideas or argument of an author, using a detailed approach. Your instructor will assign summary writing as a means to help you obtain a good understanding of the assigned readings that will prepare you for a related writing task.

Summaries can help readers who are busy and do not have time to read entire texts, because they provide them with a general overview of the key information. They help students understand their reading materials. Instructors often use summaries to assess their students' understanding of the texts that they have read and writers use summaries to better understand their reading and help them remember their main points. Writers also turn to summaries to conveniently locate sources that support their claims.

Most summaries do not contain many quotations and, depending on the kind, they may not have any quotations. However, in some kinds of college assignments, they are required. Ask your instructor if they are needed. When you use quotations in your summaries, choose those that express one of the author's main points in interesting language. Otherwise, just summarize. Use quotations when necessary, so you avoid plagiarism. You don't want to present the writer's words as though they were your own.

Most summaries also contain paraphrases of an author's words. When you **paraphrase**, you express the author's words in your own.

Insider Tip

A deep understanding of the reading will enable you to critically engage with the course material in preparation for later speaking and writing assignments involving active thinking and analysis.

Chung Liu, a writing student, states:

"Pay attention to the visuals, titles, headings, and topic sentences of your readings. They'll help you identify the main ideas to discuss in your summary."

A WORD OF CAUTION

You will need to learn the rhetorical and linguistic features and conventions of the particular types of summaries that your instructors ask you to write. Remember that these features and conventions often vary across disciplines.

One Method for Writing Your Summary

When writing a summary, here is one possible method you might use. The following steps may be helpful to you.

Insider Tip

Knowing how to paraphrase and use quotations will help you complete your summary assignment.

1. Read the original text and make sure that you understand the main ideas. The author's thesis and the topic sentences will often give you clues. Do not be distracted by minor details. Most students find it helpful to read the text at least three times. It can be very helpful, when reading challenging text, to read the text through the first time to get the overall picture of what the writer is saying and then to break the reading passage into parts, underline key terms and ideas, and look up words that are central to understanding the text. At this point, you might even want to reread the passage and write one-sentence summaries of each main idea and/or each main part on a separate sheet of paper. When rereading the texts, many students like to highlight, underline, or copy quotations that they might use in their summaries.

2. Outline your text on a separate sheet of paper without looking back at the original text. Use key words and phrases. Some students like to use their one-sentence summaries to help them outline. Others find it helpful to list the key points that they want to include in their summaries instead of outlining the text.

3. Write a one-sentence summary of the main point of the entire passage. Many students like to choose the main idea from their outlines to be the topic of the first sentence of their summaries. The one-sentence summary should contain the central idea or thesis of the original text, the title and date of the text, and the author's full name. If the article appears in a magazine, newspaper, or book, include the name of the magazine, newspaper, or book.

4. Decide on the appropriate order for the rest of the information in your outline. You may wish to organize the information in a different order from the way it appears in the original text.

5. Without referring to the original text and referring only to your notes, write your summary in your own words. Do not plagiarize. To prevent plagiarism, many students at this point like to use only those words, phrases, and grammatical structures that they understand.

6. Use the author's name more than one time. Your reader should be aware at all times whose work you are summarizing.

7. Look your summary over and ask yourself if there are any unnecessary words or phrases that you can omit. Your summary should only include the main ideas, not the details. It also should not contain your opinion in any part of the summary.

8. Reread the original text. Reread your summary. Ask yourself if your summary sufficiently reflects the information and ideas as the author presents them in the original text.

9. Revise, edit, and polish your summary as necessary. Your summary should include all the elements of formal, academic writing.

Santiago Gonzalez, a writing student, advises:

"Learn to identify the author's memorable words and blend them into your summaries. That's what I did and it helped to make my summaries interesting. When writing summaries, there's no need to quote words that you could easily paraphrase."

Brandon Li, a writing student, states:

*"Do you know what helped me write my summary the most? Writing list of key words in the reading passage and finding out how the writer used these words. I compared the writer's use of the words with the ways other writers used them by looking at sample sentence in an online Longman's dictionary. I also use Google a lot, I look for **'sample sentences'** and write the word. I also found writing one-sentence summaries very helpful."*

Important Details

- Include the title and date of the original text and the author's full name.

- Include the author's thesis and main points.

- Refer to the author by his or her full name the first time and by his or her last name thereafter. Never refer to the author by his or her first name only.

- Use your own words.

- Be brief.

Getting Started

Start your summary by clearly identifying the title of the work you are summarizing, the author's name, the genre or type of writing, and the argument or key point in the present tense.

The Dos and Don'ts of Summary Writing

Dos

- **Do** be careful of word choice.

- **Do** keep reminding your readers that you are writing a summary by using signal phrases such as *the article suggests* and *the author argues*.

- **Do** use the present tense.

Don'ts

- **Don't** include your own ideas, opinions, or interpretations in your summary.

- **Don't** include unnecessary details.

- **Don't** complete just one draft of your summary. You will need to polish it by revising and editing it. Sometimes when you condense information, the resulting sentences lack cohesion. When revising your summary, make sure to add meaningful connections between sentences.

Minjoo Kyung gives this advice:

"Give yourself more than a few hours to complete the summary assignment. The more time you give yourself to read and write the text, the better you'll understand the text and summarize it.If you draft your summary and then put it down for a while and come back to it later, you'll have an easier time revising it and will be able to get rid of unnecessary details and add transitions between sentences. Whenever I revised my summaries, I always try to think of my instructor. My main goal was to communicate my ideas in a way that would make sense to her. I always took a long time to polish my summary. I made sure to follow MLA guidelines and correct grammar, vocabulary and spelling errors. I even read it out loud to try to catch the fixed expressions that I might have used incorrectly. My efforts paid off. I had no trouble doing well on the summary assignment."

Zhang Yan offers this suggestion about the length of your summaries:

"The length of your summaries will vary. The length depends on how long the reading is that you are summarizing and what your purpose of the summary is. When I first came to the US, all the paragraphs I wrote were over a page in length. Then my instructor told me that the paragraphs for most writing assignment would probably be less than a page. I started writing paragraphs of about a half page, all focused on a single idea. That helped me complete the writing assignments in which I had to support claims. "

Self-Evaluation Questions

When writing your summary, you may find the questions below helpful.

- Did I include all the original text's important ideas?
- Did I omit all unnecessary words and phrases?
- Does the summary read smoothly, with good transitions?
- Would a reader of my summary who had not read the original text get a clear idea of the text?

Verbs that introduce the author's ideas/opinions/thesis:

conclude	suppose	deny
emphasize	maintain	assert
suggest	claim	question
believe	contend	challenge
show	demonstrate	illustrate
add	argue	debate

Insider Tip

Before writing the first draft of summaries, many students find it beneficial to write a list of useful words. When they don't know how to use the words, they search for sample sentences from the web and study how the words are used.

Sample Summary

In her article "Bilingualism May Be Good for the Brain," which appeared in the Los Angeles Times on February 27, 2011, Amina Khan reports that, while public schools are moving away from bilingual education, neuroscientists are increasingly finding evidence that bilingualism is good for the brain. According to the writer, this benefit is not limited to one age group but continues over the span of a lifetime. For example, children who speak two languages are better at multi-tasking than children who know only one language, bilingual adults do a better job than monolingual adults prioritizing information, and bilingual elderly are able to delay the symptoms of Alzheimer's disease. Khan explains that these positive effects of bilingualism are a result of having a brain that is continuously managing two or more languages. A bilingual person's brain is constantly deciding which language to use, even when speaking to a group that knows only one language. This constant back-and-forth between two language systems, according to Khan, means repeated exercise for the prefrontal cortex, the part of the brain responsible for "focusing one's attention, ignoring distractions, holding multiple pieces of information in mind when trying to solve a problem and then flipping back and forth between them." The author emphasizes that this doesn't mean bilinguals learn better than people who know only one language. However, this constant exercise of the prefrontal cortex does keep the brain more agile, helping bilinguals multitask effectively, process information rapidly and ignore distractions, giving them cognitive advantages over people who speak only one language. Khan ends by noting that since schools are more interested in getting children to use English than helping them become bilingual, parents who want their children to enjoy the benefits of being bilingual should continue to speak their native language at home.

Peer Review

Name of writer: _____ Name of reviewer: _____

Checklist for Summary

Important Details

___ The title and date of the original text and the author's full name are in the first sentence.

___ The author is referred to by last name only after the first sentence.

___ The title of the original text is cited correctly.

___ The author's thesis and main points are in the first couple of sentences.

___ The summary is written in the present tense.

___ The summary is the appropriate length.

Evaluation

1. Does the writer clearly state the author's main point and supporting points? ☐ Yes ☐ No

2. Does the writer omit unnecessary details? ☐ Yes ☐ No

3. Does the summary contain the writer's opinion? ☐ Yes ☐ No

4. Does the summary read smoothly and use transitions? ☐ Yes ☐ No

5. Does the writer mention the author's name more than one time? ☐ Yes ☐ No

   If yes, how many times? _____

6. What verbs does the writer use to introduce the author's ideas/opinions/thesis?
   For example, Smith writes/states/believes/asserts/suggests/criticizes/explains/argues…
   List them below.

   _____

7. Does the writer include one quotation from the original text and explain it? ☐ Yes ☐ No

   If yes, does the writer follow the three steps for integrating a quotation as described in this chapter?

   Step 1: Introduce the quotation using a signal phrase such as ☐ Yes ☐ No
   Smith writes or *He claims that.*

   Step 2: Give the quotation using proper punctuation.
   (Commas and periods go inside quotation marks.)

   Step 3: Follow up the quotation with a sentence that explains it
   or comments on it. ☐ Yes ☐ No

8. Would a reader of the summary who had not read the original text get a clear idea of the text?

Explain:

9. Other Comments:

Reflecting on Summary Writing

Think about the **genre** of summary writing. (Remember that **genre** refers to the type of writing.)

- **Structure:** How is the summary you wrote organized? Does it have a beginning, middle, and end? How are the key points arranged?

- **Audience:** Who did you write your summary for? Yourself or your instructor? What were some of the conventions you followed when writing for this audience?

- **Language:** What grammatical structures did you use to paraphrase the writer's ideas?

- **Tone:** What is the tone of the summary? Is your tone academic or informal? Serious or funny? What language did you use to communicate this tone to your readers? Complex sentences? Academic words?

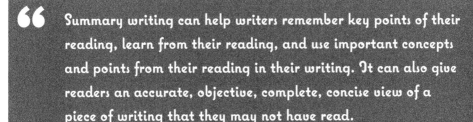

> Summary writing can help writers remember key points of their reading, learn from their reading, and use important concepts and points from their reading in their writing. It can also give readers an accurate, objective, complete, concise view of a piece of writing that they may not have read.

Reading Comprehension Questions

1. What is the goal of informational writing?

2. Why are definitions important?

3. Why might you include the definition of a key term in the introduction of an essay?

4. What is an effective method of writing an extended definition? Using the term economic recession (or another term assigned by your instructor), describe the combination of methods you would use to explain this concept.

5. What is the goal of summary writing?

6. What should a one-sentence summary contain?

7. Why don't summaries contain personal opinions?

8. How do you refer to the author or authors of an article when summarizing the article?

9. What tense should you use when writing most summaries? Why?

10. What are six verbs that you can use to introduce the author's ideas, opinions, or thesis statement?

Using and Writing Short, Formal Definitions

Directions: Complete the chart with the missing information.

Term	Classification	Distinguishing Feature
poodle	is a type of dog	
diabetes		that affects how your body uses blood sugar (glucose)
	is a sport	played in a four-walled court with a small, hollow rubber ball

Directions: Write a complete definition using the sentence frame from page _____ for each term above.

1. poodle: _____

2. diabetes: _____

3. _____ : _____

It is often thought that student success might depend on the extent they can use informative writing effectively, including definitions and summaries, to explore the academic world around them and advance their understanding of a range of academic topics.

Argumentive Writing:
The Writing Process and Finding Your Way

by Christie Sosa and Gina Ruggiero, with excerpts from Anita Fischer and Omaima Zayed

CHAPTER THREE

Finding Your Way: Argumentative Writing

Much of the writing you do in your college courses will be argumentative. This type of writing not only can give factual information but also can present a well-reasoned point with supporting ideas. When you write an argumentative piece, you make a point and support it based on your own reasoning, expertise, and understanding of a topic. Argumentative writing can include narrative analyses, persuasive letters, podcasts, policy pieces, newspaper editorials, opinion articles, essays, and books. The purpose of argumentative writing is generally to get your readers to consider your view seriously, convincing them of its validity.* This can involve stirring emotions or changing your readers' beliefs, sometimes beliefs that readers do not want to change. Among your primary goals is getting your readers to be receptive* to understanding your view.

The language you use will depend largely on the ways you represent yourself to your readers. You'll need to consider your approach to making yourself seem informed and knowledgeable, opinionated, factual, or academic; your readers; the form of your argumentative text (for instance, its structure and style); and the context in which you write. When writing effective argumentative texts, you'll want to understand your topic and support your claims thoroughly, for example, giving facts, data sources, statistics, expert testimonials, quotations, or examples when appropriate. When writing most academic arguments, you'll want to be professional and authoritative.*

You may want to assert yourself as an expert. In some types of argumentative writing, it will be useful for you to investigate both sides of an issue and present counter views when appropriate and then refute those ideas in an effort to persuade your readers to be receptive to it. Informal argumentative writing can contain slang, begin sentences with *and* and *but*, and contain sentence fragments. Writers use language in this way to make their writing seem friendly or engaging. But formal argumentative writing generally does not contain slang or sentence fragments.

*validity
*(uncountable noun): in writing, **validity** is based on what is reasonable and logical*

*receptive
(adjective): being willing to consider new ideas or understand someone else's opinions, being open or responsive to ideas or ready to understand them

*authoritative
(adjective): showing a lot of knowledge about a subject

You can organize argumentative text in different ways. You will want to announce or introduce your supporting details within the text. You will also use language to convince readers that they should be interested in your topic and engage your readers' attention. You can use short, simple sentences to emphasize key points and long, complex sentences to slow readers down and make them reflect on your points and supporting details.

If you are an international student, you may be familiar with many aspects of US-American writing, but unfamiliar with many others. You might even find some aspects counter-intuitive to you. Every culture has different writing and communication styles, and they are all valid in particular contexts. However, in order to succeed at college, you need to be aware of US-American approaches to making an argument and structuring argumentative text, and then find a balance between using these approaches and structures while simultaneously making creative, interesting choices and developing your very own voice in your writing.

Tips and Techniques for Writing Drafts and Structuring Arguments

This part of the chapter will get you started composing your argumentative writing assignments. It'll give you tips and techniques for writing drafts and structuring your papers.

Writers have their own ways of starting, writing, revising, and ending particular pieces of writing. You must find your own way of writing them whether you're simply writing a short response to a question about your opinion or an argumentative paper on smoking.

The Writing Process—What is it?

The writing process simply refers to the steps you take to write something. When writing an argumentative piece on free speech, you unconsciously take steps to compose it. Before actually writing, you may list your ideas or even draw a chart. Some of you may even skip this step and begin writing a "first draft"—a term you've likely used all throughout your academic career. After revising the content and editing one or more times with the help of your instructor's comments, you end up with a "final" draft. You're probably very familiar with this process and even comfortable with it. However, as you begin writing at the university level, you may find that the process you have learned is ineffective in meeting the demands of your assignments or you may find that the process only works for some types of writing or that some of the steps of the process work and others do not. You'll most likely need to develop a new writing process (or processes) that vary in accordance to your particular needs and preferences as well as your writing assignments, the texts you write, your readers, and the context in which you write.

You will find that you will need to vary your approach to each writing assignment depending on the requirements, subject matter, purpose, and genre. Just as your writing will vary, the approach you take must also vary, given your audience, your own needs and purpose, and context of the particular assignment.

Why is the writing process important in writing argumentative pieces?

If you've ever received a comment from your instructor telling you, "Be more specific" or had an instructor point to a line and ask you, "Is this your thesis?"—don't worry, we all have. These types of comments and questions are given because what you're writing is likely too simplistic or vague* and maybe even unclear.

*vague

(adjective): not specific because the writer has not given enough details or does not state exactly what she or he means

You can modify your writing process by spending more time on pre-writing and drafting to avoid these common problems regarding vagueness and lack of specificity. A modified writing process can help you address the assignment and reflect your deep understanding of its topic.

Each step of this process is described in detail below. This is often referred to as the *writing process*. Please note that as you develop your writing skills by writing more, you will likely develop your own writing process for different types of assignments, often loosely modeled after these steps.

Prewriting

Although students often struggle the most with concluding a paper, starting an argumentative paper is a different and, at times, more difficult task. Prewriting is similar to gathering ingredients for a recipe—you're simply getting everything you need. You may or may not use everything. In fact, you may not even know how much of something you will use. In writing, this translates to getting all of your ideas down on paper. Like all the ingredients you've gathered, you may or may not use everything. But, by writing all of your thoughts down (even the ideas you think are irrelevant or somewhat off-topic), you are giving yourself more material to work with to develop an interesting and reflective response.

The following include different pre-writing techniques. Take the time to experiment with each one and don't be afraid to develop your own.

LISTING

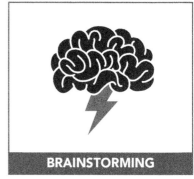

BRAINSTORMING

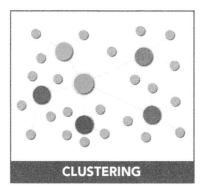

CLUSTERING

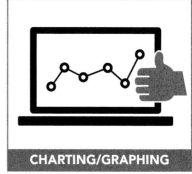

CHARTING/GRAPHING

Discussion

Insider Tip

You can use Do/ What charts to help you understand your writing assignment.

Another useful prewriting technique is discussing ideas with friends, peer tutors, writing specialists at the Writing Center, classmates, and instructors. Discussing writing prompts may force you to consider two sides to the claims you and others make as well as various perspectives on a writing topic. You can also see if others understand your interpretation of a prompt. Discussing prompts also gives you the opportunity to seek clarification regarding your ideas and ask for assistance in strengthening your claims and providing evidence to support them. Talking to others will help you identify your message and figure out what you're really trying to say. After you have a good idea of what you will write about, you can, with the help of others, begin to generate useful lists of words, phrases, and fixed expressions to use in your papers.

"Draft Zero"—A Rough Draft

After you've gathered all your ingredients, you begin to group them. For example, when you bake a cake, you mix all your wet ingredients and all your dry ingredients in separate bowls. In other words, you're beginning to combine some of your ideas because of their obvious connections. Perhaps you've been asked to analyze the effects of exercising before going to work. You may group your ideas by mental effects, physical effects, etc. But still, in a "zero" draft, your thesis may and likely will not be apparent just yet. You have an idea of what you want to say, but you're still figuring out **how to make your point and what evidence does this best.**

Draft 1—Working Draft

You've combined most of your ingredients. You've decided what shape you want your cake to take (your general organization and message). In fact, you may be even be baking your cake at this point. You've thought a lot about the occasion for the cake and who it's for (audience), which has helped you eliminate some ingredients or add different ones. Similarly, in the writing process, you will choose what to include in your paper after you clarify the "occasion" (and take into account such factors as the prompt, your purpose, and the points you want to make) and you consider who will read your paper. You'll consider what the relevant audience already knows about the topic, needs to know, and might find disagreeable.

In other words, your first draft looks nothing like your "zero" draft. You have made immense progress by eliminating, modifying, or adding some of your ideas and you have a well-developed understanding of *what* you want to say and *how* you want to say it, but are still aware that you still may make minor to somewhat major adjustments to your ideas and thesis.

Xizhu Yan – a former writing student, states:
Usually, I like to start with relating my topic and ideas to my own life because it is easier to develop ideas and a unique perspective from what I'm familiar with. Also, talking to my teacher and friends gave me more unexpected ideas.

Draft 2—Working Draft

Your cake is baked and now you must decide how you're going to combine your cake layers and begin considering how you will decorate it. Throughout your academic life, your second draft may have been the "draft before the final draft," and this may be the case as well for some of your university classes. However, in *writing* courses, this is often *not* the case. Many of you will end up writing many more drafts before you complete your final paper. In fact, some of you may find the cake you baked turned out to be a disaster—perhaps you forgot an ingredient, got the flavor wrong, or overcooked it. In such extreme cases, you will have to start over.

However, perhaps you simply changed your mind. While waiting for your cake to bake, that is, for your instructor and possibly classmates and others to give you feedback, you suddenly came up with a brilliant idea and it doesn't fit with your current draft. In this case, your paper will undergo some major changes. Don't be afraid to make changes. Oftentimes, these changes will lead you to a complex, thoughtful response that brings you closer to finishing.

Draft 3—Working Draft/Final Draft

As mentioned above, draft 3 often means final draft to you. If that is the case, then what you do to your final draft is the similar to decorating a cake. You're checking for grammatical and punctuation mistakes—anything that is distracting. You're also turning to *Longman's Dictionary of Contemporary English* to make sure you're using words effectively. You make sure you've formatted your paper correctly and have spelled your instructor's as well as your own name correctly. You're putting the final touches on your cake. You've frosted it and now you're making sure you didn't miss a spot.* As mentioned before, in a *writing* course, draft 3 may still be a working draft, especially if you made major changes to draft 2.

Draft 4 and Subsequent Drafts—Working Drafts/Final Draft

Once a paper is written, it is often revised and edited several times before it is close to being completed. Depending on how difficult a piece is to write, your draft 4 may still be a working draft. Or, this may very well be your final draft and again, you are simply polishing up your paper, that is, checking for formatting or grammatical errors.

Li Yi, a writing student, warns:

My preliminary drafts are chaotic because I write down all the ideas I have. It has a lot of grammar mistakes and no transitions between any two paragraphs. These problems are reasons why we need to write more drafts. In my next draft, I organize my thoughts. I make sure that my topic sentences are clear. I make sure all my quotations are well explained and make sure my evidence supports my thesis. All these things are learned from drafting. When I finish my final draft, I can see that my essay is totally different.

Kaly Ngo, a writing student, argues:

Discussion and outlining are the most useful for me when developing ideas for a paper. Discussions are engaging and they create momentum in the thinking process for an idea. Outlines remind me what needs to be included and keep my papers focused.

Things to Remember

The writing process is messy. Remember the cake. Have you thought about who the cake is for and what those individuals are expecting, given all their experience with previous types of cakes? Have you considered what they have found agreeable or disagreeable about the past cakes they have eaten? Before all the ingredients are put together, and even while you begin to combine them, you may well have a mess. It's not clear how it's going to turn out, and only after much work can you begin to see how it's going to turn out and make adjustments accordingly.

Another thing to remember is that although you may have been writing three draft papers for most of your academic career, know that at the university level, many of your papers will need to be revised more than three times.

At times, it is not necessary or even possible to follow this prescribed process for *all* types of writing. In truth, you will naturally develop your own writing process. In order to do that, you will need to experiment with prewriting and the steps described above, finding which approach works best for you.

A WORD OF WARNING:

Although the process of writing a paper has been compared to the process of making a cake, keep in mind that the writing process is actually much more complicated. It does not involve step-by-step directions, specific ingredients, or precise measurements. Every text you write will be different and the procedures and processes you use to write texts will vary. However, consciously considering the procedures and processes will help you develop the habits of good writers.

Yeng Lor, a writing student, explains:

Drafting is a writing process that links ideas together to form a purposeful and reflective analytical essay. I learned that writing multiple drafts enables me to gather more ideas in helping me write and develop my ideas. Revising helps me recognize my errors. Also, drafting gives me time to organize and structure my essay properly. When taking the time to revise my paper meticulously, it allowed me to rephrase my sentences better and make them flow smoothly.

Getting to the Nuts and Bolts: Organizing Your Argument

Begin an Argument

The best introductions are usually written when you yourself discover a personal connection with the topic and you are invested in writing about it and helping your readers find their own connections with it. However, there are specific strategies for starting many types of writing. You can begin your writing with sentences that engage your readers. You can also vary the way you engage them, announce the topic of your writing, and orient them. In writing an introduction to a text-based paper, you might find hooks* helpful.

*hook

(countable noun): a device writers use to make readers interested in their writing

Using a hook, such as an anecdote (a story), a quotation from the text, a thought-provoking question, dialogue, or a statement to make people think can capture the readers' interests. Below are some hooks written as models for an argumentative text.

A WORD OF WARNING

The use of famous quotations or cultural proverbs as an opening is generally not recommended. Defining words that people generally know or stating information that is common knowledge is also an ineffective way to start an introduction.

Anecdote (Telling a Story)

A a personal narrative (a story based on personal experience) might help readers relate to the topic of the writing and find it memorable.

Example

In the classroom where I tutor, a five-year-old boy is fighting with the letter E. With knees bent and shoulders cocked, he is poised on his bench as though ready to pounce. His whole being is devoted to this singular, monumental task. I focus on him over the din of the classroom. I see the blunt pencil caught in his grip, and I realize that an entire process is beginning again. Tens of thousands of years of evolution are being re-enacted right in front of me.

– Wegman, Jesse. "Six Days: On Learning a New Alphabet." *The Atlantic Monthly.* May 1999.

In introducing the essay, the author tells the story of a child trying to master the letter E as a way to move into her discussion of her own experience learning a new language.When telling a personal narrative to support a claim, keep in mind the purpose the story by asking yourself, "Am I telling the story in a way that is relevant to the point I am trying to make?"

Quotation

Starting an introduction with a well chosen, insightful quotation related to your topic can also serve to engage your readers' interest in the topic. One student wrote a paper on gender differences and opened it with a quotation from Katherine Hepburn.

Example

"Sometimes I wonder if men and women really suit each other. Perhaps they should live next door and just visit now and then."

A Statement to Make People Think

Beginning with a statement that explains the significance of your writing engages the readers' attention. This is especially the case if the statement is an interesting one.

Example

Peer pressure often can influence children to behave badly, especially if there is just one bully in the group.The writer went on to discuss the problem of bullying.

A Startling or Interesting Statistic

A statistic that your readers can relate to and find interesting or surprising can be an effective hook.

Example

Identity fraud is the fastest growing crime in the United States. In 2004, over nine million Americans, or approximately one person in 24, became victims of identity fraud or identity theft, at a cost to the economy of 52.6 billion dollars (*2005 Identity Fraud Survey Report*). Because many cases of identity fraud and identity theft may go unreported, the numbers could be even higher. Identity theft is a serious problem that claims millions of innocent victims, and the government must implement better regulations to help put an end to this crime.

Key Point:
The length of your paper matters. If you are writing a very short paper, you will not have much space to write long, engaging sentences to introduce your topic and engage your readers' interest. Beginning your paper with a long anecdote or even a quotation that requires an explanation might not be appropriate.

Some sage advice: *some introductions that you used when you wrote essays in high school or university admissions tests will not work in college courses.*

Helpful Tips

- Try to avoid these types of openings:

  - Dictionary definitions such as "Webster's dictionary defines…"

  - Broad general statements such as "X is a very important issue facing America today…" or "Throughout history…"

- Make sure that the relationship between the quotation you choose and your topic is explicitly clear to your readers. Beginning with a quotation from Thomas Edison that is only indirectly related to your topic is ineffective.

- Don't use the same opening strategy again and again. Beginning every piece of writing you do with a quotation or definition gets old. Mix it up. Find the hook that works best for the particular text you are writing. Some types of texts do not require hooks.

- Do not rely on the introduction openers recommended here.

- Finally, be aware that instructors' opinions often vary in terms of the types of hooks they want their students to use. Talk to your instructor if you have questions about how to introduce the topic of your writing.

Once you've got your readers interested in what you are saying, you'll want to provide enough background information to help them know where you are headed in your writing. If you are writing about a text, you'll generally need to refer to the type of genre you are writing about (e.g., a play, novel, article), the name of the text, and the author. You'll usually identify the title, author, and genre of the text. That is sometimes referred to as **TAG** (for **t**itle, **a**uthor, and **g**enre). TAG sentences often start with a prepositional phrase:

Example

In (type of genre and name of text) by (author), (x happens).

As part of the TAG or right after the TAG, you will generally include a brief statement that summarizes the text and provides background information, including the point, issue, problem, or conflict it addresses. This statement often will lead into your thesis.

Advice for Writing Effective Thesis Statements for Argumentative Writing Assignments

A thesis is a statement, usually one or more sentences, that summarizes the main (debatable) point or claim of a persuasive argument or literary analysis and is developed, supported, and explained by means of examples and evidence.

Before you write a strong thesis statement, determine what kind of argument you are writing and what kind of thesis you will need. In your courses, you will often be asked to write a persuasive argument or an interpretive analysis of an academic reading that contains an arguable claim. Both types of writing are arguments.

Your thesis statement should be specific. It should cover only what you will discuss in your paper and should be supported with specific evidence. It should provide a specific, arguable claim that reflects your position and is a clear response to the prompt. To produce an arguable claim, it may be useful to imagine that you are trying to convince an imaginary audience who does not agree with you.

The Function of a Thesis

As you begin writing a persuasive argument, imagine sending your readers on a road trip to a place where they have never been before. In your thesis you will need to give them clear navigation instructions to help them reach the destination. There may be several routes you can send them on, so you are in charge of providing them with step-by-step reminders that confirm that they are on the correct path. These are your topic sentences, which refer back to the original purpose stated in your thesis. Without such navigation, your readers are likely to get confused, lost, and uninterested in your argument, which may appear to them like a string of random ideas without a specific destination.

Rethinking the Thesis Statement

Traditionally, the thesis statement is given at the end of the first paragraph of a paper. However, there is no fixed rule for the placement of the thesis statement and its placement may change depending on the assignment. Your topic may change as you write, so you may need to revise your thesis statement to reflect exactly what you have discussed in the paper. You will probably need to modify your thesis once you have a complete draft to make sure that your paper does what your thesis says it will.

In generating a thesis, you might become locked into a formula of stating your main idea in a single sentence. This can rule out the possibility of developing complexity of thought. An interesting thesis

Insider Tip

Anita Fischer, an instructor, provides this useful tip: Instead of simply listing three points in their thesis statements, as students are sometimes taught, think about the relationship among those points, or the story they tell, and write that for your thesis.

A thesis statement is not just an explanation of what your essay will be about.

Key Point:

Your professors expect you to come up with original thesis statements of your own and not use thesis statements that have been used by others.

goes beyond the simple and obvious and can be articulated in more than one sentence. Since the function of a thesis is to outline and structure the essay's entire argument, it will probably be the most difficult part of the essay to write. It may well need to be developed in more than one sentence—often in two or more.

This is not an example of a thesis statement because it introduces a very general topic (cruel behavior) and does not give enough information to the reader about what the writer will argue.

This is **NOT** an Example of a Thesis Statement:

This essay will be about why the children behaved cruelly toward Margot. (This is not a thesis statement.)

A thesis statement advances your interpretation of the topic or issue you are discussing.

This **IS** an Example of a Thesis Statement:

The children behave cruelly toward Margot because they sense that she is different and so they ostracize her.

Possible Steps for Writing a Thesis Statement

Some kinds of writing, like persuasive essays, commonly use thesis statements to communicate to the readers what the writer will be arguing. Sheridan Baker, from the University of Michigan, has suggested following these steps when writing a thesis statement:

1 Identify the topic of your writing. What are you writing about? Altruism in the United States? The effect of diligence in attaining success in language learning?

2 Take a stand. To do this, you can ask a question. Next, take a stand. This is your position. To know what your position is, answer the question.

- Are people who live in cities in the United States altruistic or self-serving? *Preliminary Thesis Statement:* People who live in cities in the United States are self-serving.

- Can diligence help students obtain success in learning language? *Preliminary Thesis Statement:* Diligence can help students become successful in language learning.

3 Discover the rationale. Why is the position a reasonable and correct one? You can use a sentence with a "because" clause to explain the reason.

- People who live in cities in the United States are self-serving because the government does not tend to award them for altruism.

- Diligence can help students obtain success in language learning because it provides them with practice writing.

4 Use a qualifier, a word, phrase, or clause that limits your claim. One way to qualify or limit the claim you make is by using an "although" clause.

- Although many people who live in cities in the United States are for the most part self-serving because the government does not reward altruism, they do in specific situations engage in acts of altruism.

- While diligence builds students' overall success in language learning because it provides them with practice writing, diligent students who spend hours in their dorms studying and not interacting with others do not always develop oral language fluency.

A WORD OF WARNING

Make sure you do not become dependent on the steps for writing thesis statements given above. You will find that the steps are useful for some types of argumentative writing and some assignments, but not other types of writing and assignments.

Thesis points that predict body paragraphs are optional. They can vary in number and can enrich an essay provided that they do not overlap with each other and are not formulaic. Phrases like "as the passage, my personal experience, and my observations of others show" are too formulaic.

Example

- Thesis statement: "Malcolm Gladwell's *The Tipping Point* should be required reading for students because it is informative, engaging, and full of examples."

- **Revised** thesis statement: "Malcolm Gladwell's *The Tipping Point* should be required reading for students because it informs readers with lots of examples while still being engagingly written enough to hold students' attention."

What is a Paragraph?

A paragraph is a group of sentences that has a single focus. The sentences are related to one another. Each paragraph should have an overarching main idea and consistency in thought. The main idea of the paragraph is generally expressed in the topic sentence* or sentences, which usually appear toward the beginning of the paragraph.

Insider Tip

In academic writing, try avoid using words that lead to over-generalizations, such as "always" or "all the time," since these words have a tendency to make your writing less credible. Instead, try using words and expressions such as generally, most of the time, frequently, in most cases, usually, or generally speaking. The same goes for when referring to a group of people. Try alternating the use of words such as "the vast majority of people," "most people," "a large number of individuals."

*topic sentence

(fixed expression – noun): a sentence that states the meaning of the entire paragraph and that often, though not always, appears at the beginning of a paragraph

Subsequent sentences support your topic sentences. The body paragraphs of an argumentative paper support the claim/s in the thesis statement. While paragraphs can vary in length from one sentence to many, in writing assignments, your paragraphs will end up about a half a page or so in length. What's important is not how long your paragraph is, but how well it develops and supports your topic sentence, for instance, offering enough concrete evidence to support the point you are trying to make. You may find it helpful to think of the structure of a paragraph as a **paraburger**.

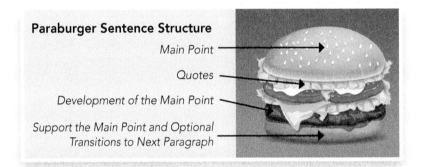

Paraburger Sentence Structure

Main Point

Quotes

Development of the Main Point

Support the Main Point and Optional Transitions to Next Paragraph

The top bun contains your main point. Your development of the point is contained in the main meaty ingredients and constitutes the largest part of the paraburger. Your quotes are considered the ketchup, mustard and mayonnaise, because though they can make your burger tasty, a little can go a long way. The bottom bun can relate the topic sentence to the statements that support the main point of your paragraph and can provide a transition to the next paragraph.

A WORD OF WARNING

While the *paraburger* approach to paragraph structure works for many kinds of academic writing, you will find that it is not the only approach. Use the best kind of paragraph structure that makes sense, considering, for instance, your purpose as the author, the text you are writing, your readers, and the context of your writing.

Paragraph Length

Experienced writers usually use a combination of both short and long paragraphs, depending on the complexity of the ideas in their paragraphs. Paragraphs usually have a minimum of three sentences. However, paragraphs with complex ideas may be lengthier. There is no rule as to how many paragraphs should be in a paper because this varies from assignment to assignment. Throughout high school, many students are taught to write five-paragraph essays. However, at the university level, your instructors will usually expect more sophisticated writing with more than just five paragraphs. They usually expect you to figure out how many paragraphs are sufficient to say what you want to say.

Order Matters

Get into the habit of asking yourself, "Is this sentence relevant to the idea of this paragraph?" Every paragraph should have a main idea that is typically stated in a topic sentence. To maintain cohesion, all sentences within a paragraph should relate to this main idea. For example, if you are writing a paragraph on why nuclear power plants are an efficient, clean way of generating energy, it will be out of place to then to go on to discuss the reasons you decided to come to college. How you order your sentences matters. Order your sentences in a way that best supports your topic sentences. Here are just a few common ways:

- Chronological
- Cause and Effect
- Clarification (The first sentence is broad, a general statement follows it, and the subsequent sentences explain the general statement with details.)
- Compare/Contrast

Paragraphs that List Ideas in a Laundry List* Fashion

To impress academic readers of the sophistication of your ideas and the complexity of the content of your paragraphs, you will most likely want to avoid a simple listing of ideas in a laundry list fashion and using words such as *first, second,* and *third* to list them.

*laundry list:
(fixed expression; noun, informal): a list of a lot of different things, unrelated and random (appearing without any order)

Example of "Laundry-List" Paragraph

Moon cites several different studies that support of the argument that humans are givers and takers, but these studies are flawed. First, his argument is not logically well constructed in that he does not consider the contextual variables that affect giving and taking. Second, Moon ignores data indicating that those people who give the most are those who have the most to give and the least to lose by giving. Third, his evidence does not support his overall conclusion that individuals cannot change over time, sometimes being givers and sometimes being takers. Fourth, Moon provides only research on givers or takers and overlooks the many people who both give and take. Further, the author disregards relevant historical data that indicates that those who take and do not give often became successful emperors, presidents and prime ministers. Additionally, it is questionable whether the same findings would hold true for all types of people in all situations.

Insider Tip

When you write paragraphs that synthesize your argument for assignments, avoid presenting your points in a laundry-list style.

Synthesize* the information as much as possible and order it in a way that will support your topic sentence and convince your reader of the credibility of your claim.

***synthesize**

(transitive verb): to combine ideas together by connecting them

---

***analysis**

(uncountable and countable noun, plural – analyses): a careful examination of something in order to understand it better

---

Convincing analyses of someone's writing go beyond mere description or summary to examination and explanation.

Example of a More Thoughtfully Composed Paragraph

The evidence cited by Moon does not support his overall conclusion that givers become highly successful and takers do not. His argument is not logically well constructed in that he does not consider the contextual variables that affect the extent to which individuals give and take over time, related, for instance, to their finances, talents and intellect. Moon also ignores data indicating that those people who give the most are those who have the most financial resources, talents and intellectual gifts to give and the least to lose by giving. Because he provides only research on givers or takers and does not examine the patterns of individuals who both give and take (most of us) and the contextual variables affecting shifts in these patterns, he fails to account for most of the data. Additionally, his evidence does not support the overall conclusion that individuals cannot change over time, sometimes becoming givers and sometimes becoming takers, as the nature of their finances, talents and intellectual prowess change. And because he disregards time as a critical confounding variable, he also disregards relevant historical data that indicates that those who are takers often became emperors, presidents and prime ministers. In brief, it is questionable whether his findings hold true for all types of people in all situations.

Analysis in Writing

Generally, analysis* goes beyond mere description. It involves examination, explanation, evaluation, and argumentation of a point.

Analyzing Others' Writing to Support Your Claims

In preparation for future university writing, you will need to learn to move from summarizing a reading to analyzing it to support your claims. This is a skill that allows you to be more creative in your writing because, unlike summarizing, you are offering the readers your observations and making a strong point, or highlighting something that the reader might find striking, noteworthy, or important. These types of considerations may go far beyond your opinion. When analyzing, it is your job to develop a point based on the reading. You now have a "voice" about the reading. Furthermore, it is your job to convince your readers that they should agree with your point. You do this by formulating a strong thesis statement.

Analysis means to break something down into smaller parts and to examine the parts to see how they affect the whole thing. For example, if you take a bicycle apart, you could analyze how each of the parts (brakes, gears, chain, etc.) contributes to making the whole bicycle work smoothly when you are riding up a steep hill. It's the same with a written text. You might read a text and be able to answer the "What" question (What is this reading about?) very easily because you understand the vocabulary. However, just describing what is in the reading does not help you answer "how" or "why" questions ("How is the author convincing me and why does the author want me to believe his or her perspective?"). To answer these questions, you need to analyze the text or break it into parts and examine smaller things like the kinds of verbs the writer uses to convince the reader of his or her position, or kinds of adjectives the writer uses to make the reader feel certain emotions, or the kinds of details the writer includes to communicate his or her motive for writing about this topic. Each small

way the writer uses language affects the "big picture" or the overall message he or she is trying to communicate to the readers. When you analyze a text, you are breaking it down into smaller parts to find the answers to these "how" and "why" questions. Learning how to analyze the writing of others can help you become a more effective writer.

Analysis does not equal description. It goes beyond that. It goes beyond summarizing to understanding and examining the real relationship between ideas. Your analysis must convince the readers— even those who disagree with your view—that your argument has been carefully thought out. It must be cogent, persuasive, and believable because of its clear presentation.

Consider this explanation of analysis from The University of California-Irvine Center for Excellence in Writing and Communication:

> Analysis involves a certain amount of creativity because you have to connect smaller bits of language or ideas back to larger parts of language or ideas in a way that reveals something unexpected, where you create connections that we might not see from just looking at the larger or smaller pieces by themselves. It's also about finding unexpected contradictions: Do some of the parts seem to go against what the whole stands for? When you put some parts in relation to others, are there tensions and conflicts that we wouldn't see from just looking at the surface? Above all, analysis is not just summary or simply stating what is obvious.

Source: Schoenbeck, Rob. "What is 'Analysis' and Why Does My Writing Instructor Keep Asking for It? Part I." *UC Irvine Center for Excellence in Writing and Communication*. 1 Nov. 2013. Web. 31 Aug. 2015.

Insider Tip

Even if you don't have a lot of knowledge about literature or language, you can still make interesting and effective observations if you just focus very closely on part of the reading and point out something that your readers might have missed.

> Your job in analyzing others' writing and using it to support your own claims or points is to use "rhetorical" tools effectively.

According to Abraham Romney and Daniel Gross, the term **rhetoric** refers to "the art or set of techniques, used for effective communication" (6). When analyzing a reading, your job is to analyze the "rhetorical" devices used. This means you must analyze the ways writing techniques are used in specific ways to convey meaning or persuade readers, sometimes asking readers to consider new or different perspectives. Does the author present logical ideas and evidence to appeal to the audience? Does the author appeal to the audience's emotions? Does the author appeal to readers by seeming to be an authority on the subject of the text or someone who is likeable, credible, and worthy of respect? To develop the habit of thinking rhetorically about the books and other texts you read, ask yourself this question:

How do the authors try to convince their readers to believe what they believe or see things in a certain way?

Remember:

- You are writing about **your** points.

- You are the authority, so you can critique or talk about the authors' style, tone, or use of language. What techniques do the authors use to persuade the readers to believe something or see something in a particular way?

- Your argument is an informed opinion. You don't have to agree with the author, but you do need to be sure that you defend your opinion throughout your paper.

- You need to persuade the readers about what you believe about the text/prompt.

- How does the author persuade the audience to believe his/her argument or make the audience open to trying to understand it or see it in a new light?

- Do authors use informal language, questions, specific pronouns, or words to build a relationship with their readers, engage their attention, or make their ideas memorable or interesting?

- Good writers don't summarize information or examples from the reading. Good writers explain how the information and/or examples support the thesis.

- You need to do the same. Explain how your information and examples obtained from the text support your thesis.

If you focus on even a few of these suggestions, you will show that you are taking chances to be more creative and analytical and you will be that much more prepared for college writing. Give it a try. You may be surprised at your ability.

In argumentative writing, conclusions should briefly restate the thesis (without copying it verbatim) and go on to clarify why the thesis should matter to the reader. An element to avoid in a conclusion is to make additional points that were not mentioned earlier and seem off topic (afterthoughts). In addition, ending with an imperative or "you" as part of a direct appeal to the reader is not appropriate in most types of academic argumentative and informational writing that you do. Anita Fischer, a writing instructor at a major U.S. university, provides useful suggestions for writing conclusions for the argumentative writing you do in college.

Conclusions *By Anita Fischer*

An effective conclusion lets your reader know that your argument is now over and then gives it additional meaning. It's the last thing your reader reads so you want it to have an impact. Just repeating your thesis and main points is very boring to your academic readers because they can remember what they just read.

Instead of repeating what you have already stated, here are some **conclusion tips** to better impact your readers:

- Don't start with "In conclusion,…" It's awkward because it's like an announcement. Instead, use your words in such a way that your readers would already get that it's your conclusion without you having to announce it (see below).

- Restating your argument is a good way of beginning your conclusion because it reminds your reader of your overall point, signaling the end of your essay. But don't just repeat your thesis, which is boring. Instead, rephrase or recap your thesis in a different way. For example, using the revised thesis example from above, a concluding paragraph might begin: "Every student would benefit from reading Malcolm Gladwell's *The Tipping Point* because they would learn a lot and never be bored."

- Once you've reminded your reader of your main point, don't just repeat what you've already pointed out in the essay. Instead, to have an impact, give them a reason to believe your argument is important and then expand on that a bit. Here are some suggestions:

    - Explain how your argument affects you: "As a student myself, I know I have grown a lot by reading Gladwell's ideas…" (follow with examples of how you have grown).

- Explain how your argument can affect your reader: "Students can learn a lot not just about the information and ideas Gladwell presents, but also how to write them out logically..." (follow with why it's important for them to write logically).

- Explain why your argument is meaningful to society: "Gladwell's idea of the tipping point is an interesting thing for everyone to think about because..." (follow with a couple of reasons and examples). Or: "It's important to consider the overall pattern of events happening in the world and in our lives..." (follow with why that matters).

- Anything else that gives your readers something to think about, care about, or do, based on what you have just argued in your essay.

- If you ask a question in your conclusion, be sure to answer it. Otherwise, your reader might come up with his or her own answer, and not the one you want, thereby weakening your impact. Example: "Shouldn't everyone want to read a book like this? Yes, because the more we understand how our actions create consequences, the more we might think twice about them." If the answer to the question wasn't there, a reader might be tempted to say, "No, they shouldn't! It's hard and boring! I have better things to do than to read this required book." But the answer gives them something meaningful to consider.

A WORD OF CAUTION:

When you write nearly all types of academic texts, you'll want to avoid falling back on the familiar writing strategies and writing structures and *templates** that you were taught earlier. You may have used them when preparing for college admissions writing tests and when composing high school essays. You'll be doing different types of writing and you'll need to organize your writing differently. In general, college instructors will not accept five-paragraph essay templates.

*template

(countable noun): something that is used as a model for writing; a fixed way of writing that does not seem creative or original

Your instructors will remind you not to use formulaic approaches to writing. They'll ask you to develop original thesis statements and vary the approach you take to writing—considering many variables— including your communicative purpose and objectives, your audience, your message, the context in which you are writing, and the genre or type of writing that you are composing. They'll say, "*Five-paragraph essay writing is discouraged in my courses. I want you to organize your writing in a different, more thoughtful and original way.*"

Reflecting on Argumentative Writing

Think about the genre of argumentative writing. (Remember that **genre** refers to type of writing.

Structure: How is the argumentative piece you wrote organized? Does it have a beginning, middle, and end? How are the key points arranged?

Audience: Who did you write your argument for? Yourself, your instructor, or someone else? What were some of the conventions you followed when writing for this audience?

Language: What grammatical structures did you use to present your argument?

Tone: What is the tone of your writing? Is your tone academic or informal? Serious? Authoritative? Passionate? What language did you use to communicate this tone to your readers? Complex sentences? Academic words?

*genre

(countable noun): a type of writing with distinct characteristics and conventions; examples of genres include plays, novels, poetry, definitions, and arguments. Genres help writers accomplish specific tasks and purposes.

Reading Comprehension Questions

1. Why are audience considerations so important?

2. If you were writing a paper arguing for the need to reduce pollution, what would you need to know about your readers?

3. What language features can you use to convey a tone of formality and seriousness in your writing?

4. What language features can you use to convey a casual tone?

5. What is diction and why is it important in college writing?

6. How important is it to use synonyms in your writing?

7. What difficulties do you have using synonyms appropriately? Why do you have these difficulties? What can you do to overcome these difficulties?

8. What are the advantages and disadvantages of using a thesaurus?

9. What are three examples of vague or very general words in English?

10. What can you do to improve your diction?

Activity

Directions: Compare the two paragraphs below and explain why one paragraph is informal and the other is academic.

Passage 1: Informal English
Main premise: The government should introduce tighter gun controls

Jack Springer thinks that the government should have the right to own a gun but I don't agree with him. People like him should think that the government is stepping on our democratic rights when it stops gun ownership. They think that most people who own guns are responsible guys who keep the guns for sport and recreation. They also think that the police are unable to stop violent crime and we need guns to protect ourselves. But I think he is wrong. I agree with Josephine Bluff who thinks that guns increase the amount of crime in the community. I also think that human life is worth more than giving shooters the right to go shooting on the weekend. And I also think that many of the guns that are kept around the house end up being used in violent domestic disputes or teenage suicides.

Passage 2: Academic English
Main premise: The government should introduce tighter gun controls

Jack Springer maintains that the government should have the right to own a gun. This position asserts that the government is infringing on our democratic rights when it restricts gun ownership. People who own guns, so the argument goes, are responsible citizens who keep the guns for sport and recreation. It is further contended that the police are unable to stop violent crime and we need guns to protect ourselves. However, as Josephine Bluff states, guns increase the amount of violent crime in the community. Moreover, human life is worth more than giving shooters the right to go shooting on the weekend. In addition, many of the guns that are kept around the house end up being used in violent domestic disputes or teenage suicides.

Adapted from: Bill Daley, 1997 http://wwww.eslplanet.com/teachertools/argueweb/inform.html

An Informal Passage to Improve

Directions: The two paragraphs below on October Sky are written by a student named Carol Jacobs. They are informal. Make them more academic.

1. Cross out the bolded words that are not needed. For example, delete words like I think and kind of.

2. Find two contractions and replace them.

3. Replace underlined words with formal academic English ones from the word bank below. Make sure to add them to the chart below the passage. See the example.

Word bank: students, hence, malignant, moreover, enormous, friends, mathematics and science, however, father, his classmates, effect, well-liked, compassionate, what, impressive, explains

Paragraph 1:
Miss Freida Riley died on Tuesday, August 5, 1969 at the age of just 31 years old. **What is up with that? In my perspective,** she wasn't just a typical teacher. She was <u>cool</u> and <u>awesome</u>. She taught <u>kids</u> <u>stuff</u> at Big Creek High School in West Virginia during the late 1950s and early 1960s. <u>But</u> **I think** she **kind of** suffered from Hodgkin's disease, a <u>bad</u>, sometimes fatal disease, characterized by the enlargement of lymph nodes. She was a <u>nice</u> teacher who offered constructive feedback and useful advice to her students. She had a positive influence on students like Homer Hickam, Jr. and his <u>pals</u>.

Paragraph 2:

The 1999 movie production of *October Sky* shows that Miss Riley leads Homer to believe that he can do <u>things guys</u> cannot. **In my view, I believe** she makes Homer realize that he is capable of leaving his small town. <u>And</u> **I think** she also makes him believe he is capable of thinking independently and doing what he is most passionate about, building rockets **and things like that**. Her opinion is that he shouldn't necessarily do what his <u>dad</u> tells him. <u>So,</u> she <u>says,</u> "Sometimes you really can't listen to what anybody else says. You just gotta listen inside. You're not supposed to end up in those mines." Miss Riley's remarks indicate her <u>gr8t</u> confidence in Homer's abilities to make the right decision concerning whether or not he ends up working in rocketry or in mining.

Informal	Academic	Informal	Academic
cool	well-liked	bad	
awesome		gr8t	
kids		nice	
stuff		pals	
But		things	
And		guys	
dad		says	

Analysis allows you to be more creative in your writing because, unlike summarizing, you are offering the readers your observations and making a strong point, or highlighting something that the reader might find striking, noteworthy, or important.

Being Aware of Your Readers and Considering Stance

By Arnie Seong and Sei Lee

This chapter will help you become more aware of your readers when you write arguments. It will also help you develop strategies for presenting your positions to readers who hold views different from your own. You'll learn how to choose your words carefully to create an objective, academic tone.

What Other People Think Is Important

Until now, most of you have thought of writing as simply assignments you must complete for courses. Your central concern has often been your grade. In college, however, you are learning how to write effectively for **all** of your courses and even for more public audiences. Whatever your major, you will often need to rely on writing in order to get other people to view you as knowledgeable or trustworthy, understand your view of something, or consider what you want them to do. You'll need to write papers to show your professors that you have a thorough understanding of assigned readings and lectures and are capable of synthesizing information and coming up with a new, interesting way of interpreting information that can potentially advance knowledge. In the future, you may end up needing to write an email asking someone to reconsider your request, write a report expressing your observations of an issue, or publish a magazine article explaining to others why global warming is a major concern.

In each of the cases above, audience considerations are critical. Every piece of argumentative writing has an audience, and the extent to which you understand your audience largely determines how effectively you are able to communicate your ideas. No matter how rationally or passionately you make your argument, it will be less effective if you do not have an accurate understanding of your readers. Rather than seeing university writing assignments as just something you need to do for a grade, think of your writing assignments as opportunities to hone* writing abilities that will help you get others to take you and your ideas seriously.

*hone

(transitive verb): to improve your ability to do something, especially something you are already good at

Considering Your Readers When Writing Arguments

Considering your readers involves understanding what your readers expect and what they think is important, and then modifying your writing style and content to address their expectations and concerns. You do this because you want your readers to be open to* understanding your perspective.

*to be open to + something

(verb phrase): to be willing to consider or accept something (for example, a new idea or perspective)

Ask yourself this question, "How can I make my argument appeal* to my audience so that they will take me seriously and be receptive to considering my views?"

*appeal

(verb): to make something interesting or attractive

When you consider how to make a claim more effective, it's better not just to think about the logic or evidence supporting your claim. To make your claim, explanation, or interpretation effective *for particular readers*, it's good to consider much more.

Writing for Specific Readers

Though taking into account your readers when you are composing arguments might seem complicated, remember that you already understand the concept of audience awareness intuitively in everyday life. If you take any time at all to choose your clothes in the morning, or if you ever speak differently when speaking with friends instead of, say, your professor, you are aware of the people around you. However, you might not have had much practice thinking about your readers when you write. The following are a few steps to help you.

STEP 1: Identify your reader.

We tend to be intuitively* aware of our audience in everyday life.

Before addressing a topic, try focusing on the types of beliefs, attitudes, and prejudices your readers might have. For example, you may be writing a paper on global warming but some of your readers might not believe that global warming is a problem, or you may be writing about the virtues of female protagonists but some of your readers may not respond positively to such protagonists.

*intuitively

having an understanding that is based on a feeling rather than on knowledge or facts

STEP 2: Identify the arguments and evidence that your readers would most likely find appealing.

You'll want to explore these types of questions:

- Is the audience likely to have existing opinions about the topic?
- How familiar are the readers with the topic, how much background information do they need to understand it, and what kinds of information do they need?
- What kinds of arguments and language are needed to prompt readers to become receptive to considering ideas?
- What do the readers care about in relation to the topic being presented?
- Which style of writing will be most appropriate?

You may want to consider the answers to these questions and even shape your message to the particular needs and purpose of your writing and your readers. For example, if your audience is likely to disagree with your point of view and, as a result, not even consider it, you may need to figure out how to overcome your readers' reactions to your view in order to persuade them to consider it. You might, for example, need to address counterarguments, make concessions (that is, admit that the readers are right about some things), give them new information, and approach the topic in a way that they are unlikely to have thought much about before. You may, on the other hand, take a different approach and instead of tailoring your writing to the readers, try to get your readers to become the types of readers you want them to be.

STEP 3: Identify the most appropriate tone and style of writing for your readers.

Your answers to the questions in Steps 1 and 2 should also give you an idea of how you should address your readers—the tone* you will use. Your tone in writing is very similar to your tone of voice in speaking. Just as you would speak more formally to your instructor than to your younger brother, you should also write more formally to your instructor.

Changing the tone of your writing for your readers is important because your tone reflects your feelings about the topic and your attitude towards your readers.

Most types of writing have a default* tone and style – a tone and style that writers use most of the time in a given kind of writing.

- Example: You can change the default settings on your computer to suit your needs.

Newspaper articles, for example, are usually formal and informative rather than casual or opinionated. *Academic arguments are typically formal, serious, and respectful rather than casual, humorous, or sarcastic.*

If you are unsure of what the appropriate tone and style for a writing assignment is, you can always ask your instructor. Another effective way, however, is to try to imagine that you are *saying it, face to face,* with your readers, and imagine how they would react. Are they more likely to be open to considering your ideas if you explain them in a specific way? What if you describe them in another way?

*tone

(singular, uncountable noun): the general feeling or attitude expressed in a piece of writing or speech

*default

(adjective): the way in which things are done unless you decide to change them

STEP 4: Keep thinking about your readers while you are writing.

This is the most important step. The whole time that you write, try to imagine that your audience is reading your paper. What would they say? What objections or counterarguments might they have? What evidence is going to be most needed? How can you make your audience care more about what you are saying? Would they be offended by the way you have written a particular sentence? Are they likely to understand what you are saying or follow your line of reasoning?

You should avoid using overly complex grammar or difficult vocabulary that your readers will not understand and that does not contribute to your writing effectiveness. Using unnecessary, complicated language usually will not make your writing sound more intelligent; instead, it could make you sound like you are hiding something or pretending to be more academic than you are. In some disciplines, like the Humanities, clearly reasoned thinking and critique as well as complexity may be valued above clarity. However, many US-American readers value clarity in writing over everything else. They want to know your main idea first. In the types of arguments you write in college, you are wise to focus on clarity throughout your writing and explain your main points clearly and logically, piece by piece.

Insider Tips

Writing to US-American Readers:

In general, US-American readers tend to expect most kinds of argumentative academic writing to be formal, direct, and to-the-point. Some cultures prefer academic writing that gradually unfolds to its main point and involves the reader in a process of discovery, but most US-American readers tend to want, from the beginning, to know the overarching* main point. They tend to want a guided tour rather than a treasure hunt.*

*overarching
(adjective): including or influencing every part (of your paper)

*treasure hunt
(countable noun): a game in which you have to find something that has been hidden by answering questions that are left in different places

Insider Tips:

In writing, just as in everyday life, you have the ability to choose how you present yourself and your argument to your readers.

When you are writing, try to remember that your job as a writer is to reach your audience. Nothing else that you do will matter if you are not reaching your readers.

Being aware of your readers requires that you think of many different kinds of things. The core questions here are these: "How can I make my readers consider my ideas seriously and be receptive to them?" This section has covered some of the most important factors that you need to consider as a writer, but your writing tasks in the future will require you to think of new ways to think about and address your readers. Part of the fun of writing is trying to reach your readers in new ways. This often leads to writing that is fun to read and write.

David Bartholomae, writes that expert writers can *"imagine how a reader will respond to a text and can transform or restructure [change] what they have to say"* (p. 8).
Source: Bartholomae, David. "Inventing the University." *Journal of Basic Writing* 5.1. (1986): 4-23.

Strengthening Your Arguments: Stance* in Argumentative Writing

In many of your courses, you'll take positions in relation to what you are writing about. That means that you'll present your positions to readers who hold different points of view on the topic of your writing. You'll need to show competence and express views in a way that your readers will be open to considering and that they find logical and convincing. You'll do this with language, among other things.

Using Diction Effectively

You will need to carefully consider diction. Diction refers to words that authors choose to use in their writing in order to create a certain "feeling" or "atmosphere." For example, a story about a teen that grew up in the inner city might include profane and vulgar language. This type of diction might be necessary in order for you to convey a sense of realism for your readers. On the other hand, if you want to produce a very different atmosphere for the same story, you may use formal language instead of profanity or vulgarity. This would give the same story a different perspective. In the same way, you may use humorous words in order to create a light and playful "feeling" or "atmosphere." Good use of diction can make your writing very persuasive. It is a subtle way for you to make readers see things from your perspective. When analyzing texts, be mindful of your use of diction to persuade readers and careful of your own use of words.

Word Choice: What is it and Why is it Important?

In academic writing, your choice of words is extremely important, perhaps more so than in other types of writing. However, you, like many of your classmates, may have challenges with word choice. The following are two common, interrelated challenges facing students.

Limited Exposure to the Usage of Vocabulary

Students often have a wide range of vocabulary words they know the definitions of. However, they have seldom used or encountered the words in everyday speaking or writing. This makes it difficult for them to know how to use the words in their writing.

Overuse of Inappropriate Synonyms

Students often try to improve their word choice by using a synonym, sometimes by going to a thesaurus. This approach can have limitations because it overlooks the fact that words are highly contextualized. Two words can share a very similar meaning but may not necessarily be interchangeable.

So, why does word choice even matter? Using the right words can help you establish credibility, show others your knowledge, and help you build a strong connection with your readers. Using the wrong words can make your sentences sound awkward and unnatural. Although it is not easy to always know what is the "best" word for a particular sentence, this section will help you develop strategies to help improve your word choice.

Use of Specific Words

Your instructor may tell you that your words are too vague in your writing. What this usually means is that your choice of words is too broad and generic and does not really help your readers understand what you are trying to say. The following examples show how a sentence with vague words can be improved by using more specific, illustrative words.

Sentence with vague words

- Nicole knew she should stop *being so bad* at managing her money.

Sentence with more specific words

- Nicole knew she should be *more cautious with her spending*, but she could not resist splurging on buying new clothes every time she received a paycheck.

Sentence with even more specific words

- Nicole knew she should be more frugal with her finances, but she *could not refrain from frequently making spontaneous purchases* when it came to clothes.

Notice that in the first sentence it is unclear what it is that makes Nicole "bad at managing her money." Further, the word "bad" can be replaced with a more specific and sophisticated word that is appropriate for college-level writing.

The second sentence is an improvement from the first one because it identifies what it is that makes Nicole "bad" at managing her money. However, the third sentence is even better. First, instead of using the word "splurging," which is somewhat too casual, it uses the expression "frequently making spontaneous purchases." Also, instead of the word "cautious," which is slightly open-ended, "frugal" specifically refers to being cautious with one's money.

Minjie Zeng, a former writing student, advises:

It was very difficult for me when I want to imply and present my own ideas in my writing since I did not have a vast vocabulary in my mind. Before, I often used "small," "big" or "bad" to describe everything in my writing; however, those words cannot fully represent my ideas, emotions and attitude. Now, I try to use more specific words such as "enormous" or "gigantic" instead of "big." In this way, I am able to create a more specific image in my writing, but also deliver my perspective to the audience.

 Every piece of argumentative writing has an audience, and how well you understand your audience determines how effectively you are able to communicate your ideas. No matter how rationally or passionately you make your argument, it will be less effective if you do not have an accurate understanding of your readers.

Reflective Writing

CHAPTER FIVE

What is Reflective Writing?

Reflective writing asks you to think about and assess something you have done or learned. Your writing has a clear line of thought, and generally uses observations or examples as evidence to back up your ideas. The purpose of reflective writing is to help you think deeply about your experiences and learn from them.

Writing your thoughts down enables you to think about them and make connections between what you are thinking, what you are being taught, and what you are going to do with what you have learned. If you don't reflect on an experience, you may forget about it and not learn from it. Your feelings and thoughts that come from reflecting on experiences can lead to powerful generalizations that can help you tackle new situations.

Reflective writing has the potential of building: 1) your **metalinguistic** abilities that enable you to think about language and analyze its use, and 2) your **metacognitive** abilities that enable you to analyze and control the cognitive or mental processes involved in learning. Your metalinguistic abilities enable you to talk about language. They allow you to describe the best language forms to use in specific situations, for instance, to get someone to do something for you or to engage in a conversation. Without these abilities, you cannot identify the language errors in your sentences or consciously apply grammar rules to improve your writing. You could still use language, but you would not be aware of how you are using it or be able to analyze its use. Your metacognitive abilities allow you to analyze the ways you learn and process information and your own learning processes. Without these abilities, you would not be aware of the specific strategies and behaviors that help you learn productively. You would not be able to analyze those that you can use to support positions thoughtfully and purposefully, meeting particular situational demands.

meta-

The Greek prefix **meta** *refers to a discipline or subject at an abstract level and describes or shows an awareness of the activity that takes place or is discussed in that discipline or subject.*

In writing courses, you'll be developing both your metalinguistic abilities and your metacognitive abilities. You'll write about your experiences in completing a variety of writing assignments, interpreting and evaluating course readings, and developing language. Your instructors will assign reflective writing to help you explore your own learning, discover new ideas, and set learning goals for yourself. They'll also assign it to help them assess where you are in your learning so that they can help you, for example, by providing you with additional resources or by giving you specific types of instruction. Throughout the course you'll learn techniques for writing reflective pieces mainly for yourself but also for your instructors and classmates.

Your instructors may ask you to think about your writing, reading, and language learning processes in general or in a particular context. You may be asked to think about your intentions regarding rhetorical* elements such as audience and purpose to help you make specific goals for your writing. You may be asked to describe your decisions regarding the use of language features such as word choice, pronoun reference, and verb tense. You may be asked to explain your invention, drafting, revision, or editing processes, as well as your thought processes in developing ideas. You may also be asked to discuss what you might want to do with what you have learned from a reading or writing assignment in future communicative situations.

*rhetorical

refers to "a comprehensive art, or set of techniques, for effective communication"

Romney, Abraham and Daniel Gross. "Why Rhetoric?" In The Anteater's Guide to Writing and Rhetoric (UCI Composition Program). Plymouth, Michigan: Hayden McNeil, 2014. Print. 1-13.

You might reflect for many reasons in many ways, for example, in a blog, a short in-class writing assignment, a personal log, a letter, or a journal.

Writing to Learn and Discover: Journal Writing—Mini Reflections

In class, you write a weekly journal entry about your own learning behaviors and processes. In your journal, you need not be concerned about grammatical correctness or writing style. Seize the opportunity to play with language. You can use language to learn, develop your thinking, and explore your perception of reality, writing primarily for yourself. You do not risk anything when you do not follow conventional rules of grammar. You may share your reflections with your instructor and classmates, but only to explore your ideas. Your instructor will not be judging your writing style or language use. The writing tasks that you are given are designed to enable you to discover connections and patterns, raise questions, and address concerns. You need not revise nor edit your journal entries, though you may if you like.

You'll want to work on your journals on a regular basis throughout the course and develop a habit of writing down your insights. Reflecting on your writing, reading, and general language development, even in short mini self-reflections, will help you become aware of your learning strategies, routines, and behaviors. Your instructors may not remind you to keep up your journals. The responsibility for completing them without reminders is yours. Your journals are assigned the first day of class and are due at the end of the course.

Your journal will consist of the following:

1. Ten or more dated entries*

2. Additional commentary*

Entries: In many classes you will be required to write one entry each week. Entries are often one to two paragraphs in length, but you can write longer ones if you like. You may address the prompts below, use your instructor's assigned prompts, or come up with prompts of your own. Don't forget to date each entry.

Commentary: Make a section or sections in your journal for comments. Whenever you have insights about your language development, language use, writing, or readings, jot them down in your journals. The commentary sections of your journals can include lists, sentences—complete or incomplete, and even diagrams or pictures.

*entry

(countable noun): a piece of writing in a diary

*commentary

(uncountable noun) writing that explains something

Suggestions:

Add screenshots of pieces of your writing, the reading, your notes, or the websites you go to for additional language practice or instruction and then incorporate and discuss them in your journals.

Add photos of something related to one of your reflections and incorporate and discuss them in your journals. You might take a picture of your favorite pen, or a book that has been instrumental in your language learning.

When writing reflective pieces, you'll use the first person "I," because you want to refer to your mental state to discuss what you believe, know or are thinking about. Although instructors may discourage you from using expressions such as *In my opinion* in specific types of academic writing, you should feel free to use such expressions in your journal writing. Here are a few: *In my view, From my perspective, It seems to me that…, I would argue that…, I do not believe that/agree that…, I am convinced/unconvinced that…*

Prompts for Journal Writing

Reflections on Writing

1. Describe the purpose(s) of your writing and the effect(s) you want it to have on your readers. Explain who you think the readers are.

2. Describe your process of working on a particular writing assignment. What kind of planning did you do? What steps did you go through, what changes did you make along the way, what decisions did you face, and how did you make the decisions?

3. How did comments from your peers and the instructor help you? How did any class activities related to the assignment help you?

4. What have you learned about organizing a paragraph? What strategies do you use to avoid digressions?

5. What have you learned about writing thesis statements? What do you do to make sure that your evidence supports your thesis statements?

6. Explain how you have learned to make your writing cohere (stick together) in subtle (not easily seen) ways, without depending on transition words like *furthermore* and *also*.

7. What has helped you become more skillful at identifying evidence for claims and incorporating the evidence effectively?

8. What did you find easy or difficult about a particular writing assignment? Why did you find the assignment easy or difficult? Explain your process of writing the assignment. What pre-writing tasks did you do and how did they help you?

9. Explain how you respond to criticism of your writing from your instructor, Writing Center peer tutors and writing specialists, classmates, and others. Describe specific feedback on your drafts and your reaction to this feedback.

10. Analyze the types of feedback you give your classmates on their writing. How much time does it take you to provide fair, substantive feedback that helps your classmates improve their writing? What specific kinds of feedback do you think are the most helpful to classmates? Why?

11. Explain the types of revisions you make that help you improve your writing. Do you reorganize your writing, move sections, delete sections, or rewrite entire sections? Do you return to your reading to search for additional evidence to support your main points? Do you end up throwing away drafts and starting from scratch?

12. What improvements do you want to make to your writing or the way you approach writing assignments now? Why?

13. Analyze how you use what you are taught in your writing courses.

14. What information or kinds of help do you need to strengthen your writing? How can you obtain this information or help?

15. What are you going to do next to strengthen your ability to write a particular genre (type of writing)?

Reflections on Nonfiction Reading

1. Analyze how you prepared to do your reading. For instance, did you look for a quiet place where you could concentrate, try to obtain background information about the reading, prepare to annotate your reading, set reading goals, or survey the text before reading it (e.g., checking the publication date, author, title and table of contents, section parts, and publisher's blurb if available)?

2. Explain how you check to make sure you have understood what you have read. Do you use summarizing techniques, online dictionaries, classroom discussions or something else?

3. Describe and analyze what you do to read text critically. Explain your note-taking techniques and the types of questions you ask yourself when reading.

4. What does the reading make you think about? Does it help you understand some aspect of your own life or the life of someone whom you know well?

5. What did you find interesting about the author's ideas? Did you come across any **"aha"** moments while you were reading? An "aha" moment is a moment when you learn something insightful or new and interesting. What are the aha moments in the reading and why are they important to you?

6. Does the author have a **hidden agenda** or a secret purpose that she does not tell her readers about and that she is trying to advance? Can you **deconstruct** (take apart) any of the author's ideas to criticize them? Do any of the author's ideas need to be qualified or elaborated on to make better sense or provide a more credible view?

7. What do you think is effective and ineffective about the language that the author uses to reveal her attitude? Does the author appear informal, friendly, scholarly, condescending, or emotional? Does the author seem to know what she is talking about?

8. Analyze the way the author chooses to organize the text to unpack her ideas. Do you think some parts of the text could be better organized in a way that is easier for you to understand or that makes the text more interesting?

9. How does the author use language? For example, how does the

author string sentences together? Does the author mostly use short sentences or long ones? What about sentence fragments? Can you identify places where the author uses very long, rambling sentences to express complicated ideas or uses very short sentences or fragments to catch the reader's attention or appear friendly? Are parallel structures used to express methodological thinking? What about word choice? Does the author use an abundance of very short words or an abundance of multisyllabic words or does the author switch between the use of basic everyday words and academic words? Why?

10. Analyze how the writer uses cohesive devices to increase the cohesion of her writing. How effective is the writer in making her text cohere?

11. Describe and analyze the author's presentation of claims and use of evidentiary support.

12. Analyze the ways the author helps the reader understand key ideas and remember them. Does she use graphics, pictures, repetition, synonyms, emotional or memorable language, interesting stories, startling statistics, or something else?

13. What strategies have you been using to improve your reading comprehension? What strategies might help you improve more in the future?

14. When approaching a text that is written in English for an American audience, what is a bigger obstacle to your understanding of that text: your not understanding English or your not understanding cultural concerns that are relevant to the interpretation of the text? Are language and cultural concerns ever related? How do you usually try to address linguistic and cultural concerns that affect your interpretation of your reading?

Prompts for the End of the Course

1. Think back about where you were at the beginning of the course. Assess your strategies for understanding challenging readings, and completing reading assignments. Assess how your competence as a reader has **evolved** and changed.

*to evolve

(intransitive and transitive verb): to develop and change gradually over time

2. Describe how you have been able to use the reading strategies that you have learned in this course in other courses. Give specific examples. In what ways did this course help you complete reading assignments for your other courses?

3. What strategies helped you?

4. What strategies for improving your knowledge of English

that you learned in this course have helped you in your other courses? Have you learned strategies for note-taking or vocabulary learning that you use in other courses?

5. Analyze the extent to which you have learned to vary your approach to reading different types of texts depending on situational demands.

6. Were you able to use what you have learned in this course to complete challenging reading assignments for your other courses? Which strategies, activities, or information helped you?

7. Analyze what you plan to do in the next few months to build on what you have learned about critical reading.

8. What types of reading do you hope to do in the next few years? What will you need to learn or do to ensure you are able to do that reading?

9. If this course **piqued*** your interest in reading critically, what do you hope to read in the next few months and what strategies will you use to read closely, analyzing and evaluating the authors' ideas?

*to pique your interest/curiosity
(verb phrase): to make you feel interested in something

Reflections on Language Learning

1. What main goals do you have for improving your English and what steps do you want to take to reach these goals? Analyze how these goals will help you become a better writer.

2. Explain the specific features of English that are challenging for you to learn. Why do you need to learn them, and what specific actions you can take to learn them?

3. How might you improve your ability to use English to complete specific writing assignments? Read particular academic texts?

4. Explain the importance of hedges (like *perhaps, maybe, should,* and *somewhat*) in avoiding over-generalizations. When do you use hedges in your written and/or spoken communication? What challenges have you had in learning them?

5. Analyze the words and grammatical structures that you use in your speech and in your writing. Explain how they differ.

6. Analyze the passive structures that are used in one or more of your textbooks for other courses. Why are passive structures used? What purposes do they serve? Do you think they are used effectively or do you think the authors should have used active constructions, e.g., to avoid unnecessary words or to make their writing seem more engaging?

7. What have you learned about the different linguistic features of

different types of writing (like summary writing and arguments)? In what ways, specifically, are they similar or different?

8. Explain and demonstrate why and how you shift verb tense when writing reflective pieces.

9. How did you learn the vocabulary you needed to complete a specific writing assignment? Evaluate the techniques or strategies that you used.

10. What did you do that helped you the most today to learn English?

11. What do you do to help yourself understand English vocabulary when you do not understand it? Analyze several techniques or strategies you use in different contexts.

12. What aspects of English do you think you need more help in developing? Be as specific as possible. Consider vocabulary, grammar, discourse and rhetorical aspects of language use. Consider oral and written communication as well as digital literacy—the knowledge, skills, and behaviors you need in order to use a wide array of electronic devices to communicate effectively.

13. What have you learned about using language in a variety of genres (types of written or spoken communication like arguments, narratives, summaries, and email messages)? Have you become more skillful in using language in diverse genres? Which genres do you consider the most challenging and why?

14. What have you done to improve your vocabulary outside of class? Analyze the strategies you use to learn and use new words.

15. Have you experienced moments when your grammar improved suddenly? If so, why and how did this happen?

16. Have you experienced moments when your ability to speak English improved suddenly? If so, why and how did this happen?

17. What actions have you taken to improve your English language development? What actions might help you improve more in the future?

18. Are there any situations related to your using English that were difficult or seemingly impossible for you in the past, but now are not? Give a specific example of a situation. Explain why it was so hard for you to navigate that situation in the past and what you have learned to help you communicate well in the situation now.

19. Are there ever times when it is difficult for you to explain your experiences to friends or relatives at home who may or who may not speak English? If so, analyze the factors that contribute to your communication difficulties. Are the difficulties related to cultural or linguistic issues, or something else?

20. Are there any situations – public or private – in which you are not comfortable expressing yourself in English, even when you have the competence to use it well? What are those situations? Would you feel more comfortable using a different language in those situations? Why?

21. In this global world, in which more and more people are mixing or blending languages or switching between languages—using more than one language when communicating, are you able to use two or more languages when communicating with friends? If you do, how effective do you think it is to do this? Have you ever tried to mix two languages in your writing? What was the result?

22. How important do you think it is to develop strong language resources in more than one language? What do you see as the benefits of being able to communicate your ideas in multiple languages?

Prompts for the End of the Course

1. Think back about where you were at the beginning of the course. Assess your strategies learning language. Assess how your language development and ability to communicate in English have changed. What specific strategies have you used to improve your language development or ability to communicate?

2. How have you been able to use particular **"language learning strategies"** in other courses? Give specific examples. Did this course help you develop these strategies? What strategies helped you, for instance, communicate with your professors via email or in office hours, understand lectures, or develop discipline-specific vocabulary?

3. Have you been able to use the words, grammatical features, or discourse features that you learned in this course in your other courses? Which courses? If possible, give specific examples.

4. Analyze the extent to which you have you learned to vary your use of English depending on situational demands.

5. Were you able to use what you have learned in this course to communicate orally with professors, classmates, and others? Which strategies, activities, or information helped you?

6. Analyze what you plan to do in the next few months to improve your knowledge of English, building on what you have learned in this course.

Remember:

You can use your responses to the prompts listed at left when writing your instructor about your improvement in English.

71

7. For what purposes do you hope to use English in the next few years? What will you need to learn and what steps will you need to take to ensure your success?

Writing Assignments, Portfolio Cover Letters and Progress Letters that Incorporate Reflective Writing

Insider Tip

Describing your impressions of various aspects of your writing, reading, and language development as well as your personal investment in this development will prompt you to become a more reflective learner.

Remember:

Each discipline has different conventions and styles for reflective writing.

Your instructor may ask you to write a portfolio cover letter or a Progress Letter that incorporates reflective writing. These pieces of writing each involve multiple drafts, and you'll need to revise and edit them carefully. Your instructors will want you to write in an appropriate style, neither overly academic and distant nor overly informal and friendly. Talk to your instructor if you have questions regarding the level of formality you should use. Your instructor will expect to see thoughtfully analyzed ideas and detailed descriptions of examples and observations that reflect on your development as a writer, reader, and language learner. They'll expect you to explain your experiences using language to communicate and to describe the connections between these experiences and your learning. It's important to analyze your experiences and not just describe them. You'll also want to focus on those that have the most impact on your learning.

Composing Reflective Pieces for Major Papers and Portfolio Cover Letters

Linguistic and Rhetorical Considerations

When writing your journal entries, you focus on ideas and may not make time to revise your reflections. However, when incorporating reflective writing into a major paper assigment, progress letter, or porfolio cover letter, you write multiple drafts and dedicate time to revising, editing and polishing your writing. Being aware of the language and rhetorical features that are generally used in reflective writing for more public and academic audiences can be helpful. Keep in mind that these features may vary across disciplines.

Vocabulary

When writing reflective pieces for academic assignments, it is common to use the first person "*I.*"

To make concessions, writers often use these words or expressions: *Of course..., some could/might argue..., It is sometimes argued..., Admittedly, ..., and While....*

To emphasize their points, they may use words like *indeed, certainly, truly* and *definitely* that convey certainty. However, most instructors prefer that students use such words sparingly.

Writers use **action verbs**, sometimes called **strong verbs**, to help readers to visualize actions and convey **tone**, the general feeling or attitude expressed in a piece of writing or speech. Following are some commonly occurring action verbs you might use when composing reflective pieces that describe language, reading, and writing development. Recall that when writing your portfolio cover letter, you will want to convey an objective, analytical tone.

Insider Tip

When writing a progress letter or Porfolio cover letter, you substantiate* your improvement as a writer and language user and provide an objective analysis of your writing and language development. You can refer to your reflective journals for evidence that you have developed your writing and language use and that you have gained an array of effective strategies for communicating in writing. Paraphrasing or quoting relevant pieces of your writing from your journal entries can provide a useful means of documenting your learning.

*substantiate

(verb): prove the truthfulness of something

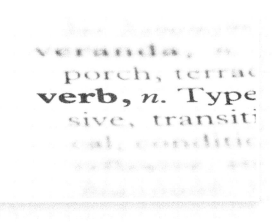

I staggered to the final exam with my friend. We *approached* the building slowly, *budgeting our time* carefully and *engaging* in a discussion of the strategies we would use to succeed.

Action Verbs

abandon	hypothesize	persevere	scatter
accelerate	identify	persuade	schedule
accuse	ignore	plan	scold
achieve	illustrate	plod	score
acquire	imitate	plunge	search
adapt	implement	polish	seize
address	improve	predict	select
adjust	improvise	prepare	shape
advance	increase	print	shield
advise	influence	process	shorten
allocate	inform	produce	shun
analyze	inspire	promote	sidestep
answer	interpret	prompt	snicker
anticipate	interview	proofread	solve
apprehend	invent	propel	spell
approach	investigate	protect	stack
appropriate	isolate	provide	stagger
assemble	jeer	provoke	start
assess	judge	pursue	study
attain	learn	push	stumble
audio-record	lecture	question	search
block	maintain	quit	strategize
budget time	manage	race	submit
chart	manipulate	raise	support
classify	mentor	realize	switch
communicate	mimic	receive	synthesize
compile	mingle	recommend	systematize
complete	mock	record	tackle
compose	model	recoup	target
construct	monitor	recruit	tease
consult	motivate	reduce	throw
control	mumble	regain	track
coordinate	needle	relax	transfer
cram	negotiate	represent	translate
create	observe	research	tutor
cripple	obtain	resist	undermine
deal	occupy	resolve	understand
decide	operate	respond	undertake
deduct	order	restore	undo
define	organize	retrieve	unify
design	oversee	reveal	utilize
determine	panic	review	withdraw
develop	paralyze	rip	
devise	perceive	risk	
diagnose	perform	rush	

In reflective writing, it is also common to replace general, commonly occurring adjectives with more specific ones to convey tone. You might use **specific adjectives**, like the ones below in Table 5.1 when composing reflective pieces for major papers and portfolio cover letters or progress letters.

Table 5.1: Specific Adjectives

General, Commonly Used Adjectives	Specific Adjectives
good	helpful, patient, friendly, knowledgable
bad	boring, rude, unfriendly, uninformed
beautiful	stunning
bad	deplorable
happy	thrilled
angry	furious
tired	exhausted
funny	hilarious
big	enormous

You will want to replace vague, commonly used nouns with specific nouns. As the previous discussion suggests, when analyzing emotions, you will probably want to avoid discussing simple emotions—like happiness, sadness, fear, and anger and instead discuss more complex ones—like euphoria, grief, embarrassment, and rage. (See Table 5.2)

Table 5.2: Specific Nouns

Vague, Commonly Used Nouns	Specific Nouns
thing	idea, gift, suitcase
person	young woman, a Sudanese government official, a local resident
people	Biology majors, the local business community, pedestrians.

Grammar

Unless they have an excellent reason for using passive constructions, writers often avoid using them in reflective writing. (A passive construction occurs when you make the object of an action into the subject of the sentence.) Instead of using passive constructions, writers generally use **action verbs** like those above to energize their writing. For example, rather than writing, *Each mistake that I made was corrected patiently by my tutor,* they would write, *My tutor patiently corrected each mistake I made.* Instead of stating, *I was tempted by my friends to hang out with them.*—a passive construction, they would state, *My friends tempted me to hang out with them.*—an active construction. Note how active structures make writing less wordy, as they allow writers to avoid using **be** verbs (*is, are, was, were, be, being, and been*).

Passive vs active writing

Language Challenges of Reflective Writing

Reflective writing can present challenges. You may not expect to have to spend much time revising your reflective pieces, but you'll find that revising them can very helpful.

One of your primary challenges concerns the thesis statement. Much of the writing you do in college combine elements of argumentation, reflective writing, and other types of writing. In essence, they are blended genres that combine elements or argumentation, reflective writing and other types of writing. When composing, you focus on the theme—a message or a key idea that you want to convey to your readers. The theme is not the topic. To identify a theme, it is sometimes helpful to generate a list of the topics you will cover in your reflective piece. The list of topics often includes abstract nouns – like diligence, courage, perseverance, hope, identity, and so forth. Think of the topic as the **What?** of your writing, and the theme as the **So What?** Your theme statement is the same as a thesis statement. It states your main message about your experiences and their relationship to your reading, writing, and/or language development. The following are some examples of thesis statements:

Examples of Thesis Statements

In my opinion, taking responsibility for language learning is the most important thing I did to improve my English since it determined the amount of time I spent studying English and created opportunities for me to practice it.

Although friendship can benefit English language development—increasing my exposure to English and opportunities to use it, it can also prevent it because the particular friends I made this last course distracted me from studying English, limited my experiences using English, coerced me into ditching classes, and made fun of me when I made mistakes using English.

You may also grapple with making your paragraphs unified. You'll want to make sure that you exclude irrelevant information and sentences that do not support your topic sentences.

Part of your difficulties making your paragraphs cohere may come from your need to learn transition words (also called time markers) like *first, next,* and *after that)* and adverbial time clauses (like *My roommate always disturbed me when I was writing my papers.)* that create complex relationships between events and indicate when events take place. You'll want to use transition words appropriately and have a good reason for using them. Most instructors will tell you **not** to rely on transition words like *furthermore* and *also* to convey cohesion, but instead use a variety of cohesive devices.

Incorporating dialogue can make your writing lively, but doing so may be challenging if you are still learning to punctuate dialogue and incorporate it into your writing as a device to support ideas and add key information. Consulting a grammar reference book or the online materials that your instructor provides you can be helpful.

The *enormous* rock climbing challenge both *thrilled* and *exhausted* undergraduate students.

You'll also want to pay attention to verb tense. When reflecting on events that occurred in the beginning of the course, you'll probably need to shift from the present tense to the past. For instance, you might state:

> *"Looking back to my first experiences at college, I **now realize** that I **did** not force myself to ask others for help with my writing. I spent too much time studying in my dorm room, so I did not practice using English. Now I've learned to reach out for help and spend time making friends and interacting with them in English."*

When reflecting on whether a strategy that you used in the past will benefit you in the future, you'll need to shift tenses. *"Next course, I'd like to be able to edit my writing by myself. I **will use** some of the strategies my instructor **taught** me to rewrite sentences that contain run-on sentence errors."*

When reflecting on how strategies and behaviors have changed over time, you may need to use the present perfect. You might write: *"I **have** already **applied** what I have learned about hedges to avoid making over-generalizations in my writing."*

John Wang, a former writer student, states:

"Reflective writing helped me learn to express my own opinions of my writing. Saying what I believe used to be hard for me. What helped me the most was trying to write a paragraph about my language development each day."

> 66 Reflection helps you to develop your intentions (purpose), figure out your relation to your audience, uncover possible problems with your individual writing processes, set goals for revision, make decisions about language and style, and the list goes on. In a nutshell, it helps you develop more insight into and control over composing and revising processes. And according to scholars such as Chris M. Anson, developing this control is a feature that distinguishes stronger from weaker writers and active from passive learners. 99

Source: Giles, Sandra. "Reflective Writing and the Revision Process: What Were You Thinking?" *Writing Spaces: Readings on Writing.* Volume 1. Eds. Charles Lowe and Pavel Zemliansky. Parlor Press, 2010. 193. http://www.parlorpress.com/pdf/giles--reflective-writing-and-the-revision-process.pdf

Suggestions of Stages to Encourage Deeper Reflection

- **Description**
  What happened? What are you going to reflect on? Don't make judgments yet or try to draw conclusions.

- **Feelings**
  What were your reactions and feelings?

- **Evaluation**
  What was good or bad about the experience? Make value judgments.

- **Analysis**
  What sense can you make of the situation? What was really going on?

- **Conclusions (general)**
  What can be concluded, in a general sense, from these experiences and the analyses that you have undertaken?

- **Conclusions (specific)**
  What can be concluded about your own specific, unique personal situation or ways of learning?

- **Personal action plans**
  What are you going to do differently in this type of situation next time? What steps are you going to take on the basis of what you have learned?

Source: Adapted from Gibbs, Graham. *Learning By Doing: a Guide to Teaching and Learning Methods*. Oxfrod: Further Education Unit, Oxford Polytechnic, 1988.

Reflecting on Your Portfolio Cover Letter or a Major Paper Assignment Calling on You to Incorporate Reflective Writing

After you have completed writing your portfolio cover letter or a major paper assignment that requires reflection, think about the characteristics of reflective writing:

- **Audience and Purpose**
  Who is your reflective writing for and what is its purpose in your writing? Is it for you, your classmates, your instructor, or someone else? What are some of the conventions you followed when writing for this audience? Did you use your reflections to support your claims?

- **Language**
  What grammatical structures and language features did you frequently use when writing this type of genre? Did you use the present tense or the past? Did you use personal pronouns?

- **Tone**
  What is the tone of your reflective writing piece? (Recall that tone refers to the general feeling or attitude expressed in your writing.) Is your tone academic or informal? Serious or funny? Formal or informal? What language did you use to communicate this tone to your readers? Complex sentences? Academic words? Did you use specific verbs and adjectives or general ones?

> 66 *Writing your thoughts down enables you to think about them and make connections between what you are thinking, what you are being taught, and what you are going to do with what you have learned.* 99

Reading Comprehension Questions

1. Is metalinguistic awareness more important than cognitive awareness? Why?

2. Is reflecting on your writing development necessary or helpful in improving your writing? Why?

3. What are the characteristics of a diary or journal entry?

4. Why do you think it is appropriate to use "I" in most kinds of reflective writing?

5. How can your reflections show your instructor that your competence as a writer has evolved over time?

6. When authors write books, they often have a secret agenda. What is a secret agenda and why would authors want to advance such an agenda?

7. What is a good way to deconstruct an author's ideas to criticize them?

8. How can you use the prompts when writing to your instructor about your progress learning English or improving your writing?

9. What are action verbs and why do writers use them?

10. Why do writers try to replace vague nouns like "thing" with more specific nouns?

> If you don't reflect on an experience, you may forget about it and not learn from it. Your feelings and thoughts that come from reflecting on experiences can lead to powerful generalizations that can help you tackle new situations.

Business Letters, Cover Letters, and Resumes

By Benjamin Duncan

College students need to know how to write professional, polished business letters, resume cover letters, and resumes. Students' ability to express themselves clearly and effectively in writing significantly affects their employment and promotions. Those who are unable to write effective business letters, cover letters, and resumes may make a poor impression on others that prevents their advancement. They may not be seriously considered for the jobs they want. On the other hand, thoughtfully constructed business letters, cover letters, and resume help students gain the serious consideration that they deserve.

Design and format are critically important in making good first impressions. Effective print business letters generally use readable typeface and fonts. Formal stationary is often used with conservative colors. You will want to use formal language and organization. The language should be concise. In other words, you will need to get to the point quickly. Try to avoid informal expressions and inappropriate language, such as contractions and abbreviations, when you are writing a business letter.

Recognizing the language expectations of the business letters and the people you send them to is fundamental to your success in writing your letter.

Table 6.1 on page 84 provides a partial list of some of the differences between formal, academic and informal English. When you write your business letter, you will want to include only formal, academic language.

Table 6.1: Informal and Formal English

Informal	Formal (Academic)
First Names / Informal Greetings Hey Peter, What's up Jenny?, Yo Dave!	**Titles and Formal Greetings** Dear Ladies and Gentlemen:, Dear Prof. Jennifer Hartings, Dear Mr. David Black, CEO of SEO Corp
Contractions can't, she'd, I've, you're	**Complete Forms** can not, she would, I have, you are
Abbreviations Thanks, exam, VP, asap	**Complete Forms** Thank you very much, examination, vice president, as soon as possible
Commands Send the report today!	**Polite Requests** Would you mind sending the report when you have the time, please?
Overuse of Pronouns without Referents She and he went there to see it, you know?	**Pronouns Referents** She and he, Melissa and Dan, went there, the movie theater, to see it, The Killer Bees, you (you) know?
Simple Sentences I like flowers.	**Longer Sentences** When the warm spring weather approaches, Dave enjoys a picnic in the park; I, however, merely enjoy the beauty of budding flowers.
Basic Vocabulary good, bad, make, get	**Advanced Vocabulary** beneficial, detrimental, construct, acquire
Idioms chicken, beat around the bush, cat got your tongue	**Exact Speech** easily intimidated, indirect speech, reserved
Slang Chilling, I'm beat, hanging out, killing me, stuffed	**Standard Vocabulary** Relaxing, I'm tired, chatting with friends, causing me severe frustration, full from eating
Phrasal Verbs put up with, take out, do away with	**Singular Verbs** tolerate, remove, replace
Lack of Consideration for Reader I have a big problem that you need to fix immediately! It's very serious!	**Full Consideration for Reader** There is a small difficulty that requires your consideration if and when you have the time. It's a tiny concern, but of great importance to me.

The most common structure of business letters is that using a blocked format, with the content of the letter on the left and no indentation* of paragraphs and with one inch margins all around. You will need to include your own address, then skip a line, and then provide the date. After that, you will skip one more line to give the address of the person to whom you are addressing. When you use letterhead that provides your address, you do not need to give your address again.

You will skip another line before the salutation (an expression of greeting like Dear Mr. Jones), which should be followed by a colon (:). Then, you will write the body of your letter, with no indentation at the beginnings of paragraphs. You will skip lines between paragraphs.

After writing the body of the letter, you will add the closing, followed by a comma. You will leave three blank lines before typing your name and title (if applicable), all to the left. Finally, you will sign the letter in the blank space above your typed name.

*indentation

(count noun) A space left between the left-hand margin of a line of type or handwriting and the beginning of a sentence or quotation. The beginnings of paragraphs in college essays are usually indented.

Business Letter in Block Format

Study the organization of this business letter in block format.

Yolanda Jenkins
Some Corporation • 768 North Alvarado St. • Memphis, TN 35000

Reservations Manager
Falsehood Hotel
99 Main Street
Los Angeles, CA 90000

November 2, 2016

Dear Reservations Manager:

I am writing this letter to confirm a reservation that was made two weeks previously under the name Yolanda Jenkins. The reservation is for three nights, November 24-26 of this year and is for two persons: Ms. Jennifer Royals and me.

I would like to confirm an airport pickup and a room with air-conditioning and private bathroom. We will be attending the Computer Conference that is being held in Hollywood that week.

If you do not mind, would it be possible to arrange a room at the back of the hotel? I am afraid that the room I was given last year sat atop the lobby and was quite noisy during the early morning hours.

Thank you for sending me the maps and directions to your facilities, which I received this morning. They look most convenient and well-organized. Unfortunately, I will not be arriving until after 10 p.m. the night of November 24, so I am taking the time now to confirm these arrangements. If any difficulties arise, please contact me at 019-555-5555.

I look forward to meeting you in person in the upcoming week.

Sincerely,

Yolanda Jenkins
Yolanda Jenkins

Another common structure of a business letter is that using indented paragraphs. You can more information about how to write a formal business letter and sample business letters in both block and indented formats at this website: http://www.writing.wisc.edu/Handbook/BusinessLetter.html

Insider Tip

Highlight your skills in the cover letter. Since first impressions count, make an impressive first impression by writing a professional letter. This letter is an opportunity for you to highlight your accomplishments and your ability to communicate well.

Insider Tip

Cover letters, which can also be sent electronically, should be very readable. Four or five short paragraphs usually works well. If you use letterhead for your cover letter, it should also be used for your resume. In general, you'll want to use the same paper and font in your resume that you use in your resume cover letter.

Cover Letters

When you apply for almost any position, you will need to write a cover letter. Resumes generally include a cover letter in which you ask to apply for the position. A cover letter briefly introduces you and your qualifications to a future employer and is typically attached to the first page of your resume.

The content, format, and tone of application letters will need to be modified according to the position, the person reading your letter, and your own personality. This means you will want to ask those who have had experience in your field to provide you with feedback on your letter and to suggest revisions. If you have a career center on your campus, that office can provide valuable guidance.

The suggestions below apply to writing most cover letters. Large computer analyses of cover letters have helped us to describe several elements shared by successful job applicants. The following example shows these elements.

Name

Address • Telephone Number • Email Address

Date

Dear (Correspondent's Full Name Preferred):

1) A brief self-introduction
   a) Work/study/life experiences are highlighted as they relate to the position for which you are applying
   b) Desired job title is clearly stated alongside one or two key reasons for the desired outcome
2) A brief discussion of your background
   a) Current job/study position is stated or expected end of current employment/graduation date is explained
   b) Summary of degrees, certifications, honors, awards, experiences that differentiate the candidate from other applicants is given
3) An expression of confidence in your abilities to fill the position
   A statement indicating that you look forward to desired next steps (such as a: follow-up interview, telephone call, or online meeting) is given

Sincerely,

(Your Signature – 4 lines)

Your Name Printed

Enclosure (Your resume is included.)

As you read the model, look for the key components and underline any language that effectively "sells" the candidate and her qualifications to the perspective employer.

Mimi Marshall

55 Some Dr. • City, State, Country, Zip code • (555) 555-5555 • mimi@some.com

July 6, 2016

Peter Rogers
Project Manager
Building Block Co.
3234 Main Street,
Beverly Hills, CA, 90210

Dear Mr. Rogers:

In the interest of applying for the telecommunications manager position within your organization, I ask you to consider my knowledge, skills, and experiences. Currently, I am a student of Some University, majoring in business and minoring in communications. My undergraduate coursework has included extensive study of marketing strategies, business management, and microeconomics. I also possess advanced proficiency in computer coding and giving power-point presentations. I seek a challenging position where I can further develop my managerial knowledge and experience.

My background includes four years of English language study in the U.S. which has added to my appreciation to live and work in international settings. I expect to obtain my B.A. in Business Administration from Some University on July 29, 201... For the past two years I have interned at ABC Consulting Company, working closely with the manager of international sales. Some of my accomplishments include:

• Maintaining a 3.6 or above GPA for the past four years.

• Assisting employees with sales presentations to international audiences

• Learning how to organize and budget for long-term work goals.

• Awarded first prize in university debate competition.

My business knowledge experience, diligence, and creativity have contributed to a number of successes. I am confident that I will be able to provide an immediate and immeasurable benefit to your company as well. The enclosed resume outlines my credentials and accomplishments in greater detail.

I can be contacted anytime at the email address or phone number listed above. I look forward to meeting and speaking with you in person.

Sincerely,

Mimi Marshall

Mimi Marshall

Enclosure

Identify the four elements previously described. in this cover letter.

Mohammed Abdul, a writing student, argues:

"I addressed the letter to the recipient by looking her name up at a company website. I was careful to spell her name correctly. I wanted to make a good impression on her. It would have made a terrible impression if I had misspelled her name."

Angelica Hermoso, a former writing student. advises:

"To grab my recipient's attention and make a great impression on him, I began my cover letter with an interesting first paragraph that explained why I was writing."

Resume

A resume is a detailed description of your background including your education, your work experience, your training and certification, the major groups that you are associated with, and your personal references.

As you read the following resume, label what you think are the parts that are usually included in a resume. Underline words or phrases that you believe may commonly appear in a resume.

Note that the top of every page has your name, address, telephone number, and email address just in case someone wants to contact you. Resumes include dates of employment, contact information, degrees, and certificates earned. After each work experience, state the title of your position and give a brief description of your duties. You may also want to highlight certain accomplishment or responsibilities.

Dan Doozelman

55 Madeup Dr. • Memphis, TN, USA 38150 • (555) 555-5555 • dan@some.com

Fiction High School, Memphis, TN
Graduated top 10% of class, June, 2015

Some University, Boston, MA
Expected to graduated cum laude, B.A. Business, December, 2016.

ABC Consulting Company, 999 Cloud St, Boston, MA, 02115
September 1, 2015 – currently employed

Director: Dr. Carl Barbary (555) 555-5555 (Office phone)

Intern. Responsible for assisting managing director for the northeast region. Duties include preparation, implementation, and development of sales strategies for company products.

- Implemented sales marketing strategies

- Performed research on staff training techniques

- Executed a customized testing process for new products

Photography Fixing Company, 7 Main Lane, Memphis, TN, 38155
May 2, 2010 – January 30, 2014

Manager: Benjamin Argall (555) 555-5555 (Office phone), 09/99-05/01.

Part-time employee. Worked part-time in a photography lab assisting customers with the printing and editing of digital photos.

- Developed reliable work habits

- Successfully applied organizational methods

- Improved group communication

     Business Management Methods. Training class led by Some University Department of Business. Business Management Methods Certification received 05/15.

     Business English Writing. 100-hour intensive training class in resume and formal business letter writing led by Roger Sinclair. Training completed 01/14.

Intern of the Month. ABC Consulting Company, 10/2015.
National Honor Society Academic Scholarship. Some Univeristy, 9/2011 – 12/2014.
Student Action for the Environment. Some University. Vice President, 9/2012 – 7/2013.
Fiction High School Newspaper, Managing Editor. ABC Consulting Company. 06/10.
St. Maybe's Children's Medical Clinic. Boston, MA. Volunteer health worker, 08/09-12/10.

References

Betsy Ross	Former Employer	(555) 555-5555	bross@some.com
John McDougal	Former Co-Worker	(555) 555-5555	jmac@some.com
Oprah Itzy	Long-Time Friend	(555) 555-5555	oitzy@some.com

Five Resume Mistakes

1 Sending resumes that have grammar, vocabulary, and punctuation mistakes

2 Listing skills and experiences that are not relevant

3 Using pictures or too much artsy or colorful background

4 Including inspirational quotations

5 Including unnecessary personal information (I like to workout in the evenings, I own my car)

Reading Comprehension Questions

1. What is the primary purpose of the sample business letter? Where does the purpose appear in the organization of the letter?

2. Read the following informal letter. Underline words or phrases that make the writing more informal than formal.

Hey Mimi,

wassup! i heard u moved into a new apartment in LA. that's really phat! i bet u are loving it there :) I miss u, so that's why i decided i would spend my vacation with u in LA can u believe it? i'll be coming to visit next week and i'd like to crash at your place for a few days and nights. watcha think? is it possible? if so why don't u send me an email or give me a call – you got my number but just in case here it is again 555-5555. can't wait to see u, sister.

Jo Jo
555-55555
P.S. Can Mason join me when i come? U remember we had math class together last year, he wants to come to LA. Watcha think?

3. What specific details is the author requesting in the sample business letter? Where do these details appear in the organization of the letter?

4. What are the specific arrangements, dates, orders, etc. that the author wishes to confirm in the sample business letters on page 85? Where are these arrangements explained?

5. How does the author end the business letter?

6. What specific language makes this a formal letter?

7. What are the characteristics of an effective cover letter?

8. What are the components and characteristics of an effective resume?

9. How can you write a cover letter that impresses the people you send it to?

10. How can you write a resume that impresses the people you send it to?

Jay Fong, a former writing student, remarks:

"Even in my first year of college I started thinking about obtaining internships and getting a job in the summer months. I put together a great resume with the help of friends and a kind instructor who helped me proofread my resume. By my second year of college, I had already landed a great internship."

Writing Activities

Writing Activity 1

On a separate sheet of paper, try writing a business letter (1 page, single-spaced). Imagine you are working at a business and need to request a shipment from a second business run by your partner. The details of the letter are up to you, but remember to include formal language and a polite request. Include the business's address and a formal greeting and conclusion.

Writing Activity 2

On a separate sheet of paper, try writing a business letter (1 page, single-spaced). Imagine you are writing to a business in Asia or the Middle East to schedule an upcoming visit. You will want to confirm arrangements, meeting dates and times, and hotel reservations. You may choose to adapt and combine some of the previous activities from this chapter.

Writing Activity 3

On a separate sheet of paper, write a cover letter (1 page, single-spaced) for a future job you may wish to apply for. Your cover letter may be shorter than the model above, but you should highlight your best qualities and qualifications for the position.

Writing Activity 4

On a separate sheet of paper, write your own resume (1-2 pages, single-spaced). Your resume may be shorter than the sample resume given in this chapter, but you should highlight your work and education qualifications and additional extracurricular activities, certifications, and awards.

> ❝ Those who are unable to write effective business letters, cover letters, and resumes may make a poor impression on others that prevents their advancement. They may not be seriously considered for the jobs they want. On the other hand, thoughtfully constructed business letters, cover letters, and resume help students gain the serious consideration that they deserve. ❞

Communicating with Email Messages

Making the Most of Email

The use of computer-mediated interaction is changing the way communication takes place. You'll find that many of your instructors offer face-to-face office hours, and some offer virtual office hours. All will expect you to communicate with them by email and read your email daily.

Emailing Your Instructor

If you can't go to your instructor's official office hours, it's a good idea to send a specific question to your instructor in a short email message. Don't send your entire paper or ask your instructor to download a paper or print it for you. Just cut and paste a few sentences or a paragraph from your paper that you are having difficulty with and ask your instructor not for general help but very specific help. Your instructor will probably respond right away if you write a short request or ask a particular question.

Kaixin Zhang, a former writing student, advises:

"If you write well-written short email messages, requesting very specific information about your paper, your instructors are likely to respond. If you write general questions, like 'How can I write this paper?,' you probably won't get a quick response."

Emailing professors is not the same as emailing your friends. Every act of communication involves a person who communicates, a message, and an audience—all in a specific context. You are now in the context of the university. As a student, you need to send emails to professors to ask questions or turn in work. The way you write your email to a professor should be very different from the way you write to your friends. The following are a few tips that might help you when you email professors.

Insider Tip

There are many ways to express your needs and raise questions in an email message. The above statements are just examples of some you might use. Take time to express yourself well.

- **Use your university or official email account and not your personal email account.** Some students email from their personal email accounts written in their first languages. When you email your professors from your personal account under the name of "김진희" while using your English name *Michelle* in class, it can create some confusion.

- **Include a greeting.** Unless you have a very friendly relationship with your professor and know that professor quite well, you should probably not address your professor *Hello* or *Hi*. The best greeting is generally *Dear* _____. If you do not know how your instructor wants to be addressed, then just write *Dear Professor*, or you can add the professor's last name after the word "Professor," for example, *Dear Professor Smith*. Remember that because Professor is a title, you need to capitalize the *P*. If the professor tells the class to use his or her first name, then you can write the first name after *Dear*, such as *Dear Lily*. Only do this if the professor gives permission to use his or her first name. If you are not comfortable addressing instructors by their first name, then write *Dear Professor _____[last name]*, or *Dear Dr. _____ [last name]*, Do not use *Mr.* or *Mrs.* when writing email messages to professors.

- **Sign your complete name at the bottom of your email.** Professors get dozens of emails a day from students. They don't remember all your email addresses, but they try to remember your names. It's also considered proper etiquette to sign your name, even if your email address has your name. You can close your email with *Thank you* or *Thanks for your attention to this matter* or something positive and pertinent to the content of the email message. If you do, put a comma after these words, skip a line and add your complete name. If you end with the word/s *Sincerely*, *Best*, or *Best wishes*, make sure to put a comma after the word/s. Then skip a line and add your complete name. Make sure to write your first name first. If you go by an English name in class, you should use your English name when you communicate with your professors. Indicate an appropriate subject on the subject line. Make it clear and brief. Don't leave the subject line blank. Give your message a title that you can put on the subject line so your professors can go through emails more efficiently. If you know that your instructor teaches more than one class, it is helpful if you include the number of your class or section. Here are two examples of appropriate email subjects:

  English 201 Thesis Statement Question
  Academic Writing Section 20039 Portfolio Letter Question

- **Use standard written English.** That means you need to follow the standard rules of spelling, punctuation, capitalization, grammar, and style (no slang) in your emails. If you are used to texting on your cell phone, it may seem natural for you to use an informal tone emailing your professors. For instance, you might say, Sorry. Can't come to class tomorrow. *Email me about the HW.* or *Visit U in yr office on Tues.* or *Check out my first essay and send me your comments.* It is not appropriate to use texting abbreviations and informal language in email communication with your professors. Remember that your professor will form an opinion about you based on the email message you send.

- **In general, avoid being accusatory, demanding, or whiny.** An *accusatory* remark indicates to your professor that you believe she or he has done something wrong. A *demanding* remark will make your professor think that you expect a lot of attention or expect to have things done exactly the way you want them, regardless of the difficulties that may cause your professor or classmates. A *whiny* remark will make your professor think that you are unhappy and complaining, possibly about the professor or your class.

- **Try to keep your email message brief and to the point.** Professors appreciate specific questions rather than general or complicated ones.

- **Keep in mind your audience.** Your professors get many student email messages each day. You'll want your instructor to react positively rather than negatively to your email message. Your instructor's reaction is important. Your instructor helps you to improve your English in general and writing in specific, grades your assignments, and may letter write a letter of recommendation for you. You'll most likely get a positive reaction from your instructor if you follow university email etiquette (Table 7.1).

Insider Tip

If you want to look professional, go to the Webmail options and adjust your email setting so that your full name will show (instead of your email address) whenever you send an email. You have no idea how much easier this makes it on the professors.

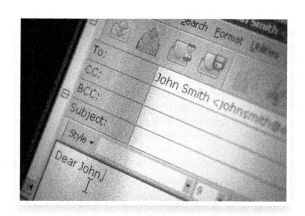

Table 7.1: Email Etiquette

Avoid these types of statements	Instead, use these types of statements
Check my homework.	I appreciate your checking my homework when you have time.
See me in your office tomorrow.	Would it be possible for me to see you in your office tomorrow?
Look at my homework in the attachment.	I know most professors do not accept homework that is sent via email, but I am sending you mine just so you know I completed it. I will make a copy of it and bring it to you when the class meets.
You did not open my email.	I am resending my email message that I sent you earlier, as you may not have received it.
You were not in your office.	I stopped by your office, but I did not find you. Would you have time to see me next week?
You did not correct my homework.	Would you have time to review my homework this week or next? I realize I made many mistakes. I have tried to correct these mistakes by myself after reviewing my homework with a peer tutor, but I am concerned that I may have overlooked some errors. I would appreciate any help you can give me.
I feel so bad and I am so sorry I make mistakes and will not do so ever again.	Thank you for pointing out my mistakes. I learned a lot from your help.
I could not come to class because I was sick last night and I had to take medication and then I could not get up in the morning and I have a headache now.	I missed class yesterday because I was sick. I received the homework from classmates and will complete it on time. I will bring a doctor's note to class this Monday.

A WORD OF WARNING

Most instructors don't appreciate when students email them to request course syllabi and notes that the instructors have already given in class or that students can obtain easily from classmates.

Li Min, a former writing student, warns:

"Don't expect your instructors to read and to reply to your emails immediately. Give your instructors at least a day to reply."

Wang Tao, a former writing stdent, advises:

"Don't send email messages to your instructors asking them questions that you can find the answer to easily yourself."

Reflecting on Email Messages

Think about **email messages**.

Structure: How do you organize your email messages to instructors? Do they have beginnings, middles, and ends? How are the key points arranged? What about when you are writing messages to your friends?

Audience: What are some of the conventions you follow when writing to instructors? Do you follow different conventions when writing to friends?

Language: What grammatical structures and language features do you often use when writing email messages? Do you use the present tense or the past? Do you use personal pronouns?

Tone: What is the tone of the messages you send your instructors? Is your tone academic or informal? What language do you use to communicate this tone to them? Complex sentences? Academic words? What is the tone of your messages when you write your friends? What language do you use to communicate this tone to them? Is it serious or funny? Formal or informal?

Example of an Effective Email Message:

Subject Line: Emily Li – Absence 9/22/16

Dear Professor Jones,

I was unable to attend writing class yesterday (Thursday, September 22). I understand from a classmate that I missed a lot of information and an important assignment. This is just to let you know that I plan to get notes from my friends concerning the information you covered on Thursday. I already got the assignment from a classmate and will hand it in next week on time. I look forward to seeing you in class this Tuesday.

Thank you,

Emily Li

Student ID 4567800
Writing 24 – Tuesday and Thursday

Example of an Ineffective Email Message:

Hi Mr. Smith,

I was sick with a headache last week and felt so bad that I just stayed home and missed your class. Yeah, not good. So don't lower my grade cuz I don't turn in my next assignment on time. Sucks to be me!!!!! Not my fault I was sick and missed so much stuff in class. I'll drop by your office. You can tell me what you covered in class and give me the assignment. Hope I didn't miss too much.

Em

Michael Yan, a former writing student, cautions:

"When I first started emailing my professors, I made a bad impression on them. I didn't spell check or proofread emails. I ignore those red squiggly lines that mean there was something wrong. Once I started sending better messages, I notice my instructors responded to my request carefully. Some of my professors are now telling me what a good writer I am – just because I know how to write email messages well."

Reading Comprehension Questions

1. What should you do if you can't go to your professor's office hours, but you have a question about an assignment?

2. How many email messages is appropriate to send a professor in a single week? Why?

3. What might happen if a student sends a professor lengthy email messages that contain many questions?

4. What are three differences between the email messages you write to friends and the email messages you write to your instructor?

5. What is an appropriate greeting to use in the email messages you send your professor?

6. Can you ever use your professor's first name (and not last name) in an email message? In what situations?

7. When do you use the title Mrs.? Would any professors be offended if you used that title to address them? Why?

8. What makes an email message seem demanding?

9. What makes an email message seem whiny?

10. Professors don't expect apologies when you miss a class. If you are sending them an email message about missing class, they often want to know that you are taking responsibility to make up the work you missed. They won't like it if you suggest how to grade missed work or blame something or someone for making you miss class. Given this, what types of information would you put into an email message to a professor concerning an absence?

11. Which of the sentences below is too demanding and which one is respectful?

    a. "Get back to me as soon as possible."

    b. "Please advise me at your convenience."

66 The use of computer-mediated interaction is changing the way we think about communicating. You'll find that many of your instructors offer face-to-face office hours, and some offer virtual office hours. All will expect you to communicate with them by email and read your email messages daily. 99

CHAPTER EIGHT

Narratives

By Christie Sosa and Tina Matuchniak

N arratives can be interesting, cogent, compelling, and memorable. They can also constitute an important type of evidence. As a college student, you may be asked to write narratives in a number of your courses. You may also be asked to write narrative essays when you apply to graduate school, since many colleges and universities request narrative essays as part of their admissions application.

What is a Narrative?

Narration, the telling of factual and imaginary stories, creates a clear picture in the readers' minds of a story, with a setting, characterization and plot. Narratives contain artistic, thoughtfully written language, often having a rhythm and flow. Short stories—such as fairy tales, mysteries, romances, horror stories; personal essays and letters; diary entries; biographical works; and travelogues all contain aspects of narrative writing. Their basic purpose is to entertain, though they may also be written to teach, inform, or even change attitudes.

The Introduction

The opening sentences of your narrative should grab your reader's attention. Your readers should feel compelled to continue reading to the end. How you choose to open your narrative depends on your personal style of writing and the story you tell.

In a **narrative**, a theme or purpose runs through your story, though you usually do not state the theme or purpose directly. Instead, your characters, setting and plot help develop the theme throughout the story. When you begin a **narrative essay**, you should know the purpose of your story and craft a thesis, which may or may not appear in the first paragraph. As with your opening sentence, the placement of your thesis depends on your writing style and the story that is being told.

Insider Tip

In a narrative, it's important to properly introduce and establish the characters by showing how they are rather than telling. To do this, give special attention to the dialogue and actions of the characters to ensure they reveal key characteristics or personality traits pertinent to the story you're telling.

Your introduction also includes details and information that will help your reader understand your story. You might explain where the story takes place and when, or introduce the main and provide some relevant information about them. Such background information will help the readers understand your thesis statement.

The Plot

After writing a captivating introduction, you'll begin to develop the plot, that is, the sequential events of the story. You might find it easiest if you organize the events chronologically, adding smooth transitions between paragraphs. However, depending on your purpose, you may organize events in a different order.

> **Rising action**: the development of conflict and complications in a literary work
>
> **Climax:** the turning point in a literary work
>
> **Falling action:** results or effects of the climax of a literary work
>
> **Resolution or denouement:** end of a literary work when loose ends are tied up and questions are answered

Climax and Conclusion

The events of your narrative should end in a dramatic moment called the climax. The climax often reveals the point at which the protagonist changes, for better or worse.The climax should remind the reader of the thesis or main point of the story. It should be reiterated, though perhaps in a nuanced or subtle way, in your conclusion.

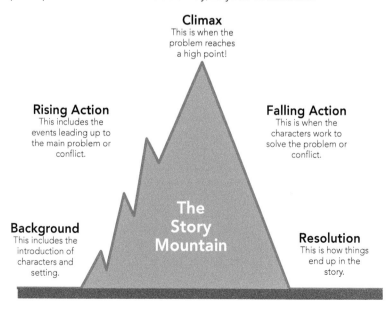

Climax
This is when the problem reaches a high point!

Rising Action
This includes the events leading up to the main problem or conflict.

Falling Action
This is when the characters work to solve the problem or conflict.

Background
This includes the introduction of characters and setting.

The Story Mountain

Resolution
This is how things end up in the story.

What Language is Used in Narratives?

The language that you use in your narratives and narrative essays depends largely on the audience and purpose. Informal narratives can contain slang, begin sentences with *and* and *but*, and contain sentence fragments. Formal narratives, which include, for example, narrative essays for graduate school or a job, cannot.

In general, narrative writing is creative. It's common to use different figurative language tools such as **metaphors, symbolism,** and **personification** to help communicate a theme. (See Chapter 9.) These features along with other linguistic features—including alliteration, repetition, synonyms, word families, pronouns, and transition words can contribute to the cohesion of your writing.

You will want to use a variety of sentence structures that vary in complexity (for example the use of relative clauses, parallel structures, rhetorical questions, and lists of nouns and adjectives), as well as structures that convey **hyperbole** or **deliberate exaggeration** to make your writing dramatic as in the sentence, *Grief and pity and sorrow ran over him like a tanker.* You can use a variety of sentence beginnings (for example, with participles – *Jumping with happiness, she sprinted to the finish line* or with adverbs – *Quickly, the cat pounced on the unsuspecting mouse*).

You may also want to pay attention to **verb tenses** when writing narratives. Although there are variations, most writers begin narratives with the present tense to announce their topics with hooks (see below) and make general truth statements. They switch to the past tense when describing the elements of stories and then back to the present tense when writing their conclusions. You will want to generally avoid the passive voice, using action verbs to show what is happening.

As seen in this example, you can use adjectives and adverbs for **vivid imagery**, often to evoke the five senses (sight, sound, smell, taste, touch): *The enormous dark cloud loomed threateningly above the small village, engulfing it in doom before bursting, soaking it in a torrent of incessant rainfall.* You can also use adjectives to describe contrasts: *Her evil blood drenched her pure white wedding gown.*

You will also want to use a variety of words in your narratives. You may want to use **emphatic words** (*certainly, truly, definitely*) that convey certainty, **onomatopoeic words**, words like *buzz*, with sounds imitating their meaning, and use **specific words** (like *orchid*) instead of general words, like *flower*. You'll probably want to use **academic words**, like *maintain*, which are used across subject areas, and **content-specific words**, like *chlorophyll*, infrequently compared to everyday words.

Strategies to Help You Write Your Narratives

1. Vivid Descriptions

Replace general words with specific, vivid ones. (See Chapter 5 for a more detailed description of the types of adjectives, adverbs, and verbs you should use.)

General Adjectives and Nouns	Specific, Vivid Adjectives and Nouns
bad food	foul-tasting, rancid fish

Notice how author Amy Tan uses vivid adjectives and nouns in her short story, "Fishcheeks."

"a slimy rock cod [fish] with bulging eyes"

"tofu, which looked like stacked wedges of rubbery white sponges"

"rumpled Christmas packages"

2. Showing, Not Telling

What does showing not telling mean? It means using vivid details and words to help your readers imagine the situations you describe. See the examples below.

Telling	Showing
I was in a bad car accident.	The glass shattered, leaving me bloodied, in a pile of twisted metal.

3. Dialogue

To develop the plot, it is helpful to use interesting dialogue. When writing dialogue, each speaker gets his or her own paragraph, mimicking a real conversation. Consider the example below.

When I was eight, my father dragged me into my bedroom after I lit a folded pile of his shirts on fire. I sat on the edge of the bed, not looking up, my hands folded mannerly in my lap.

"What's wrong with you?" he asked.

"Nothing," I said.

"You lit my shirts on fire, boy? Where'd you learn that?"

"Daycare."

"What? Daycare? You learned how to light shirts on fire at daycare?"

I froze and looked up at the ceiling, trying to backtrack. I actually learned how to light matches by watching him light his pipe, but I could not tell him that.

4. Time Order Signals and Adverbials of Time

Use Adverbials of Time (Table 8.1) and other Time Order Signals (Table 8.2) to organize the events you describe chronologically.

Table 8.1: Adverbials of Time

Adverbials of Time	Sentences
By + time	By nine o'clock, the streets were crowded.
At + time	At around one, the excitement grew.
After + time	After twelve, the people went home.
Before + time	Most people arrived before or at nine.
After + noun	After an hour, the parade passed by us.
Before + noun	Before the parade, everyone was excited.
During + noun	During the parade, everyone had a good time.

Table 8.2: Time Order Signals

Time Order Signals	
Words	**Phrases**
First, Second, Third, etc.	Before beginning the lesson,
Later,	In the morning,
Meanwhile,	At 12:00,
Next,	After that,
Now	The next day,
Soon	At last,
Finally,	Until I met you,
Then	By the time I graduated,

Insider Tip

In MLA, commas are required following long introductory prepositional phrases. Many writers also use them after shorter prepositional phrases and words like *later, meanwhile, next,* and *finally.*

5. Use action verbs, sometimes called strong verbs (Table 8.3). See page 74 for a list.

Table 8.3: Action Verbs

Common	Action Verbs
break	crash, fracture, tear
confuse	befuddle, flummox, bewilder
laugh	chortle, chuckle, crack up, giggle, howl, snicker
leave	abandon, back out, desert
say	claim, cry, moan, shout
walk	stride, jog, meander, stagger, stumble

6. Verb Tense

Generally use the present tense when you are giving background information about your story in the introduction, describing the setting, establishing the theme of your story, or writing a thesis statement (in a narrative essay). You also use the present tense at the end of your narrative or narrative essay if you are describing general truths or the moral of your story.

7. When and While

Use *when* to introduce a simple past action.

I was studying when the doorbell rang.

Use while or as to introduce the past progressive action

While I was studying, the electricity suddenly went out.

8. Name your characters and give details about them and the setting.

It is more interesting for your readers if you include details about the characters, for example, their names, the setting, even naming the towns and cities you refer to.

Henry Wu, a former student, warns:

"My instructor would not grade my narrative because he said he could not understand it. That's because I did not name my characters and I did not give any background information about the setting to help him understand my narrative. In China I did not have to name my characters or give the reader so many details about the setting."

9. Include sensory words such as the ones in the chart below to help you provide interesting details and examples in your writing (Table 8.4).

Table 8.4: Sensory Words

Sight	Sound	Touch	Taste	Smell
bleary	bellow	balmy	appetizing	acrid
blurred	blare	biting	bitter	aroma
brilliant	buzz	bristly	bland	aromatic
colorless	cackle	bumpy	creamy	fetid
dazzling	cheer	chilly	delectable	foul-smelling
dim	clamor	coarse	delicious	fragrant
dingy	clang	cold	flavorful	moldy
faded	crackle	cool	flavorless	musty
faint	creak	crawly	gingery	nidorous
flashy	grumble	creepy	luscious	odiferous
gaudy	gurgle	cuddly	nauseating	odor
glance	hiss	dusty	palatable	odorless
gleaming	howl	feathery	peppery	old
glimpse	hush	feverish	piquant	perfumed
glistening	jabber	fluffy	refreshing	pungent
glittering	mumble	furry	ripe	putrid
gloomy	murmur	fuzzy	rotten	rancid
glossy	mutter	gooey	salty	rank
glowing	rant	greasy	savory	reeking
grimy	rave	gritty	scrumptious	scent
hazy	roar	hairy	sharp	scented
indistinct	rumble	hot	sour	smell
misty	rustle	icy	spicy	spicy
peer	screech	limp	spoiled	steno
radiant	shriek	lumpy	stale	sweet
shadowy	shrill	moist	sugary	waft
shimmering	sizzle	oily	sweet	whiff
shiny	snarl	powdery	tangy	
smudged	squawk	prickly	tasteless	
sparkling	squeal	scratchy	tasty	
streaked	swish	shivery	unappetizing	
striped	thud	silky	unripe	
tarnished	thump	slimy	vinegary	
twinkling	whimper	slippery	yummy	
	yelp	spongy	zesty	

10. Conversational Style

Most types of narratives are written with informal forms of English. Contractions, informal language, slang and idioms can be used to enliven your writing and keep your readers engaged.

Your Turn

Work with a partner to complete the chart below. You can use a dictionary to assist you. The first one has been done for you.

Formal	Informal	Slang/idiom
Act decisively	Take charge	Take the bull by the horns
Gentleman	Man	
Contented	Pleased	Happy as a clam
Diminutive	Small	Itty bitty
Beverage	Drink	Booze
Authentic	Real	Legit
Unintelligent	Dumb	Airhead
Instigate	Cause	Make happen
Consider	Think about	Take a look at
Impart	Share	Pass on
Convert	Become	Turn into
Arrive	Reach your destination	Get here
Concur	Come to an agreement	Work out

Use the space below to list some of the informal words, slang, or idioms that you hear every day. With a partner, discuss how you would change them to more formal English expressions.

What challenges am I likely to encounter when writing a narrative or narrative essay?

Particular challenges for many multilingual students include understanding the principle of *showing not telling*; incorporating dialogue, quotations and paraphrasing; varying sentence structures—especially those with participles, prepositional phrases, and gerunds; switching between verb tenses; establishing cohesion (e.g., through transition words and other more subtle linguistic features like sentence complexity and pronouns); maintaining pronoun consistency; and using vivid and specific vocabulary and fixed expressions (including word phrases like *all of a sudden*; not *all of the sudden*; *on the other hand*, not *on the another hands*, two word verbs (like *call on* for *visit* and idioms like *kick the bucket*).

If you are an international student who has lived in the United States for a short time, you are likely to experience some challenges learning how much background the reader needs to understand their stories, the types of stories that are interesting and appropriate to share with US-American readers, the words to use to express their intentions, and even the structuring of narratives.

Fortunately, all students bring to the task of writing narratives many resources. You already have much knowledge of narrative writing and have developed a rich repertoire of stories and story-telling devices. Your life experiences and knowledge of the world increase your opportunities to brainstorm and interact with classmates about your narratives and put your ideas on the page.

The following papers won awards at the writing contest of a major university.

Worship
by Victoria Chiang

I never understood the meaning of worshiping my ancestors. The only thing I did was mimic the my relatives worshipping them. I did whatever they did. Every Chinese New Year, my whole family would get together at my home in China. My cousins, aunts, uncles, and their children came over to cook and talk. In my house there was a small room with a table where somewhat had put my grandparents' statues. After we were done cooking, we presented delicious food to these statues and then we burned incense. "Why?" I wondered. "How can they eat the food?" I was so confused. I asked myself again and again, "How can the statues eat the food we give them?"

When my dad called everyone to assemble, all the people would stand in front of the statues of my grandparents and wait to worship them. This was a tradition we always did in my family, especially on my dad's side. He was very serious and knew all the rules of worshiping. Then, everyone would grow quiet as we began to light incense. Each person held the incense in their hands, closed their eyes, and then murmured some words. They would ask questions of my grandparents and show concern for their well-being in heaven.

They would also tell them how their own lives were going. At this time, I would secretly open my eyes to observe what everyone was doing. "Can grandparents really hear us?" asked myself. And inside my heart, I was confused again. I thought the actions my relatives took made no sense and they sounded funny. I could not understand why they were worshiping my ancestors as they were. "Why did we have to talk with those who had already passed away?" I wondered.

When my sister and I were still young, we always got our father angry about not showing adequate respect when worshiping. "Do not laugh when worshiping!" My father said. He was really serious when facing these statues. No one should ever laugh or joke around in front of them. I remembered there was one time when I was around seven years old, my sister and I were worshipping, and we were so hyper that day and excited about the get together that we got carried away talking and rough housing. We were having so much fun that it make it hard for us hard to control ourselves or to stop laughing when everyone started burning incense. When everyone closed their eyes, my sister unexpectedly turned to me and made a funny face. I knew I should not laugh, but she was so funny that I could not hold in my laughter anymore. My dad was so angry, and he made us kneel down for almost an hour to punish us for not being respectful of our ancestors.

Since I have grown up, I have come to understand the meaning of worshiping. "Grandma, Grandpa! I'm back from Irvine," I scream whenever I arrive home. After moving to America to study, whenever I go back home to China, the first thing I do is tell my deceased grandparents that I am safe and I have returned. Every time when any of the members in my family go on a trip, we naturally go to the room and inform them. Sometimes I even tell them the interesting things that have happened on me. I am glad there is someone I can talk to, and I know they are somewhere in heaven listening to me.

Inside my heart, I was confused again.

1°C
by Jiani Hu

Old, gray walls, thick tiles on the top, and wet air. This was my memory of my grandparents' house when I was a child. I usually went to my grandparents' house on the holidays. There were no fancy Crayon Shin-Chan cartoons or models of F1 which were my favorite. I had a TV at least, so I watched TV a lot, and my grandma always looked at me with a kind smile. She liked going to the tiny, smelly market with me. The numerous heads of cabbage she bought cost 2 yuan, and my colorful lollipop cost 6 yuan. "Pick whatever you like," my grandma always said.

Sometimes my grandfather wanted to play my favorite sport, table tennis, with me. I loved playing it, even though he could only play for 15 minutes while I could play for an entire hour without losing my breath.

I liked my grandparents, but I just didn't like living in their house in the countryside since it was kind of boring to me. In Summer, after returning from the market in the late afternoon, grandma always asked me to take the first shower and then have dinner comfortably in the air- conditioned living room. I enjoyed my rural life and liked the tasteless shower water. Later, when the cold winter came, I hardly went out unless it snowed. Sometimes I was afraid that the house would collapse when I heard the howl of wind. Winter was much more boring to me, and a strange thing happened. Grandma preferred to go to the market alone, and Grandpa played table tennis with me more

often. That was fine. It was so cold outside and going to the market didn't interest me a lot. Instead, I preferred to play table tennis at home. In the afternoon, when I was going to take a shower, my grandma suddenly stopped washing vegetables and said, "I feel so cold, let me take a shower first." I was surprised, but I was okay with that. However, Grandma tried to take a shower before me everyday. When I was confused, I asked her why and her answer was always that same: that she felt cold. "Did my grandma still love me?" I asked myself. To me, this question was even more difficult to answer than answering a question about the result of eighty-two minus twenty-seven. Then when winter turned into summer again, once more Grandma let me take the first showers again.

One afternoon during a winter holiday, I went to visit my grandparents. My grandma didn't come back home at the usual time, and I was somewhat happy because I could take the first shower finally. However, when I was taking the shower, I felt something I had never felt before. The water was cold, and it was a colder than I had ever felt before. Later, when grandma came back home and learned that I had already taken the shower, she said, "I don't need to take the first shower today." Maybe because she knew I had already taken the first shower, she said no longer needed to take the first shower that day. I was surprised because I thought that coming back from the market would make people feel much colder. I didn't think about what had happened much. On the second day, I took the shower second as usual, and I felt the water was warmer. It was warmer than it was yesterday. Suddenly, I thought I figured it out. My grandma took showers before me in the winters because in that simple way, the temperature in the bathroom would be higher by one degree centigrade, so I would feel warmer when I took a shower. Although there was no heater in my grandparents' old bathroom unlike my parents' house in the city, I felt much warmer at my grandparents' home.

Suddenly, I thought I figured it out.

Lights Out
by Heaven Howse

Pure darkness took over my eyesight as I stepped inside of my home after performing at my school's Friday night football game. I held my hand out to guide me through the hallways, so I would not run into anything. I felt a presence in the house; however, it only made me become more frightened. Nevertheless, the palm of my trembling, yet sweaty hand bumped into a slim figure. My mother's rich coffee colored skin blended in with the darkness, but I noticed the harsh red glow in her eyes.

After running into my mother, I was too tired to make conversation, so I floundered my way to my room. After attempting to turn on the lights, I failed. I couldn't get them on. I stopped bothering with the lights and decided to plug my phone into one of the sockets by my bedroom window. However, my charger did not connect to my lifeless cellular device. So, I changed out of my clothing and laid down quietly in the dark and let sleep take over for a short while.

When I awoke from my slumber, I recognized that I was still trapped in darkness by a blackout. As I walked out of my room I noticed that there were multiple lifeless candles melting around the house. I could hear voices coming from the other room and could tell that my younger and older brothers were home. I made my way into the living room and flopped myself on our black out-of-date leather couch next to my younger sibling, who was holding a camping light. I tried turning on the television, but nothing appeared to be working. The television set stood blank and all of us sat silently in the living room. However, my mother broke the silence. When I found out my mother could not pay the electric bill and that was the cause of our misery, I was devastated. How would I make conversation with my friends about the new reality shows that were coming up? I wouldn't even be able to turn on the TV to watch them? Was I going to be behind on my shows? Was I going to miss out on everything new? How was I going to ever be able to charge up my phone? No technology? This power outage and my mother's inability to pay the electric company made me feel that I was at the end of my life. Nonetheless, we continued to sit around the burning candles and flashlights just as if we were going to perform a ritual. It felt unusually bizarre without the lights on.

"You do not need electricity to have a good time," my mother said.

I groaned at the sound of her cheerful, but melancholy tone. I threw my flashlight, causing it to make a ringing thud when it landed on the ground. My mother stood next to me, looking confused because of my actions. She hastily got up from the floor as if she had forgotten something in the other room. The next thing I knew screeching noises sounding like a cat clawing its nails on a dry metal cat scratch came from my mother, who was madly looking through the livingroom cabinets.

"Found them."

"Found what? What are those for?" I asked.

She came back with a stack of UNO cards, which is a card game. That night she taught my siblings and me how to play the game of UNO. We remained playing throughout the night and my mother continued to win as though she was a scammer at a casino in Las Vegas, NV.

It was the seventh time that my mother was going to win and my oldest sibling decided it was my mother's last time. He ended up pulling a "draw 4" card on her, so she could not win. The look on her face was in essence that of a circus clown carrying a knife to frighten children away. While noticing my mother's ludicrous expression, my brother began laughing, with a loud chuckle that turned into snorting like a pig rolling in mud. We continued to play the game, completely forgetting that our power was turned off as we enjoyed each other's company.

Whenever my mother could not afford to keep the power on, it became tradition to play a card game and forget that we were even struggling during the time.

It was not until before I moved away from my mother that I was able to appreciate how being away from electricity can bring you closer to the people around you. During my first midterm week in college, my friends and I took a break from studying. When they began to turn off their laptops, a wide grin appeared on my face. I brought out the UNO cards.

Reading Comprehension Questions

1. Why is it important for college students to learn to write narratives?

2. What does the setting include?

3. When you introduce characters in a narrative, what helps the reader understand them?

4. Does the information in a narrative essay always have to be true? Why?

5. What is the difference between showing and telling?

6. How can you make your narrative interesting?

7. Which three strategies discussed in this chapter do you find most useful in writing a narrative? Why?

8. What advice would you give a friend for punctuating dialogue in a narrative?

9. What do you put into a concluding paragraph of a narrative?

10. Read the university students' stories. Describe their strengths and explain which story you like the best and why.

> Narration, the telling of factual and imaginary stories, creates a clear picture in the readers' minds of a story, with a setting, characterization and plot. They can be interesting, cogent, compelling, and memorable.

Rhetorical Analyses:

The Literary Analysis and Analysis of Informational Text

By Rose Jones and Robin Stewart

This chapter explains what rhetorical analysis is and provides guidelines and tips for writing rhetorical analyses. Although you will not be writing many rhetorical analyses in college, should you be asked to write them, you will find this chapter useful. The rhetorical analysis is particularly valued in composition and literature courses.

When you write a rhetorical analysis, you are basically writing a type of argument about something that you have read. You write about particular attributes of a text to support an argument about the strategies or devices that a particular author uses to produce a specific effect on an intended audience. This often requires that you use terms like **tone** and **style** that you have learned earlier in literature classes. You defend your argument, drawing on evidence from the text and when appropriate, secondary sources like books and articles.

What is Rhetoric?

Rhetoric is the art of communicating with a specific purpose in mind, usually to create a specific effect on the reader. An author's purpose may be, for example, to entertain, to inform, or to persuade readers. (See Chapter 4.)

When you analyze rhetoric, you'll examine the way in which writers use rhetorical devices in particular ways. Writers who are trying to entertain, for instance, create a mood of enjoyment and pleasure by incorporating words with multiple meanings, alliteration, satire and irony. In contrast, writers who are trying to convince readers of something provide arguments and supporting evidence. Your main goals in analyzing rhetoric are to identify, understand, and analyze the effectiveness of particular rhetorical devices and the ways these devices achieve a desired effect on readers.

Insider Tip

Useful sentence frames to use when discussing images are these:

The image of _____ reveals...

The [violent] imagery of the piece emphasizes...

The images of the _____ evoke [sorrow]....

When writing a rhetorical analysis, you'll refer to literary terms (such as *character*, *theme*, *setting*, *rhyme*, *point of view*, *alliteration*, *symbols*, *image*, *figurative language*, and *protagonist*) to support your points. Here is the way in which one writer uses the term *images*:

> Adrienne Rich uses vivid *images* to demonstrate a feminist perspective in the poem "Aunt Jennifer's Tigers."

A rhetorical analysis of nonfiction often begins by analyzing or taking a critical look at the **rhetorical situation**—that is, the **context** in which the writing was created (for example, the participants; the time and place; the cultural, social, political, and economic environment or conditions). It often examines the kinds of **appeals** authors make. In rhetorical analyses, an ***appeal*** refers to the ways in which writers use rhetoric to make readers accept something as right or proper by saying things that are directed towards the reader's reasoning, emotions, attitudes, etc. They might use such sentence frames such as those below to discuss the writers' appeals.

Sentence Frames

When _____ states _____ he/she appeals to the audience's _____ by _____.

This is an effective way to persuade the audience because

_____.

Rhetorical analyses of argumentative texts analyze the extent to which writers make an appeal to the readers' sense of **reason (*logos*)**, **emotions (*pathos*)**, or **authority (*ethos*)** (Table 9.1).

Table 9.1: Sentence Frames for Rhetorical Appeals

Appeals	Sentence Frames
Logos (reason)	The writer's argument shows that _____
	The writer uses examples facts/statistics/etc. to support her point that _____
	The writer reaches the logical conclusion that _____
Pathos (emotions)	The author appeals to the emotions of the reader when stating _____
	The author makes the audience afraid of the consequences, and so sways their opinion when she states _____
Ethos	The writer establishes his authority by _____
	The writer's reputation as a scholar is renowned because _____
	The writer makes himself sympathetic to the audience by _____

What is Fiction Writing?

Works of **literature**, or **literary texts**, such as plays/dramas, novels, short stories, and poems, are **fiction**. Fiction writings are also referred to as literary texts. **Non-literary**, or **informational, texts**, such as essays, speeches, textbooks, articles, and travelogues, are nonfiction.

Writers use fiction to tell a **story** that they imagine. While sometimes inspired by real events or people, the characters and the events in the story do not correspond to real individuals or actions. They are constructed to illustrate features of the human or social condition. Stories often describe the **conflicts** of a **protagonist**, or main character, in a specific **setting**. Informational texts, on the other hand, seek to explain or provide instructions using language that explicitly explains some fact, theory, or process.

Authors explore their ideas by inventing a **plot**, or series of events, experienced by a set of **characters** over a specific **time** period in a specific **location**. Science fiction and fantasy describe normal people in extraordinary circumstances to test the potential and the limits of human nature as we know it.

Literary texts often contain **allusions*** or specific references to previous works. They often experiment with traditional **styles** and **conventions**.

Because literature is a form of communication, it contains all of the basic features that rhetorical analysis describes: an author, a message, and an audience. However, unlike other forms of communication, such as informational essays, literature can employ a wider range of creative techniques to convey a given message. In addition, literature is often more complex, subtle, and indirect in both its means of communicating a given message and the possible content of the message itself.

*allusions

(plural count noun): something said or written that mentions a subject, person, etc. indirectly; An example of a literary allusion: In Elliot's poetry, we find many allusions to the human body.

Inference

Inference is a literary device used commonly in literature and in daily life. It refers to making logical deductions or conclusions based on evidence and reasoning. When you deduct something, you use your knowledge or information to understand something or form opinions. When you read nonfiction writing, you nearly always need to **infer** the writers' thoughts and hidden messages. Nonfiction writing rarely has an explicit thesis or argument, though sometimes it has a **moral.***

*moral

(countable noun): the lesson to be learned from a story or experience

A good example of a story that has a moral is Aesop's famous fable of "The Tortoise and the Hare." In the fable, a tortoise challenges a hare to a race. The hare laughs at the tortoise and is so confident in his superior speed that he decides to take a nap during the race itself. But when he wakes, he discovers that he has slept too long and that the tortoise, who has been giving consistent effort throughout the race, is almost at the finish line. The hare frantically tries to catch-up, but he's too late: the tortoise wins. At the end of the story, Aesop provides the following moral: "slow and steady wins the race."

Theme

A **theme** is a central idea that runs throughout a literary text. It is a unifying idea, image or motif, repeated or developed throughout a work. Most fiction writing contains themes—a lesson, message, or key idea that the writer wants to communicate to a reader.

Reading for Intention

The goal of a rhetorical analysis is to develop and support arguments about **authorial intention**. This just means what writers plan or aim to do in their writing. Writers of rhetorical analysis must clearly identify the thoughts and feelings the authors want their readers to have. In addition, they must evaluate how the details of the writing represent the authors' strategies for producing these thoughts and feelings.

Rhetorical Analysis of a Literary Text

Like other types of argumentative writing, literary analysis contains these basic components: *an introduction,* with an interesting hook, statement introducing the text you are analyzing, and thesis statement; *body paragraphs*, containing your evidence and supporting your thesis statement; and a conclusion, giving your essay a sense of completeness, and often giving your readers a useful insight related to your thesis statement. Refer to Chapter 3 on argumentative writing more information about the organization.

Here are some basic tips for writing a literary analysis:

1. Use the literary present tense.

2. When in doubt, generally use the third person (no I or you) and leave yourself out of the analysis. Some instructors may require or allow the first or second person in an informal analysis. Ask your instructor if you are unsure whether to use I or you.

3. Do not summarize the plot. Analyze it.

4. Include a clear thesis statement with an arguable claim that addresses a meaningful aspect of the text.

5. Use literary terms like **alliteration, character, imagery,** and **plot**.

6. Use quotations and paraphrases as evidence to support your thesis statement, but do not use too many quotations and paraphrases. The majority of your paper should consist of your own ideas and be written in your own words.

Components to Consider When Writing a Rhetorical Analysis of Literature

1. Biographical Background

Knowing specific details about the author of a literary text can provide insight into the text's function or purpose. **Biographical background** refers to the time period in which the author lives or lived; the author's upbringing and family relationships; and his or her education, social status, gender, religion, major life events, etc.

2. Historical and Cultural Context

When writing your rhetorical analysis, it is important to consider **cultural and historical contexts** pertaining to the text you are writing about. Literary texts often reflect unique cultural and historical values

Insider Tip

When writing a rhetorical analysis of a literary text, ask yourself:

1) What are the author's intentions?

2) What is he or she trying to accomplish?

3) What effect does he or she want to have on the reader?

that can be quite different from our own. For example, in order to understand why Elizabeth Bennet and Mr. Darcy, the lead characters in Jane Austen's *Pride and Prejudice*, act the way they do in the novel, we first have to understand the nature of the English class-system in the 18th century. The cultural and historical context motivates Mr. Darcy's cold, sometimes arrogant behavior. Assumptions about how women were supposed to be subordinate to men that were common in England in the 18th century explain why Elizabeth Bennet cannot express her feelings directly throughout the novel.

Author biographies or **autobiographies**, articles on your assigned texts written by **literary critics**, and **social histories** covering the time period the text was originally published can all be useful in understanding and writing about the historical and cultural context. They can provide you with the information you need to write a successful rhetorical analysis. As you do research for your rhetorical analysis, you should ask yourself some of the following questions:

- What were the political, religious, social, and moral values shared or debated during the time period the text was written?

- What were the important historical events that occurred around the time of the text's writing that might have influenced the author?

- Can you find any reactions to the literary text?

- Can you find any evidence of the literary text's success or failure to reach an audience? How widely was the text distributed? How many copies did it sell? How many times was it reprinted?

Finding answers to these questions will help you gain knowledge of a text's original audience, which will enable you to evaluate how the author succeeds or fails in his or her strategies to address reader expectations. You will need to ask your instructor if you need to include a works cited page.

*elegy

(count noun): a sad poem or song: a poem or song written for someone who is dead

*sonnet

(count noun): a poem made up of 14 lines that rhyme in a fixed pattern

3. Genre

Genre refers to the types of literary texts. Certain **conventions**, or established and expected features, define each genre. The main literary genres include **drama, poetry, novel,** and **short story**. These conventions establish the purpose or function of the text, and form. Within each genre are specific **subgenres**, which are crucial to understanding how a particular work is structured. For novels, for instance, there are **romance** novels and **graphic** novels; for dramas, **tragedies** and **comedies**; and for poetry, **elegies*** and **sonnets***.

4. Characters

Characters refer to the individuals or figures, human or non-human, around whom the central action of the story takes place. In a drama or play, novel, or short story, the main character, also known as the **protagonist**, is the **hero/heroine** of the story who must undertake some kind of journey or quest and, in the process, undergo some kind of personal change, growth, or transformation. There are often many supporting characters. They help the protagonist along on his or her journey. The main villain or challenger to the heroic figure, also known as the **antagonist**, is often contrasted with the hero or heroine. This is done as a way to highlight the heroic qualities of the main character and to help move the plot along to its climax or peak, and ultimate resolution.

Characterizations of the characters in a story (that is, the way in which a writer makes the characters look in a book, film, or play) allow the author to support his or her arguments about the various themes in his/her work. The writer might characterize the protagonist as having many weaknesses, or the writer might characterize the protagonist as behaving in a moral and honest way. Characterization allows the author to manipulate the audience's response, for example, creating a more sympathetic or critical audience response toward the main character (Table 9.2).

Insider Tip

If you are having difficulty discussing characterization in your rhetorical analysis, try using the chart on this page.

Table 9.2: Characterization Sentence Frame

Literary Term	Definition	Sentence Frame
characterization	the portrayal of people through actions, description, physical characteristics, or dialogue	_____ is characterized as_____, which is surprising because_____ The characterization of _____ as _____ reveals that _____ She characterizes her opponent as _____ are portrayed as _____in order to_____

5. Plot

A **plot** is the sequence of events in a literary work. Most often plots are driven by some form of **conflict** that the protagonist faces. A text's **dramatic arc**, or the development of the central conflict, normally proceeds through a few basic stages. The plot finally reaches a **climax**, or the point at which the conflict is greatest, before reaching some form of **resolution,** in which the protagonist either successfully or unsuccessfully deals with the conflict.

The events of a plot can be arranged in a variety of sequences. The most basic is **chronological sequence**, in which the text develops the action from beginning to middle to end. However, many authors present the events of the plot out of the chronological order, either to build suspense or to develop the text's central theme in unexpected ways. Most literary texts actually begin **in medias res**, a Latin term meaning "in the middle of things." The text may then depict events that happened earlier in time through a **flashback**, or jump ahead to an event in the future through a **flash-forward**. Though these arrangements may be difficult to follow at first, they can become clearer through careful re-readings of the text. As you consider the details of a plot—its central conflict and resolution, its sequence, and the events of the larger story that the author chooses not to depict—ask yourself how these elements reflect authorial intention and produce specific effects in a reader.

6. Setting

Setting refers to the time, place, and social environment in which a plot unfolds. Settings can be important for creating a certain mood or **atmosphere** in a literary text, because where and when an author chooses to set a story has a profound effect on the nature of that story's characters, conflict, and development, all of which can represent strategies for how the author wants his/her reader to think about the text's central themes. As an example, consider the film *Titanic* (1997), one of the most successful romantic movies of all time. At the center of the film is the love story between Rose, an upper-class woman played by actress Kate Winslet, and Jack, a working class man played Leonardo DiCaprio. The conflict of the plot concerns the love relationship between two young people is destined to fail because of social barriers imposed on them by others. The barrier that Rose and Jack encounter is their difference in social status, and the unfairness of this difference in social status becomes one of the central themes of the film.

James Cameron, the film's director, might have chosen any number of different settings for the story of Rose and Jack, so why did he choose to set it on the Titanic? The sinking of the Titanic is a well-known historical event, regarded as an example of how wealth and power, which the ship was thought to represent when it was originally built, does not always triumph against the forces of nature, in this case, the iceberg that caused the ship to sink.

7. The Narrator and the Author

Sometimes the **narrator** is confused with the **author** himself or herself. This is a common mistake. Unlike the author or writer of the story, the narrator **is** a character in the story. The author, on the other hand, is the **creator** of the work.

James Li, a former student, cautions:

"Do not confuse characters' (in fiction or drama) or speakers' (in poetry) viewpoints with authors' viewpoints."

8. Tone, Figurative Language, and Irony

Tone

Tone in a rhetorical analysis of a literary text often refers to the feelings associated with a description, which can be either the narrator's feelings about what he or she is describing or the feelings that the writer wants the readers to have, as the readers imagine the things that the narrator has described.

Allen Jay, a former writing student, advises:

"Don't confuse voice (personality) with tone (attitude). Also don't write: 'This piece shows that the author uses tone when expressing himself.' or 'The author's voice is revealed in the piece. All writers use tone and voice. It is better to describe the author's tone more specifically. 'The author uses images of children crying to reveal his sorrowful tone.'"

Amanda Patterson lists 155 words to consider in analyzing writer's tone. (See http://writerswrite.co.za/155-words-to-describe-an-authors-tone.) Table 9.3 contains just a few from this list.

Table 9.3: Tone Analysis

Tone	Meaning
Absurd	illogical; ridiculous; silly; implausible; foolish
Accusatory	suggesting someone has done something wrong, complaining
Acerbic	sharp; forthright; biting; hurtful; abrasive; severe
Jaded	bored; having had too much of the same thing; lack enthusiasm

Figurative Language

Figurative language, or imaginative language, is an important part of what makes literary texts literary. **Similes**, or comparisons using *like* or *as*, and **metaphors**, or comparisons without using *like* or *as*, are part of what makes literary texts interesting, surprising, and insightful. Figurative language is often used to create a specific effect on an audience. (See Chapter 4.)

Irony

Irony refers to any phrase, action, or situation in which reality differs from what appears on the surface or what is logically expected. Authors use irony to inspire humor, surprise, or critical reflection. This is why it is an important element to consider when writing a . The three most common types of irony used in literary texts are **verbal irony**, **dramatic irony**, and **situational irony**.

Verbal Irony

Verbal irony occurs when a character or narrator says something that is the opposite of what is meant or expected. **Sarcasm** is a form of verbal irony. It is used to show that the tone or feeling of a speaker is different from what he/she literally says. For instance, someone might say, "What a great day," in a quiet and depressed voice. In writing, however, you cannot hear tone of voice to alert you to instances of sarcasm. You have to pay attention to the context of the dialogue. For example, imagine you read a story with the following dialogue:

Insider Tip

If you are having difficulty describing irony, try using the sentence frames in the chart on this page.

> Lisa watched as Bob suddenly tripped and landed on his face in the mud.
>
> "Are you okay?" Lisa shouted.
>
> "I'm great," Bob replied.

Although "replied" does not give the reader clues about Bob's tone of voice, the reader can infer from what has just happened to him that he must be feeling pretty far from "great."

Table 9.4: Irony Sentence Frame

Literary Term	Definition	Sentence Frame
Irony	Irony is when the opposite of what the reader expects to happen.	Ironically, … The irony of _____ reveals that… It is ironic that…

Dramatic Irony

Dramatic irony occurs when a character says or does something that the audience knows will have a different effect from the effect that the character intends. For example, in a scary movie, the audience will often see a killer go into a building, and then very soon after, they will see a character trying to escape from the killer come to the same building and say, "We'll be safe if we hide in here!" Writers use dramatic irony to inspire a variety of feelings in an audience. These include suspense, humor, anger, and pity.

Situational Irony

Situational irony occurs when events, or the consequences of an action, unfold in a way that is different from what readers would normally expect. The most famous example of situational irony is the O. Henry short story "The Gift of the Magi." In this story a married couple, Jim and Della, want to buy presents for each other but are too poor to afford anything. Each possesses only one thing of value: Jim has a gold pocket watch and Della has long, beautiful hair. Della decides to cut her hair and sell it to a wig maker. Using the money from the sale of her hair, she buys Jim a new chain for his watch. But when she gives Jim the chain, she discovers that he has sold it in order to buy her a set of combs for her hair. O. Henry uses this situational irony to explore the theme of gift giving, prompting his readers to reflect upon whether the usefulness of a gift or the thought behind it is more important.

Reading Comprehension Questions

1. What are two different types of rhetorical analysis that an instructor might ask you to write in a composition course?

2. What is the process of writing a rhetorical analysis?

3. What is usually included in the introduction of a literary analysis?

4. How do you determine which different literary elements or rhetorical devices you will discuss in a rhetorical analysis?

5. What can you add so that the reader who has not read the text you are writing about can understand your rhetorical analysis?

6. What is the role of social and historical context in a rhetorical analysis?

7. How can you determine whether to use secondary sources in a rhetorical analysis?

8. How can you determine which quotations to include in a rhetorical analysis?

9. How many details are needed to support the thesis statement of a rhetorical analysis? How can you determine which details are needed?

10. What content is generally included in the summary of a rhetorical analysis?

Writing in the Sciences:

Data Commentary and Reports

By Benjamin Duncan

The sharing of research, methods, results, and conclusions is fundamental to the development of science and technology. Students need to be confident about their research and writing and the presentation of their data and ideas. Producing a research report is one of the most essential parts of "joining the conversation" in many fields of study. A report requires careful planning if it is to appropriately fulfill the following purposes: (1) summarizing the methods and results (2) contributing to ongoing research and academic discussions in the field.

This chapter teaches you a set of skills necessary to write successful reports and to evaluate your own writing in terms of both strengths and weaknesses.

Structure of the Report

Different professors may ask you to include some or all of the following sections in your report. The sections you write for your reports will vary depending on the discipline. In most scientific disciplines, the common format includes introductions, methods, results, and discussions sections. Always consult your professor before you begin writing your report for specific requirements and expectations. Table 10.1 summarizes key features of the organizational structure commonly used to report research in a number of different scientific disciplines.

Table 10:1: Key Features of Organizational Structure

Header	Includes the name of the university, department, and course number. The title of the lab experiment is printed in bold in the center of the page. The student's name is given. Group members are listed in alphabetical order and its leader is identified. The date of experiment, submitted date, and name of the instructor and/or principal investigator are also given.
Abstract	An abbreviated form of the most important parts of the report. Usually the abstract addresses: purpose of the experiment, given facts and data, assumptions, measured data, and results or conclusions. Details are not included.
Objective	Discusses what the experiment hoped to accomplish. Typical aims include: (1) To explain observations and/or specific areas of study, (2) To improve on the efficiency or precision of previous work, (3) To show others how to replicate and validate results, and (4) To discuss the meaning of your results in the "larger conversation".
Equipment and Apparatus	A list of equipment used in the experiments is frequently included in laboratory reports. However, descriptions are usually not included. Common lab equipment, like stopwatches and scales, are typically excluded from the list.
Sample Calculations	Calculations clearly present the equations used with the data. Each section is labeled for easy identification.
Methods	This section discusses in a concise paragraph(s) the operation that was performed rather than listing the steps of the operation.
Results Data Commentary and Discussion	The results section usually includes a description of the data (data commentary) and a discussion of the findings. The data is presented in the same sequence that it was collected and each section is clearly identified. Data often include visuals (tables, graphs, charts, etc.) to identify the results discovered. The visuals include column headings with units. An original data sheet may be included in the Appendix. The discussion often begins with a brief summary of predicted results. Key results are clearly identified. Implications of the research are summarized near the end. The discussion also includes the possible causes of irregularities with the anticipated results.
Conclusions	This section discusses the results with respect to the objectives stated at the beginning of the report. Sometimes, suggestions for further study or improvements may be suggested.
References	Lists sources of material for further research by the reader. The citations are listed alphabetically by the first author's last name and may include page numbers after the name of the publisher.
Appendices	Includes supplementary material used to reinforce the material, for example, original data sheet or extensive theory.

Titles

Titles describe the content of the experiment or study and are written very clearly so that readers understand precisely what the study is about. Abbreviations and jargon are avoided as well as "cute" language. Words such as "an investigation of" or "research on" are generally omitted.

Abstracts

When writing your abstract, you discuss the most important or key points and condense it.

You include a brief description of the methods, a summary of the main ideas, and the major conclusions and significance. You will need to determine precisely how many words your abstracts should be. They often vary in length from 50 to 300 words.

Introductions

In your introduction, you explain the research problem or hypothesis you address. You also provide enough background information so that your reader understands your research. This means you will need to summarize relevant research and explain key terms and concepts. Your introduction also explains the significance of your study. Here you will want to explain that your study addresses an important question or concern, utilizes an untested population that must be studied, employs a new method or one that has not been tried before, challenges previous research, or extends research.

John Swales and Christine Feak collected large numbers of specialized lab reports and analyzed them for common language in introductions. They describe this language in *Academic Writing for Graduate Students*, 2012.

The Language of Introductions

Writers use the following expressions in their introductions. A number of them have been described by Swales and Feak.

Common Expressions Used to Establish the Importance of a Topic

- *The increasing interest in…has created a greater need for…*
- *Of particular interest is…*
- *Recently, researchers have turned their attention to…*
- *The possibility…has generated interest in…*
- *…is a classic problem in…*
- *The relationship between…is a classic problem of…*

Insider Tip

When writing the introduction, engage the reader by explaining why readers should care about your research. As appropriate, move from the significance of your research in the real world to the significance of your research in your discipline, to your methodology, and to your experiment. If you do not know if you should summarize your results and/or conclusions in the introduction, talk to your instructor.

- *The well-known phenomenon…has been a favorite topic for analysis both in…*
- *Knowledge of…has a great importance for…*
- *The study of…has become an important aspect of…*
- *The effect of…has been studied extensively in recent years.*
- *A central issue in…is the validity of…*

Common Expressions Used to Establish the Relevance of a Study to Previous Research

- While some have argued that…our study suggests the opposite.
- While previous studies suffer from…and are limited to…our study may provide alternatives that improve on the previous limitations.
- The previous studies focused on adults, ages 21-45, but failed to consider children, ages 8-16
- While many have researched this growing trend in the United States, our study examines whether a similar situation exists in South Korea.)
- However, it is not clear whether the use of…can be modified.
- The question remains whether these studies are applicable in other settings.
- This study continues the earlier research of _____ and applies the methods reviewed.

Common Language Used to Describe the Purpose of the Study

- This paper reports on the results obtained…
- The aim of this lab report is to describe…
- In this paper we give preliminary results of…
- The main purpose of the experiment reported here was to…
- This study was designed to evaluate…
- The present work extends the use of the previous lab…
- The purpose of this investigation is/was to…

Methods Section

In the methods section you explain how you carried out the study and the procedures you used. You describe the materials, subjects, and equipment (chemicals, experimental animals, apparatus, etc.) you used. (You may want to use such subheadings as materials, subjects and equipment.) You also explain the steps you took in your experiment. (These may be subheaded by experiment, procedure, etc.) Make sure that you use the past tense to describe what you *did* and provide enough detailed information—for instance, measurements, amounts, times, temperatures and concentrations—so that your study can be replicated.

Dominic He, a former writing student, warns:

"I mixed my results section with my procedures section. It lowered my grade. Ask your instructor if you need separate headings for results and procedures."

Results Section

In the Results Section, you generally explain what you observed in each experiment you did and each procedure you followed. You report the main results that are supported by your data. An important part of this section includes data commentaries.

Data Commentaries

It is not easy to predict precisely what you might need to do in the results section of your report, but here are some of the more common ways.

- Provide sufficient background for the data.
- Introduce a table, graph, diagram, etc., and help the reader locate it.
- Highlight the key results.
- Explain the significance and/or implications of key results.

When your study includes multiple results, discuss with your instructor the organization. You should organize the results logically, for example, you might organize it from the most to the least important or from simple to complex. When you include a table, do not just repeat the information from the table in your commentary on the data. Instead, be selective. Discuss the most important data and the major generalization/s that can be made concerning data trends. Table 10.2 is a sample table, and data commentary follows it.

Table 10.2: Sample Table and Data Commentary:
Sources of Acute Respiratory Infections*

Source	Percentage
Airborne viruses	87%
Food bacteria	4%
Industrial pollution	2%
Water pollution	2%
Smoke inhalation	2%
Unsterilized medical equipment	1%
Malicious poisoning	<1%
Total survey respondents	299

Note: These are not real data

Sample Data Commentary

(1) An acute respiratory infection is a health problem that affects normal breathing. (2) Although it typically starts as a minor infection of the nose, throat, or lungs, it can quickly spread to the entire respiratory system if left untreated. (3) Moreover, acute respiratory infections are contagious to other people living and working in close proximity and can be especially harmful to children, the elderly, and those with weakened immune systems. (4) Table 1, above, shows the most common sources of acute respiratory infection. (5) As can be observed from the first row, in a great majority of cases, the entry point of the virus infection can be detected, with airborne viruses being responsible for nearly 9 out of 10 reported illnesses. (6) This very high percentage is increasingly alarming, especially since with a certain amount of caution such infections are largely preventable. (7) As a consequence, we should be wary of staying in close proximity to colleagues or loved ones suffering from breathing difficulties, as the disease may spread quickly into our lungs. (8) In addition, improved airflow in work and home settings necessitates continual inspection of dirty air vents and window screens. (9) While it may be possible to lessen the likelihood of respiratory infections, our bodies are still vulnerable to airborne viruses because of the constant threat of new, quickly spreading viruses that cannot yet be identified by medical practitioners.

The purpose of the first few sentences (sentences 1-4) includes explaining what the data are about (acute respiratory infection) and establishing the importance of the dataset. The first sentences prepare the reader to understand the data in the table. Notice that the data commentary does not actually start until sentence 5.

Structure of a Data Commentary

Data commentaries usually have the following elements in the following order.

1. Summary statements

2. Highlighting statements

3. Discussion of implications, problems, exceptions, recommendations, etc.

Location + title summary   Linking as-clause+ highlight of
                                         key date

Implications of the data

(4) Table 3, on previous page, shows the most common sources of acute respiratory infection. (5) As can be observed, in a great majority of cases, the entry point of the virus infection can be detected, with airborne viruses being responsible for nearly 9 out of 10 reported illnesses. (6) This very high percentage is increasingly alarming, especially since with a certain amount of caution such infections are largely preventable. (7) In consequence, we should be wary of staying in close proximity to colleagues or loved ones suffering from breathing difficulties, as the disease may spread quickly into our lungs. (8) In addition, improved air flow in work and home settings necessitates continually inspection of dirty air vents and window screens. (9) While it may be possible to lessen the likelihood of respiratory infections, our bodies are still vulnerable to airborne viruses because of the constant threat of new, quickly spreading viruses that cannot yet be identified by medical practitioners.

Reporting and Summary Language

Many data commentary sections begin with a sentence locating the visual the writers use, followed by a verb (like *shows, provides,* or *gives*) and a summary of the data (Table 10.3).

Table 10.3: Reporting and Summary Language

Reporting Verb	Summary
Graph 5 shows…	the sources of acute respiratory infections
Table 2 provides…	details of the common causes of respiratory illness.
Figure 2 plots…	the major causes of respiratory illness over the last five years.
Figure 4.2 gives…	the results of our study on respiratory infections.

The passive voice can also be used (Table 10.4).

Table 10.4: Passive Voice Reporting Language

Summary	Reporting Verb
The sources of acute respiratory infections…	are shown in Graph 5.
Details of the common causes of respiratory illness …	are provided in Table 2.
The major causes of respiratory illness over the last five years…	are plotted in Figure 2
The results of our study on respiratory infections…	are given in Figure 4.2.

Table 10.5 provides additional data about acute respiratory infections. Consider which data you would want to highlight and what are the implications of the data.

Table 10.5: Sources of Acute Respiratory Infections, 2011-2016*

Source of Infection	2011	2012	2013	2014	2015	2016
Airborne viruses	0%	9%	26%	32%	56%	87%
Food bacteria	43%	36%	42%	36%	25%	4%
Industrial pollution	4%	21%	27%	21%	9%	2%
Water pollution	29%	15%	7%	5%	7%	2%
Smoke inhalation	7%	12%	18%	12%	13%	2%
Unsterilized medical equipment	6%	11%	8%	4%	2%	<1%
Malicious poisoning	0%	0%	2%	1%	0%	<1%
Total number of survey respondents						299

* Note: These are not real data.

Conclusions

Swales and Feak (2012) provide a list of typical ways writers conclude their lab reports.

(Un)expected Outcome

Here writers comment on whether the overall results of the experiment achieved the expected objectives.

Re-Statement of Key Results

Writers restate the most important results within the first paragraph and discuss less important results in later paragraphs.

Background Information

Writers strengthen their discussion by summarizing main points, highlighting theory, and reminding the reader of technical information.

Explanation

Writers suggest reasons for a surprising result, or one at odds with those reported in the literature.

Deduction and Hypothesis

Writers make a claim (however qualified) about the general usability of the reported results.

Recommendations

Writers advocate the need for further research or make suggestions about possible lines of future investigation.

The following is a conclusion of an electrical engineering lab report. As you read the conclusion, underline words or expressions that you could use in a report.

---

(1) In general, the experimental results agree reasonably well with the simulation predictions. (2) The gain of the hardware implementation was 0.5 dB higher than the predicted value of 46 dB. (3) This 0.5 dB deviation corresponds to a 6% error in the value of vout/vin. (4) The error could be caused by mismatches between transistors Q1 and Q2 (changing the bias current), or by an imperfect SPICE model for transistor Q3. (5) The error is larger than would be expected from measurement error for the test equipment used. (6) While the lower 3-dB frequency of the implementation agreed closely with the simulation result, the upper cutoff frequency of 1.2 MHz was significantly larger than the value predicted by the simulation. (7) The upper cutoff frequency is determined by the parasitic capacitance of transistor Q3. (8) Apparently the values incorporated in SPICE model were larger than those of the device that was used in the implementation. (9) Since the amplifier input impedance Rin depends upon the β of Q3, it is not surprising that the simulated and measured results differ from each other. (10) Both results (at 1 kHz) satisfy the prediction, and are reasonable for the transistors used. (11) Some care should be taken in interpreting Figure 7 at other frequencies. (12) Simulation results show that the impedance is resistive only for frequencies in the range $300 \text{ Hz} \leq f \leq 3 \text{ kHz}$. (13) At frequencies below or above this band, the amplifier input impedance is primarily capacitive. (14) At high frequencies in particular, the impedance magnitude is much smaller than that predicted. (15) The design and implementation of a 46 dB, 1.2 MHz bandwidth amplifier has been presented. (16) Hardware tests verified the performance of the amplifier. (17) While the amplifier performed largely as predicted, some care is needed in interfacing to the amplifier.

Reading Comprehension Questions

1. How are scientific reports organized in your discipline? If you are unsure, analyze a report from your field.

2. What is the purpose of a title?

3. How many words need to be in an abstract?

4. What do writers need to include in an abstract of a scientific report?

5. What are key expressions writers use to describe the importance of their studies?

6. What are five key expressions writers need to describe the purpose of their studies?

7. What are five expressions that are often used in data commentaries?

8. What five words or expressions are often used to describe data in a table?

9. When writing a scientific report, why is it important to number each table and include a title for each table?

10. Graphs are often used in data analyses and reports. (See below.) Study this graph and then fill in the blanks of the paragraph that follows the graph.

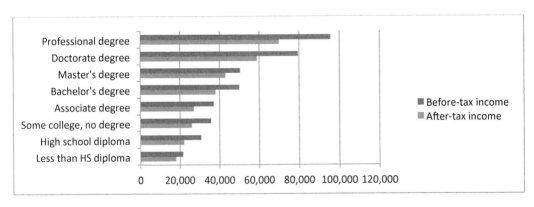

Graph 1. Median Earnings and Tax Payments by Level of Education, 2003.

Notes: Includes full-time year-round workers age 25 and older. Prices as in U.S. $. Tax payments are based on 2002 tax rates and do not incorporate the 2003 federal income reduction. Source: U.S. Census Bureau 2004, PINC-03; Internal Revenue Service, 2003.

Salary and Education

According to (1) _____, annual salary steadily (2) _____ in connection with degree of education. In 2003, workers with professional and doctorate degrees earned on average between (3) _____ and (4) _____ U.S. dollars before taxes each year. These numbers represent an average raise of (5) _____ U.S. dollars from workers with a master's degree, or an increase of (6) _____ percent. The largest group, those with only a high school diploma, earned an average of (7) _____ , and those with (8) _____ grossed an average 21,000 U.S. dollars each year. Interesting the average annual salary for both (9) _____ and (10) _____ were nearly identical at approximately 50,000 U.S. dollars. Likewise, (11) _____ and (12) _____ accumulated similar annual pay rates, albeit significantly lower than those with college degrees. As can be seen from the graph, it is evident that (13) _____

_____.

> Producing a research report is one of the most essential parts of "joining the conversation" in your field of study.

Using Sources in Academic Writing:

Quoting and Paraphrasing in Argumentative Writing

Strategies for Using Sources

What does **using sources** mean? A *source* is a person, book, or document that gives you information. When you use sources, you take others' words, information, and ideas and you combine them with your own writing. In other words, you *integrate* your sources into your writing. You might summarize them, paraphrase them, or quote words from them in a way that makes your writing more effective. In order to use sources well, you'll need to be able to do the following:

- **Understand the source.** Have a good understanding of the *source material*. Is it a book? Newspaper? Article? Is the piece meant for a particular audience? Source material refers to the publications from which you obtain information, ideas, and words for your writing. It is essential to understand the source material thoroughly, so you avoid misrepresenting it.

- **Evaluate the source.** Be able to evaluate the use of the source material, for instance, to determine which parts of it you can use in your writing to support your points.

- **Synthesize and analyze the source.** Synthesize the source material—to combine others' ideas with your own, making them into a complete whole or possibly even into a new idea and *analyze* the source material—that is, examine and think about it carefully. This makes it possible to make connections between what you and others say about a particular topic.

- **Explain the source.** Explain the critical information about the source that the readers need to understand and the relevance of the source to your writing and the points you are making.

One of the most important types of literacy you'll gain at college is **information literacy**. According to the American Library Association of the Presidential Committee on Information Literacy, *"Ultimately, information literate people are those who have learned how to learn. They know how to learn because they know how knowledge is organized, how to find information, and how to use information in such a way that others can learn from them. They are people prepared for lifelong learning, because they can always find the information needed for any task or decision at hand."*

Source: Presidential Committee on Information Literacy. *Presidential Committee on Information Literacy: Final Report.* Washington, D.C., 1989. Association of College & Research Libraries. Web. 31 August 2015

In your courses, you'll read texts and use them to support a claim in a persuasive argument and in a literary analysis. You'll learn how to integrate sources in your writing using a specific citation style guide developed by the Modern Language Association (MLA). You'll also learn how to identify the material that best supports the points you are making in your writing, where to incorporate this material, how to incorporate it, and how to analyze it to support your writing.

You'll use sources when you use quotations, paraphrases, and summarized material in your writing. While there are many different criteria you can use when choosing what source material to include in your writing, here are three important ones:

- **Useful.** How is the quotation, paraphrase, or summarized material useful in supporting a point or claim? Will the readers find it worth remembering?

- **Relevant.** How directly related is the source material to the thesis statement? Does it support a specific point you are trying to make in your writing?

- **Context-Appropriate.** Does the source material fit well in a particular place in the writing? When writing an argument, does it contribute to the development of a coherent argument? Does it make sense, given the surrounding sentences?

Li Ming, a former student, advises:

"In English writing, when I make clear connections between the source material and my point, my instructor says my writing make sense. In Chinese, when I make direct connections between the source material and my point, my teacher in China tell me my writing does not look intelligent. The reader can understand the connections without words. I don't need to make connections in a way that is very clear and direct in Chinese. It sounds better that way. If I write the Chinese way in English, my instructor get confuse and my writing does not make sense."

In this book you'll learn other criteria for selecting sources. The type of evidence from you select will be based in large part on the readers, the text you are writing, and your goals. A lab report for biology includes different types of evidence from an analysis of a short story. It will include more descriptions of direct observations than paraphrases. Social science reports will include more statistics than quotations. Your persuasive writing will mostly include very brief summaries, paraphrases, and quotations statistics as evidence of your points.

You'll want to use sources in your writing where they are necessary and helpful, and leave them out where they are not. You'll also want to follow established practices for citing sources.

One way you'll use sources in your English language or writing class is by quoting from them. The following section teaches you how to integrate quotations smoothly into your writing, address format issues concerning titles and page numbers, and use paraphrasing effectively. In Chapter 12, you'll learn about summarizing.

Insider Tip

If you are required to write a research paper in one of your courses, you could find it very helpful to talk to your English language or writing instructor and campus writing specialists. Consulting with librarians about possible sources is also an excellent idea.

Abal Hamed, a former student, states:

"I look for good source material that supports my points and forget about bad sources that gives unnecessary details."

Integrating Quotations into Your Writing

Quoting is copying word for word what another person has said and putting the words in "quotation" marks followed by the appropriate reference details. Using a small number of well-selected quotations has the potential of making your writing memorable and interesting. However, you'll want to use quotations sparingly* in many types of academic writing, because too many can undermine* your efforts to convey original ideas.

*sparingly
(adverb): using something only a little

*undermine
(verb): to gradually weaken something

Filling your writing with a lot of quotations probably won't strengthen your writing and could weaken it. Most of your papers should be your own writing and reflect your own ideas. You'll provide quotations as just one type of support for your points.

If the quoted material is at least one complete sentence, it is useful to introduce it with **signal phrases** such as *The author claims*, *Gladwell argues*, *Smith writes*, or *According to Jones*, followed by a comma.

Insider Tip

Do not use a reporting verb (*state, lament, indicate*) together with the words "According to..." One of the most common errors that students make concern statements like the one below:

Incorrect:
According to John Smith, he writes...

Correct:
John Smith writes...

Examples:

- Martha Washington, the wife of First President George Washington, **writes***, "I am determined to be cheerful and happy in whatever situation I may find myself. For I have learned that the greater part of our misery or unhappiness is determined not by our circumstance but by our disposition."

- According to Arundhati Roy, an Indian writer and activist who focuses on issues related to social justice and economic inequality, "Wars are never fought for altruistic reasons."

When the quotation is less than a complete sentence, blend it into your own sentence using the word *that*. In this case, do **not** use a comma or a capital letter.

- American philospher Robert Persig claims that "a period of creativity" is always preceded by boredom.

- American President Franklin D. Roosevelt argues that "true individual freedom" requires "economic security and independence."

Blend short quoted phrases into your sentences as smoothly as possible.

- For Helen Keller, life is either a "daring adventure" or not worth living.

- Nick Cave, an Australian musician, songwriter, author, and screenwriter claims that if you eat with cannibals, eventually you will "get eaten."

Follow up a quotation with a sentence or phrase that explains it or comments on it.

- By this, he means that if you put yourself close in a dangerous situation, you will probably be hurt.

- This shows that Dave has a sense of humor.

Three Important Steps for Using Quotations

Below are **three steps** for integrating quotations into your writing:

 Introduce the quotation using a signal phrase such as *Smith says* or *He claims that.*

 Give the quotation using proper punctuation.

 Follow up the quotation with a sentence that explains it or comments on it. Good phrases to begin this sentence with include:
In other words, These words mean that…, This suggests that…, This quotation explains that…, This is significant because…, and *In essence, the author is arguing that….*

Insider Tip

Make sure to provide your own commentary that refers to, clarifies, and explains the quotation. Explain the significance of the quotation. The reader should have a clear idea of how the quotation supports the claim you are making in your paragraph. Instead of restating what the quotation has already said, add your ideas about its relevance to your claim. If this is difficult for you, ask yourself these questions: Why did I choose this quotation and how am I using the quotation to support my claim? How does it support my argument? You may have to replace the quotation with a different one if the quotation does not support your claim.

Examples of Quotation Introductions

- According to Malcolm Gladwell in his book *Outliers: The Story of Success*, "If you work hard enough and assert yourself, and use your mind and imagination, you can shape the world to your desires" (151). By this, he means that all individuals are capable of achieving success, but they must do so through diligence, assertion, intelligence, and creativity.

- In the excerpt "Silence" from her memoir *The Woman Warrior*, Maxine Hong Kingston remembers that she "flunked kindergarten" (48). She explains that this was a consequence of her silence during her first year in an American school when she was still unfamiliar with the English language and American culture.

Kevin Zhao, a former student, advises:

"Finding the right quotation was a big challenge for me. It helped me to highlight interesting quotations when I read and then copy down the ones that were relevant to my claims. I've learned just to quote the words and phrases that I need to support my claims and leave all others out. Take time to understand the main points to make sure your quotation directly supports one of them. I always jot down those main points and keep them in front of me when I write."

Insider Tip

When analyzing quotations to support an argument, it is also helpful if you comment on your interpretation of the quotation. Commenting on your commentary will enable you to analyze quotations in greater detail. Notice how this is done in the examples on this page.

Examples of Comments on Commentary

- On March 4, 1933, President Franklin Roosevelt argued in his inaugural address, "The only thing we have to fear is fear itself." Speaking to a nation weakened and demoralized by economic depression, he wanted to convince Americans not to be afraid in times of financial difficulties. He helped them regain confidence in the United States.

- In describing the crash of Air Florida Flight 90 and a man who sacrificed his life to save others from the disaster, Rosenblatt remarks, "If the man in the water gave a lifeline to the people gasping for survival, he likewise gave a lifeline to those who observed him." In other words, Rosenblatt is suggesting that to observe such an act of selflessness and heroism gives us hope and inspiration. He teaches us that ordinary people are capable of extraordinary acts of courage.

Using Verbs to Report What Others State

Table 11.1 lists verbs you can use to introduce quotations or report on authors' ideas. These verbs are often called reporting verbs.

Table 11.1: Useful Reporting Verbs

Strength	Examples
Neutral: verbs used to say what the writer describes in factual terms	describe, show, reveal, study, demonstrate, note, point out, indicate, report, observe, assume, take into consideration, examine, go on to say that, state, believe, mention
Tentative: verbs used to say what the writer suggests (without stating directly)	suggest, speculate, intimate, hypothesize, imply, allude to, hint at, speculate
Strong: verbs used to make strong claims	argue, claim, emphasize, contend, maintain, assert, theorize, support the view, deny, refute, reject, challenge, strongly believe, counter the view/argument

A WORD OF CAUTION

The above verbs are not all interchangeable. Before selecting a verb, it is important that you understand the meaning of the verb and its grammar rules.

If you are unsure about the exact meaning of any of the verbs in the table above, consult a dictionary—preferably one that shows usage. Good ones are *Longman English Dictionary Online* and *Cambridge Advanced Learner's Dictionary*, which are both available online.

Grammar Tips for Using Reporting Verbs

Some reporting verbs may appear in more than one of the following groups.

Verbs followed by a quotation that contains a subject and a verb

Examples:

- In discussing fame, Marilyn Monroe *adds*, "Fame doesn't fulfill you. It warms you a bit, but that warmth is temporary."
- Henry David Thoreau *concludes*, "Rather than love, than money, than fame, give me truth."

add	comment	notes
affirm	conclude	points out
argue	contend	proposes
assert	emphasize	remark
believe	explain	show
boast	insist	state
claim	maintain	thinks

Verbs followed by a that-clause containing a subject and a verb

Examples:

- Alexander Pope *remarks that* "fame can never make us lie down contentedly on a deathbed."
- Immanuel Kant *affirms that* "we are not rich by what we possess but by what we can do without."

acknowledge	deny	repeat
add	doubt	reply
affirm	explain	report
argue	fear	reveal
assert	feel	say
believe	indicate	state
boast	insist	suggest
contend	observe	suppose
claim	proposes	tell
comment	remark	think
complain	remember	understand
conclude		

Verbs that are a part of fixed expressions

Examples:

- Lance Armstrong *raises the question whether* "pain is temporary."
- George R. Martin, author of "A Game of Thrones," *supports the view that* "Some old wounds never truly heal, and bleed again at the slightest word."

Remember These Useful Expressions:

- counter this view by arguing that _____
- go on to state/claim/explain that ____
- challenge the view that _____
- posit the view that ____
- raise the question whether ____
- reveal the truth about ____
- support the view that ____
- take into consideration that ____
- take the perspective that ____
- take issue with
- tell a lie about ____
- tell a story about _____

Verbs followed by a clause starting with a question word

Examples:

- Author José B. Norris *explains why* "tears shed for another person are not a sign of weakness," but instead "a sign of a pure heart."
- Sophocles asks *whether love can* "free us of all the weight and pain of life."

ask	explain	remember
decide	forget	report
demonstrate	indicate	reveal
discover	know	show
discuss	learn	

Sofía García, a former writing student, cautions:

"In English, a lot of words are used together and when you don't use them together, readers will think there is something wrong with your writing. They'll find it jarring. Sometimes they'll even tell you how much it bothers them. Using fixed expressions incorrectly can disrupt the flow of your writing. That's why it's important to spend some time memorizing them and using them in your writing. I memorized the list above, and that help me write well."

The Verb Mention

men·tion [transitive]

Definition: to talk or write about something or someone, usually quickly and without saying very much or giving details:

Example:

- His name was *mentioned*.

mention (that)

Examples:

- He *mentioned* that individuals who help others may be selfless, but he did not explain why.
- It is worth *mentioning* (=it is important enough to mention) *that* they only studied a very small number of cases.
- As *mentioned* earlier, selfishness can lead to individuals' success.
- As *mentioned* above, selfishness can lead to individuals' success.
- He *mentioned* the discrepancy between the two approaches.

– Adapted from Longman Dictionary of Contemporary English Online

A WORD OF CAUTION

Be careful when using the verb *mention*. It does not have the same meaning as "state" and is not often used to introduce quotations in academic because it introduces a minor idea. The verb mention is never followed by "about."

Zhang Min, a former writing student, states:

"Get used to using the word argue to introduce quotation when you are writing an argument. When you use it like that, it means to state, giving clear reason, that something is true."

Wang Fang, a former student, advises:

"The best pieces of advice I can give Chinese-speaking students is this: Don't expect English to work like your first language. You can't just replace one reporting verb with another in English. Reporting verbs are not interchangeable. You need to know when each one is used and how to use it."

Your Turn

No one would say the incorrect sentence below. Why? Study the correct version and the definition of the word *mention* to determine the reason.

- **Incorrect:** Did I *mention* that World War III began this morning?

- **Correct:** Did I tell you that World War III began this morning?

Next explain why *mention* is used correctly or incorrectly in the sentences below.

- **Correct:** My instructor *mentioned* that when revising my essay, I should check to make sure that the quality of my evidence is sufficient.

- **Correct:** Gladwell, the author of *Outliers*, *mentions* that the most successful musicians have often spent hours practicing to obtain success.

- **Incorrect:** In the *Emancipation Proclamation*, Lincoln *mentioned* that as of January 1, 1863, all slaves in the United States "shall be then, thenceforward, and forever free."

- **Incorrect:** The primary support for the argument that people need to work hard to obtain expertise, comes from Gladwell, the author of *Outliers*, who *mentions*, "Researchers have settled on what they believe is the magic number for true expertise: ten thousand hours."

- **Incorrect:** The dictionary *mentions* that "altruism is the principle or practice of concern for the welfare of others."

Li Qiang, a former writing student, advises:
The best pieces of advice I can give students are these:

1. *Do the work and don't rely on your instructor to do it for you. This means you've got to read this chapter very carefully, study the lists of reporting verbs and learn their grammar rules, and do all your homework. You've also got to study how professional writers use reporting verb. Take the time to highlight and analyze the use of reporting verbs when you are reading. Figure out which reporting verbs are the best to use in particular sentences in your writing.*

2. *Identify your weaknesses. Figure out what you need to learn and concentrate on that.*

3. *Practice makes perfect. The key to learning to quote is to practice quoting.*

4. *Never give up. Although learning to quote is complicated, it will help you throughout your entire time at college. Quitting is not an option. Stick to it until you can quote well.*

TAGs

The following section provides examples of incorrect and correct uses of prepositional phrases followed by helpful sentence frames for introducing titles, authors, and genres (sometimes referred to as a **TAG** (for **t**itle, **a**uthor, and **g**enre).

Insider Tip

You may have difficulty introducing titles and authors if you are translating from a different language into English or falling back on a familiar topic/comment structure that you have learned earlier. Try using the sentence frames and varying them to meet your needs. If that does not work, you might try avoiding introducing titles of words with prepositions. Example: In the book *The Red Pony* by John Steinbeck describes a young man named Tom who learns not only responsibility but also ways to face loss.

Helpful Sentence Frames

1. In the narrative _____ *(give the title of the story)*
   the author _____ *(name the author)*
   _____ *(claim/states/argues/other reporting verb)*

2. In the narrative _____ *(give the title of the story)*
   by ___ *(name the author)* ___ , *(name the character)* ___
   Verb Phrase *(tell what the character does, believes or feels)*

3. In the book ___ **Give and Take** ___
   the author **Adam M. Grant** ___
   _____ **argues that...** ___

4. In the narrative **Social Inequalities in Washington Post** ___
   by **George Wills** ___
   Verb Phrase **claims that...** ___

A WORD OF CAUTION

Sentence templates such as the ones above won't work in all contexts. Use them while you are developing good strategies for introducing titles and authors, but do not grow dependent on them and repeatedly use them in all your writing. Also, use them flexibly. Change them to fit your needs as a writer.

Incorrect and Correct Uses of Prepositional Phrases

In the Gettysburg Address, by Abraham Lincoln, is about freedom for slaves.

Prepositional phrase
used incorrectly as subject   **Predicate**

The Gettysburg Address, by Abraham Lincoln, is about freedom for slaves.

Noun phrase
used correctly as subject   **Predicate**

Source: Olson, Carol Booth, Robin Scarcella, and Tina Matuchniak. *Helping English Learners to Write.* New York: Teachers College Press, 2015. p. 53. Adapted and reprinted with permission.

Incorrect and Correct Uses of Prepositional Phrases

Directions: Write *Correct* or *Incorrect* under each sentence. If the sentence is Incorrect, rewrite it so the prepositional phrase is used correctly.

1. In the book *The Theft of Memory*, by journalist Jonathan Kozol, describes Kozol's father who suffers from Alzheimer's.

_____

_____

2. In the short story "The Medicine Bag," the author Virginia Driving Hawk Sneve describes a young boy who is confused by his grandfather's heritage.

_____

_____

3. In the article "Why Pushy Parents Do More Harm than Good," by Elizabeth Meakins, she claims that many parents become obsessive about their children's lives.

_____

_____

4. Malcolm Gladwell, in his book *The Tipping Point*, he claims that outliers are not necessarily innately talented.

_____

_____

Paraphrase Your Source

You don't always have to quote your sources. You can also paraphrase the words in sources—change their words to your own words, while keeping the same meaning. If you have chosen to paraphrase someone, do not use quotation marks, even if the material being paraphrased is a complete sentence. Paraphrases are often introduced by the word **that**.

Key Point:

Do not call a book a "novel" (fictional) if it is non-fiction (fact-based).

- James Herriot argues **that** animals are more likely to have a soul than humans since, for him, having a soul means feeling love, loyalty and gratitude.
- Abraham Lincoln writes **that** everyone has to do their own growing, regardless of how tall their grandfathers were.

There is more information about how to paraphrase later in this chapter in the section titled *Paraphrasing*.

Key Point:

In your papers, give the author's full name in the introduction to your paper and refer to him or her by the last name in the rest of the paper.

MLA Format Issues: Titles and Page Numbers

Titles

Italicize the names of long texts such as movies, books, and newspapers. Only <u>underline</u> them if you are writing them out by hand. All word processors have an *italics* option on the tool bar. Use quotation marks to indicate the name of short texts such as articles, essays, short stories, poems, and quoted parts.

- **Correct:** In *Rolling Stone*, Peter Travers states that *Rudy* is an excellent movie.
- **Correct:** In her article "Why Pushy Parents Do More Harm than Good," Elizabeth Meakins claims that many parents become obsessive about their children's lives.

Punctuating Quotations without Page Numbers

When there are no page numbers involved, commas and periods should be placed **inside** the quotation marks:

- "The theory has yet to be proven," Symes confesses.
- She says he is "as good as gold."

A question mark or an exclamation mark should be placed **inside** the quotation marks if the quoted material is a question/exclamation: "Get out of my way!" she shouted. "Why should I?" I replied. The last thing he asked was, "How much money does it cost?"

In rare cases a question mark or exclamation mark may be used outside of the quotation marks. This only occurs when the quoted material is not a question/exclamation.

- Have educators read "Please, Stop Following Your Dreams"?

Punctuating Quotations with Page Numbers

When writing a paper and quoting from a short story, article, essay, or book, put only the page numbers (no author or title) in the parentheses following the quotation marks. Put the period after the parentheses. Introduce the title of the text before you quote material from it.

- In *Outliers* Gladwell writes, "Lucky breaks don't seem like the exception with software billionaires and rock stars and athletes" (56).

- Gladwell argues that "the closer psychologists look at the careers of the gifted, the smaller role innate talent seems to play and the larger role preparation seems to play" (38).

- In Malcolm Gladwell's *Tipping Point*, he claims that outliers are not necessarily innately talented. Gladwell argues that "the closer psychologists look at the careers of the gifted, the smaller role innate talent seems to play and the larger role preparation seems to play" (38).

Adding or Deleting Information When Quoting

To clarify a part of a quotation that is unclear or out of context, or to insert a word to make the quotation flow grammatically when you integrate it into your own sentence, you can add a word or phrase in **square brackets.** This is often done to clarify what a pronoun is referring to or to change a pronoun so that it agrees with the other words in the sentence. It may also be done to change the tense of a verb in the quotation so that it suits the tense of the integrated sentence.

In *Sweet Destiny,* Amaka Imani Nkosazana states, "Everything that looks good may not be good for you. In life, we all take chances. You must carefully examine the pros and cons. People often times have certain hidden agendas. And, you might not realize [what these agendas are] until you're in too deep."

Helen Keller claims that "only through [the] experience of trial and suffering can the soul be strengthened, ambition inspired, and success achieved."

If the passage you are quoting has parts that are not directly relevant to the point or argument you are making, you can delete this information and use **ellipsis points** (three periods with spaces in between) to mark the deletion. Ellipsis points are not used at the beginning or end of a quotation because you can start or end the quotation in mid-sentence as long as you blend it grammatically into your own sentence.

- **Correct:** Abraham Lincoln writes, "Be with a leader when he is right…but, leave him when he is wrong."

- **Incorrect:** Abraham Lincoln writes, "Be with a leader when he is right, stay with him when he is still right…"

When a passage you are quoting contains words in which the author quotes another source, turn the author's regular quotation marks into single quotation marks. [" …" → ' …']

- Elizabeth Meakins writes that in many middle-class homes, "there is a pernicious growth of an unhealthy form of boundary blurring. As one mother put it recently, 'We are in the middle of exams'" (98). (Originally, there were regular quotation marks around "We are in the middle of exams.")

Author/Director

Introduce your sources by using the author's or movie director's full name and giving some brief background information about the text or movie, such as its genre. After the first reference, use the author's or director's last name. Do **not** use the author's (or director's) first name by itself.

- **Correct:** In *The Theft of Memory*, journalist Jonathan Kozol describes Kozol's father who suffers from Alzheimer's. Kozol provides a rich description of how his relationship changes with his father and how he copes with caring for him.

- **Incorrect:** In *The Theft of Memory*, journalist Jonathan Kozol describes Kozol's father who suffers from Alzheimer's. Jonathan provides a rich description of how his relationship changes with his father and how he copes with caring for him.

Prepositional Phrases Used to Introduce Texts

When writing an introduction to a text-based paper, it is customary to acknowledge the title, the author, and the genre (or type of writing) you are discussing. Typically, when you are referring to the text or the genre, you use the preposition "in," and when you are referring to the author, you use the preposition "by," as in the example below:

In the short story "The Medicine Bag" *by* Native American author Virginia Driving Hawk Sneve, a young boy is confused by his grandfather's heritage.

Insider Tip

The easiest way to identify a person's last name is to remember that it comes last. In some languages the family name is put first, but in English it is important to list the family name last. If you can't figure out which of the author's names is first and which is last, ask a classmate or your instructor, or look up the name of the author on the internet.

Remember:

Prepositional phrases cannot be the subjects of sentences.

Complete the following exercises with a partner. Share your answers in class.

Citation and Format Exercises

Exercise 1 (Citations)

Each of the sentences below contains two formatting errors. Correct them with your partner.

1. According to novelist Lance Morcan in *The Orphan Conspiracies: 29 Conspiracy Theories from The Orphan Trilogy* "Traditional journalism, where reporters deliver information in a fair way, is rapidly disappearing. This is especially evident on television where reporters become bigger than the story, delivering news almost as if they were actors".

2. In his book *Bad Dogs Have More Fun: Selected Writings on Family, Animals, and Live from the The Philadelphia Inquirer*, journalist John Grogan writes "In the English language, it all comes down to this: Twenty-six letters, when combined correctly, can create magic. They can form the foundation of a free society (152)".

3. In his farewell address of 1961, Dwight D. Eisenhower warned that the increasing amounts of money spent on defense were creating an all too powerful military. He went on to claim that "The potential for the disastrous rise of misplaced power exists and will persist".

4. In his inaugural address of 1961, Kennedy called for national unity in facing "The common enemies of man: tyranny, poverty, disease and war itself.

5. After police and other whites brutally attacked civil rights protestors in Selma, Alabama, President Lyndon B. Johnson went before Congress to demand passage of the Voting Rights Act of 1965 that would ensure that African Americans had the right to vote. He explained that "…even if we pass this bill, the battle will not be over" For Johnson, the nation still had to overcome racism.

Exercise 2 (Format Issues)

Each item below contains at least five formatting errors. Correct them with your partner.

1. In his 2015 "Atlantic Magazine" review of the best-selling book "*Give and Take: Why Helping Others Drives Our Success*" writer Jerry Useem argues that the author of the book, 33-year-old Adam Grant, a Wharton professor, offers solid evidence "that "givers"— people who share their time, contacts, or know-how without expectation of payback—are highly successful in their fields".

2. Malcolm Gladwell, author of the best-selling book, The Tipping Point, discusses the contagiousness of yawning. He writes, "just because you read the word "yawning" in the previous two sentences—and the two additional 'yawns' in this sentence—a good number of you will probably yawn within the next few minutes'. (9)

Exercise 3 (Analyzing a Citation)

Read this excerpt taken from a student essay. Then answer the questions that follow with your partner.

In "The New Way We Work" by Martha Groves, a certified accountant named Steve Wade says, "When I started in business, the people who input the information were clerks. Today, we don't have clerks. It's CPAs and MBAs who do their own inputting." Groves points out that as technology has developed, many businesses expect their employees to keep up with new developments.

1. What is the full name of the author being cited here?

2. Who is being quoted?

3. Why is the quoted person's opinion important?

4. Does the writer provide the title of the article he or she has read?

5. Does the writer name the publication where the article can be found?

6. From now on, how should the writer refer to Steve Wade?

7. Should the writer mention where this article was published?

8. Is "The New Way We Work" a book, a documentary or an essay? How can you tell?

9. Is this excerpt a good example of a quotation that has been integrated using three steps? Why or why not?

10. Do you think this excerpt is a complete paragraph? Why or why not?

Key Point:

The consequences of plagiarism are severe.

Paraphrasing

You can paraphrase to show you understand a text and can interpret it. Paraphrasing is an important tool you can use to reshape information to fit many different types of academic writing. It is an essential skill for success at the university and can help you avoid plagiarism.

How to Paraphrase

When you paraphrase, you are rewriting others' words in your own. Paraphrasing a text requires strong reading ability. You need to understand the text well, and that takes time. Try putting the text away and rewriting portions of it in your own words. Also try paraphrasing the author's words orally. By talking about the author's ideas orally, you might get a better understanding of them and be able to express them more clearly when you write them down as paraphrases. Here are some sentence frames to help you.

- So from what I understand, Murakami believes that…

- From what he wrote, I understand that…

- Can you tell me if I understood correctly? It seems that the author believes…

- When the author said…did he mean…?

Techniques for Paraphrasing

To avoid plagiarism it is often necessary to use more than one technique at a time. See the examples below.

- **Synonyms**
  Original: The unemployed suffered most greatly during the Great Depression.
  Paraphrase: Of all those who were tormented by the Great Depression, the unemployed were hurt most.

- **Circumlocution**
  Original: Early marriage laws in the southern states were discriminatory in the late nineteenth century.
  Paraphrase: In the latter part of the nineteenth century, laws governing those who could marry resulted in discrimination.

- **Phrase Reversal**
  Original: Turtle fishing was the backbone of subsistence.
  Paraphrase: The primary form of subsistence was turtle fishing.

- **Sentence Combination**
  Original: Irony occurs when the reader is surprised by the ending of a story. The author accomplishes this surprise ending by leading the reader to expect a different ending.

Insider Tip

Complete the paraphrase exercises at Purdue's Online Writing Lab: https://owl. english.purdue.edu/ exercises/28/12/33. They'll give you valuable practice paraphrasing.

Paraphrase: When the reader's expectations of the conclusion of a story are different from the actual conclusion, the author has developed an ironic ending.

- **Sentence Distribution**

  Original: Turtle fishing was the backbone of subsistence, providing meat throughout the year.

  Paraphrase: The primary form of subsistence was turtle fishing. It provided meat throughout the year.

- **Active/Passive**

  Original: Social motives play a very important role.

  Paraphrase: A very important role is played by social motives.

- **Alternate Word Form**

  Original: A manager's success is often due to perseverance.

  Paraphrase: A manager often succeeds because of perseverance.

  Original: "All those who take drugs are accomplices to murder," said Nancy Reagan.

  Paraphrase: Mrs. Reagan claimed that all the people who took drugs were accomplices to murder.

- **Negative/Opposite Forms**

  Original: I was very full after dinner last night.

  Paraphrase: I was definitely no longer hungry after last night's dinner.

- **Changing Subjects**

  Original: The boss lent Tom his laptop computer for the weekend.

  Paraphrase: Tom borrowed the boss' laptop computer for the weekend.

MLA Format

The format conventions described in this chapter are set by the MLA (Modern Language Association) and are generally followed in the fields of the humanities and arts. In other academic fields, other conventions apply, such as the APA (American Psychological Association) format in social sciences or the CSE (Council of Science Editors) format in life sciences.

Formatting Your Papers in MLA Style

The Modern Language Association (MLA), an international association of almost 25,000 professionals involved in teaching languages and literatures, sets guidelines for many aspects of scholarly communication in the humanities. One of these aspects is the format of college papers. You may already be familiar with MLA-style quotations and Works Cited lists, but informing yourself on how to format your paper's header, name block, spacing, font, indents and margins will also be very useful to you. Like your knowledge of quoting and documenting your sources, formatting your paper correctly will signal to your audience that you possess both the technical know-how and the academic experience of a 21st-century college writer.

- **Header**
  Your paper will need a header, which includes your last name, one space and the page number. To format a header in Word, go to the "insert" tab, select "page number" and select "Top of the Page" and "right align." The page number will automatically show up and change on every page. To add your last name, double-click the first page number. Type your first name and a space in front of it, and the complete header will now be visible on each page.

- **Name Block**
  Unlike the header, which is right aligned and uses only one line, the name block is left aligned and consists of the following four lines in the order shown.

  – your first name followed by your last name

  – the capitalized word "Professor" followed by his or her last name

  – your class (title and course number)

  – the assignment's due date (such as "14 October 2016" or "October 14, 2016")

- **Spacing**
  Double-space your writing assignments. There should be no extra spaces between your paragraphs. In some versions of Word, the spacing between paragraphs is automatically set to to 10 pt., resulting in large spaces between paragraphs. To correct this, highlight your entire text and click the "Layout" tab at the top of the screen. Once there, locate "Spacing" and make sure both the "Before" and "After" areas are set to "0 pt."

- **Font**
  The font to use is Times New Roman. The font size is 12. Do not use bold print. Italicize the titles of books and movies as well as the names of periodicals (newspapers or magazines).

- **Indents**
  The first line of each new paragraph should be indented by half an inch. If you hit "tab" on your key board and your indent comes out too small, there is an alternative to tabbing. You can highlight your entire Word document, go to format/ paragraph/ special/ first line and select 0.5." This ensures that your new paragraph indents are indeed set at half an inch.

- **Margins**
  Before you start writing, click "Layout," "Margins," and "Normal." The dialog box should specify that you have selected 1" margins for the top, bottom, left and right of your paper. Your computer may be set to centimeters instead of inches, so that should be 2.54 cm. If printing is required in your class, use a ruler to measure the margins of a printed page. If your printer gives you less than the 1" margins you set, you can set the margins to 1.2" or a similar increase that actually yields 1" margins on a printed page.

For more information on formatting your paper in MLA style or to download sample essays, you can visit the following reputable websites. The Online Writing Lab (OWL) at Purdue University provides an 11-page sample paper with clearly marked, helpful formatting comments.

   https://style.mla.org/formatting-papers/
   https://owl.english.purdue.edu/owl/resource/747/01/

Formatting Exercise (10 points)

In the following writing, find the ten formatting errors and write your findings on the lines below.

Header (one error) _____

Name Block (four errors) _____

_____

_____

_____

Spacing (one error) _____

Font (two errors) _____

_____

Indents (one error) _____

Margins (one error) _____

Lee, Viola

Eng 20C

Pro Scarcella

4th October 2016

Adults' Expectations of Young People

Different adults have different expectations for their kids in various situations. In Akeelah and the Bee directed by Doug Atchison, Akeelah, an eleven-year-old African American girl from a poor middle school in Los Angeles, experiences a lot on her way to win the Spelling Bee. Her mother Tanya, a full-time worker, experiences a serious of changes in her attitude towards Akeelah. In Akeelah and the Bee directed by Doug Atchison, mother's attitude changes greatly throughout the movie, which is mainly due to Akeelah's performance in the Spelling Bee. Because he thinks the child he is facing is immature and impolite, Dr. Larabee treated Akeelah cruelly when Akeelah is disrespectful to him. Adults' expectations increase with the increasing of their children's accomplishment. Adults' expectations become low when they got disrespect treat. More importantly, on children's way to success, adults' expectations can be a way to give children positive influences or negative influences.

Adults' expectations increase with the increasing of their children's accomplishment. We can see it obviously from the movie Akeelah and the Bee directed by Doug Auchison. When Tanya first knows that Akeelah is enrolled in the spelling bee competition, she shows is impatience and disapproval. In the school competition, Tanya stops Akeelah from playing spelling games and tells Akeelah to focus more on studying instead of the Spelling Bee. In the district competition, Tanya doesn't even give Akeelah a ride. However, when Akeelah wins the competition and Dr. Larabee persuades her to feel confident of her daughter, Akeelah's growth and accomplishment win her mother's confirm. Tanya realizes how incorrect she was. As a mature adult, no one will show high expectations and devote full interest in young people.

A Sample Works Cited Page

This page provides an example of a Works Cited page in MLA, 8th edition, 2016 format. Source: Purdue Online Writing Lab: https://www.owl.english.purdue.edu/owl/resource/747/12/

Works Cited

Dean, Cornelia. "Executive on a Mission: Saving the Planet." *The New York Times,* 22 May 2007, www.nytimes.com/2007/05/22/science/earth/22ander. html?_r=0. Accessed 12 May 2016.

Ebert, Roger. Review of *An Inconvenient Truth, directed by Davis Guggenheim. rogerebert.com,* 1 June 2006, http://www.rogerebert.com/reviews/an-inconvenient-truth-2006. Accessed 15 June 2016.

Gowdy, John. "Avoiding Self-organized Extinction: Toward a Co-evolutionary Economics of Sustainability." *International Journal of Sustainable Development and World Ecology,* vol. 14, no. 1, 2007, pp. 27-36.

An Inconvenient Truth. Directed by Davis Guggenheim, performances by Al Gore and Billy West, Paramount, 2006.

Leroux, Marcel. *Global Warming: Myth Or Reality?: The Erring Ways of Climatology.* Springer, 2005.

Milken, Michael, et al. "On Global Warming and Financial Imbalances." *New Perspectives Quarterly,* vol. 23, no. 4, 2006, p. 63.

Nordhaus, William D. "After Kyoto: Alternative Mechanisms to Control Global Warming." *American Economic Review,* vol. 96, no. 2, 2006, pp. 31-34.

---. "Global Warming Economics." *Science*, vol. 294, no. 5545, 9 Nov. 2001, pp. 1283-84, DOI: 10.1126/science.1065007.

Regas, Diane. "Three Key Energy Policies That Can Help Us Turn the Corner on Climate." *Environmental Defense Fund,* 1 June 2016, www.edf.org/blog/2016/06/01/3-key-energy-policies-can-help-us-turn-corner-climate. Accessed 19 July 2016.

Revkin, Andrew C. "Clinton on Climate Change." *The New York Times,* 17 May 2007, www.nytimes.com/video/world/americas/1194817109438/clinton-on-climate-change.html. Accessed 29 July 2016.

Shulte, Bret. "Putting a Price on Pollution." *US News & World Report*, vol. 142, no. 17, 14 May 2007, p. 37. Ebsco, Access no: 24984616.

Uzawa, Hirofumi. *Economic Theory and Global Warming.* Cambridge UP, 2003.

Reading Comprehension Questions

1. What is the purpose of using sources in your writing?

2. What are three steps that writers can use to incorporate quotations into their writing?

3. How many quotations should you generally use in writing? Is using six quotations in a two-page essay insufficient? Why?

4. What are three steps used to incorporate quotations into your writing?

5. What are three reporting verbs that are part of fixed expressions?

6. What word should never be used after the verb mention?

7. How can you indicate to the reader that you have deleted information in a quotation?

8. When do you use square brackets ([ ]) in a quotation? What do these brackets mean?

9. Which types of reading materials do you italicize when you are describing them in an essay? (Consider such materials as books, articles, and newspapers.) Why do you italicize them?

10. Examine the reporting verbs in Table 11.2. Circle five reporting verbs that you rarely if ever use in your writing, cross out two reporting verbs that you use a lot, and underline five reporting verbs that you would like to use more frequently.

Table 11.2: List of Useful Reporting Verbs

acknowledge	describe	note	speculate
add	discuss	point out	state
affirm	emphasize	posit the view	suggest
argue	examine	propose	suspect
assert	explain	question	support the view
believe	hypothesize	raise the question	take the perspective
challenge the view	imply	recommend	theorize
consider	indicate	refute	think
contend	insist	reject	view
claim	maintain	remark	wonder
conclude	mention	say	
deny	negate	show	

Using a small number of well-selected quotations has the potential of making your writing memorable and interesting. However, you'll want to use quotations sparingly in many types of academic writing, since too many can undermine your efforts to convey original ideas.

CHAPTER TWELVE

SECTION III: Cohesion

Writing Cohesively

By Jacob Ludwig and Robin Scarcella

What are Cohesive Devices?

Cohesive devises are words, phrases, or clauses that connect words, phrases, sentences, and paragraphs. When used correctly, they enable writers to create **cohesion**, showing the relationship or progression of ideas from one sentence to the next.

Cohesion is like glue.

Cohesion is like glue. Just as a child glues pieces of paper together to make an art piece or a tile setter sets tiles in a hallway to create a mosaic pattern, people often use glue to paste parts together, keeping the *whole* in mind. Similarly, the child thinks about the image created by all the pieces of paper, and the tile setter concentrates on the overall pattern of the tiles. When you use cohesive devises, you focus on the main point of your writing and use the devices to connect your sentences.

Why are Cohesive Devices Important?

Cohesive devices can help you organize your ideas and show this organization to the reader—clearly and logically to construct a statement, explanation, or argument. They can also help you show chronological organization, contrast, reasoning, and cause and effect. But if they are overused or used incorrectly, they can undermine your writing by, for example, making your writing seem unnatural, overly predictable, or repetitive. Cohesive devices can, when not used appropriately, even make your writing difficult to understand.

You may be familiar with many of the cohesive devices described below. Key steps for using them include understanding what you are trying to convey to the reader and choosing the appropriate cohesive devise to do that.

In this chapter you will learn that expert writers do not rely on transition words like **however** and **in addition** to make their writing stick together. They use a wide repertoire of cohesive devices to add

165

Insider Tip

The types of cohesive devices that you use will vary depending on the type of writing you compose. Each type of writing is characterized by different uses of cohesive devices. You can learn these devices by reading texts that are representative of the genre and analyzing the cohesive devices used to connect sentences. You'll find, for example, that narratives are characterized by the use of cohesive devices entailing reference and vocabulary chains, and arguments are characterized by a wide variety of devices, sometimes involving nouns and verbs that indicate cause and effect.

cohesion to their writing and they use the appropriate ones that serve their purpose. If you are in the process of learning to write academic texts and you have learned to write in a language other than English that primarily uses synonyms to add cohesion to writing, the large range of cohesive devices available in English may surprise you. You might also be surprised how frequently expert writers of English use pronouns (like **he, she**, and **it**) and sentence structure to make writing cohere. To help you learn how to use cohesive devices, this chapter provides you with useful tips and strategies on their use, provides information on the various types of cohesive devices writers use in different types of texts, discusses challenges to learning these devices as well as useful strategies for learning them, and explains the use of clause connectors and transition words as well as the problems associated with their use. Because of the difficulties students have using transition words and pronoun reference, tips and exercises for using them are given at the end of the chapter.

Using Cohesive Devices

Types of Cohesive Devices and Examples

Repetition

Repetition can make your writing redundant or can help you draw attention to your ideas. Effective writers use repetition judiciously when they have an excellent reason for doing so.

> **Why** do some people fall in love with such intensity, seemingly at first glance? **Why** do some couples ease into marriage with a level-headed friendship? And **why**, as in the case of Rayna and Mark, do so many couples seem to have opposite personality traits? (Hendrix)

Synonyms

Synonyms are words that have the same meaning. Note that the word "car" can be replaced by "Ford" (hyponym—more specific meaning). "Car" can also be replaced by "vehicle" (hypernym—a word with a more general meaning).

> One of the problems teachers face is motivating students **to work hard.** Inspiring them **to study diligently** is a necessary first step. Note that **motivating** means about the same as **inspiring. To work hard** means about the same as **to study diligently.**

Antonyms

Antonyms are words that have the opposite meanings of other words. Antonyms, often combined with negating words like not, can be effective cohesive devices.

> The student center will **not** be **open** today. It will remain **closed** until the end of the week.

Pronouns

A pronoun takes the place of a noun and agrees with the noun it replaces in number and person.

Subject pronouns *(I, you, he, she, it, we, they)* replace the subject of the sentence.

> **Dr. Hubert** did not come to campus yesterday. **She** was busy elsewhere. "Dr. Hubert" is the subject and "she" is the subject pronoun.

Object pronouns **(me, you, him, her, it, us, them)** take the place of the object in the sentence (the noun that receives the action).

> After **Ryan** got a new coat, **he** took good care of it. "Coat" is the object, and "it" is the object pronoun.

Pronouns are used to refer to previously mentioned nouns.

> **Harriet** noticed that **her brother** was sleeping soundly, and **she** was careful not to wake **him** up.

Insider Tip

*The rules for using demonstrative pronouns are complicated and can be difficult for even highly competent writers to use. You might find it safest to use the word **it** to refer to ideas and **this, that, these,** and **those** to refer to nouns. Read how authors use demonstrative pronouns in their writing and try to emulate (copy) them. Ask your instructors for advice.*

Pronouns are also used to refer ahead to nouns that will be mentioned.

> While **it** may be hard to achieve, **success** in writing can be obtained through hard work and dedication.

Articles

The definite article **the** can be used to qualify a noun that has already been introduced with indefinite articles **a** or **an**.

> When I looked out of the window yesterday I saw **a** man and **a** woman standing by the gate. **The** man was wearing a hooded jacket and **the** woman was carrying a baseball bat.

Demonstrative Adjectives + Noun/s

Another way to add cohesion between sentences through referencing is to use demonstrative adjectives *(this, these, that, and those + nouns)*. Note that this technique can result in repetition and can be most effectively used when the readers need to be reminded of the noun or nouns to which the writer is referring.

It is also effective to use demonstrative adjectives with abstract nouns, such as this view, these approaches, and this advantage. Using demonstrative adjectives in this way can help you summarize a previously mentioned idea or statement.

> The new **policy** on gun control that was enacted last night in Maryland has been highly criticized in the social media. **This policy** may be helpful in reducing gun control.

> Describing things or ideas that are **near** (in distance or time)
> Singular: **this**   Plural: **these**

> Describing things or ideas that are **far** (in distance or time)
> Singular: **that**   Plural: **those**

Demonstrative Pronouns

Demonstrative pronouns represent a **thing** or an **idea**. Demonstrative pronouns take the place of nouns, while demonstrative adjectives modify nouns.

> Many criminals were sent to prison last year. **That** will satisfy many in the community.

> <u>Note:</u> **That** refers not just to a single word but instead to the entire idea that so many criminals were sent to prison.

Word Forms

Word forms are related parts of speech like *success, succeed,* and *successful.*

> Individual **cultures** have particular values. These **cultural** beliefs are often hard to eliminate without conscious effort.

Parallel Structures

Parallel structures involve the use of matching words, phrases, clauses, or sentence structures to express similar ideas.

Example: Usually, the children spend the summer weekends **playing** ball in the park, **swimming** in the neighbor's pool, **eating** ice cream under the tree, or **camping** in the backyard.

Metaphors

Metaphors are used to describe something by referring to it as something different and suggesting that it has the same qualities of that thing. Metaphors can connect all the ideas in your paragraph.

Example: Writing in a second language is **like trying to fix a car without the parts the manufacturer specifically made.** You know how to change the part, what tools need to be used, and what the part looks like. However, if you don't have the exact part from the manufacturer, you cannot be sure if the car will run correctly or if it will run at all.

There are numerous other ways to make your sentences cohere. This chapter has presented you with many choices concerning cohesion. You will need to select the right cohesive devices for the particular text you are writing and then use them effectively. Like the tile setter who has to select the right tile to make a beautiful mosaic or the child who is putting a puzzle together, the words you select must fit your text.

Other Ways of Making Your Writing Cohere

You can also use fixed expressions, verbs and nouns indicating cause and effect, clause connectors, and transition words to make your writing cohere.

Using Fixed Expressions to Add Cohesion. Specific fixed expressions, such as those in Table 12.1, can be used to connect sentences.

Table 12.1: Fixed Expressions

go on to + Verb	Park argues that his argument is logical. He **goes on to describe…**
building on + Noun	**Building on** his argument that… Park maintains that…
so the argument goes	Gun control reduces crime. The reduction of violent crime, **so the argument goes,** leads to fewer gun-related killings.
As discussed/mentioned/ noted/ above/below/earlier…	**As noted previously,** a number of scholars have offered a different explanation.

Using Verbs and Nouns to Indicate Cause and Effect and Add Cohesion. When writing cause and effect pieces, competent writers often use verbs and nouns instead of clause connectors like **so** and **because** and transition words like **therefore** and **furthermore**. Verbs and nouns related to causation frequently occur with prepositions, and you may be confused because while the verb sometimes does not take a preposition, the noun does. You state, **"X affects Y,"** and **"X has an effect on Y."**

Cause Verbs

The verbs in Table 12.2 can all be used to indicate causation but they are **not** interchangeable. Each means something slightly different. Competent writers often use these verbs instead of subordinate clauses that begin with the word **because.** Study Table 12.2. Notice the different definitions of the verbs.

Table 12.2: Causation Verbs

Verb	Definition	Sentence
affect	to do something that produces an effect or change in something or in someone's situation	John's poor eyesight *affects* his ability to drive.
cause	to make something happen, especially something bad	The availability of guns has probably *caused* crime to rise.
contribute to	to help to make something happen	The passage of the gun law *contributed* to the well being of society.
create	to make something exist that did not exist before	The new factory will *create* more than 1,400 new jobs.
develop	to grow or change into something bigger, stronger, or more advanced, or to make someone or something do this	Her swimming *developed* her leg muscles.
influence	to affect the way someone or something develops, behaves, thinks, etc. without directly forcing or ordering them	Many factors *influenced* him to give up smoking.
lead to	to cause something to happen or cause someone to do something	Excessive irrigation of desert areas has *led* to a shortage of water.
result in	to make something happen	Poor hygiene has *resulted in* an increase in disease.
stem from	to develop as a result of something else	His headaches *stemmed* from vision problems.
trigger	to make something happen very quickly, especially a series of events	The discovery of America *triggered* the rise in influence of Portugal, France, Spain, and England.

The following verbs can all be used to describe an effect. They have different meanings and are **not** interchangeable.

account for	give rise to	promote
affect	hamper	prompt
arouse	impede	provoke
attribute X to	increase	raise
block	induce	reduce
bring about	influence	render
cause	interfere with	restrain
contribute to	lead to	results from (reason)
create	leave	slow
derive from	make	spark
develop	motivate	stimulate
enable	occur	stem from
evoke	originate in/with/from	trigger
follow from	prevent	yield
force	perpetuate	is attributed to
form	play a role in	is blamed for
generate	produce	is responsible for

Source: Wald, M. 2009. "Showing causal relationships. Getting beyond *so, because and therefore*." CATESOL presentation.

Using Transition Words and Clause Connectors to Add Cohesion

- **Subordinating Conjunctions** connect a dependent clause to an independent clause and generally appear at the beginning or in the middle of a sentence.

- **Coordinating Conjunctions** join two words or sentence elements that have identical functions and generally appear in the middle of a sentence after a comma.

- **Transitions** link and clarify the relationship between whole sentences and generally appear after a period or semicolon.

A WORD OF WARNING

The transition words below can be very challenging to learn and use accurately. Try learning a few at a time and avoid overusing them. Focus on learning their meaning, their grammatical rules, and the different ways writers use them to convey their points while making their writing cohere. Most instructors believe that transition words should be used wisely, sensibly, and carefully and never overused or used inappropriately. Learn when to use them and when not to use them.

Transition Words and Clause Connectors

Study Tables 12.3 through 12.12 to learn more about transition words and connectors.

Table 12.3: Adding Information

Transition/ Connector	Explanation	Example
and	*Coordinating Conjunction* Use a comma before a coordinating conjunction that links independent clauses.	They live in Los Angeles, *and* they study at University High School.
also	*Conjunctive Adverb/Transition* Use also to connect two related clauses separated by a semicolon; use at the beginning of one sentence to show its relationship to the previous one.	Hue loves to read fiction. *Also*, she likes nonfiction.
moreover	*Conjunctive Adverb/Transition* Use moreover to connect two related clauses separated by a semicolon; use at the beginning of one sentence to show its relationship to the previous one.	Stanford has high entrance standards. Moreover, fewer than 10% of applicants are accepted.
furthermore	*Conjunctive Adverb/Transition* Use furthermore to connect two related clauses separated by a semicolon; use at the beginning of one sentence to show its relationship to the previous one.	Los Angeles is a beautiful city; *furthermore*, its architecture is interesting.
in addition	*Transition* Use a comma after a transition at the beginning of a sentence or after a transition that follows a semicolon.	He speaks Cantonese. *In addition*, he is studying Thai.

Table 12.4: Giving Examples

for example	*Transition* Use a comma after a transition at the beginning of a sentence or after a transition that follows a semicolon.	*For example*, last summer I took classes at summer school. OR I took classes, *for example,* math and history.
for instance	*Transition* Use a comma after a transition at the beginning of a sentence or after a transition that follows a semicolon.	There are many reasons I study on campus. *For instance*, the libraries are state-of-the-art.

Table 12.5: Showing Reason or Cause

because	*Subordinating Conjunction* Use a comma after a subordinating clause that begins a sentence.	Because my brother worked until 3:00 a.m., he is tired. My brother is tired because he studied until 3:00 a.m.
since	*Subordinating Conjunction* Use a comma after a subordinating clause that begins a sentence.	*Since* he partied last night, he is skipping class this morning. He is skipping class this morning *since* he partied last night.

Table 12.6: Showing Similarity

Transition/ Connector	Function and Use	Example
likewise	*Conjunctive Adverb/Transition* Use *likewise* to connect two related clauses separated by a semicolon; use at the beginning of one sentence to show its relationship to the previous one.	English was my best subject last year; *likewise*, it is my favorite class this year.
similarly	*Conjunctive Adverb/Transition* Use *similarly* to connect two related clauses separated by a semicolon; use at the beginning of one sentence to show its relationship to the previous one.	The U.S. is a country of immigrants. *Similarly*, Canada is composed of many nationalities.

Table 12.7: Explaining or Emphasizing

in fact	*Transition* Use a comma after a transition at the beginning of a sentence or after a transition that follows a semicolon.	There are many trees there; *in fact*, it's the largest forest in the nation.
in other words	*Transition* Use a comma after a transition at the beginning of a sentence or after a transition that follows a semicolon.	They will be up all night; *in other words*, they have an important test tomorrow.
indeed	*Conjunctive Adverb/Transition* Use to connect two related clauses separated by a semicolon; use at the beginning of one sentence to show its relationship to the previous one.	Global warming has reduced the number of glaciers in the Alps. *Indeed*, there are only two glaciers left near my home town, where there used to be five.

Table 12.8: Contrasting

although	*Subordinating Conjunction* Use a comma after a subordinating clause that begins a sentence.	*Although* Americans value independence, most American families are strong. Most American families are strong *although* Americans value independence.
even though	*Subordinating Conjunction* Use a comma after a subordinating clause that begins a sentence.	I want to study Calculus, *even though* it is difficult. *Even though* it is difficult, I want to study Calculus.
but	*Coordinating Conjunction* Use a comma before a coordinating conjunction that links independent clauses.	She got an A in chemistry, *but* she didn't pass economics.
however	*Conjunctive Adverb/Transition* Use however to connect two related clauses separated by a semicolon; use at the beginning of one sentence to show its relationship to the previous one.	Class usually starts at 9:00 in the morning; *however*, today it started at 9:30.

Transition/ Connector	Explanation	Example
in contrast	*Transition* Use a comma after a transition at the beginning of a sentence or after a transition that follows a semicolon.	*In contrast* to California, Oregon has more rainy days than sunny days.
nevertheless	*Conjunctive Adverb/Transition* Use nevertheless to connect two related clauses separated by a semicolon; use at the beginning of one sentence to show its relationship to the previous one.	She loves UCSF; *nevertheless*, she will go to school at UCLA.
on the other hand	*Transition* Use a comma after a transition at the beginning of a sentence or after a transition that follows a semicolon.	Kim studies a lot. *On the other hand*, her brother never opens a book.
while/ whereas	*Subordinating Conjunction* Use a comma after a subordinating clause that begins a sentence	*While* some might support this research, others do not.

Table 12.9: Showing Choice

or	*Coordinating Conjunction* Use a comma before a coordinating conjunction that links independent clauses.	I will go to pharmacy school, or I will go to medical school.
alternatively	*Transition* Use a comma after a transition at the beginning of a sentence or after a transition that follows a semicolon.	We can host the conference at the student center. *Alternatively*, we can host it at the university club.

Table 12.10: Showing Results

so	*Coordinating Conjunction* Use a comma before a coordinating conjunction that links independent clauses.	My study group meets frequently, *so* we have received good grades.
consequently	*Conjunctive Adverb/Transition* Use to connect two related clauses separated by a semicolon; use at the beginning of one sentence to show its relationship to the previous one.	Ali is good with numbers; *consequently*, she is majoring in math.
therefore	*Transition* Use a comma after a transition at the beginning of a sentence or after a transition that follows a semicolon	She didn't get financial aid. *Therefore*, she works and goes to school.
thus	*Conjunctive Adverb/Transition* Use to connect two related clauses separated by a semicolon; use at the beginning of one sentence to show its relationship to the previous one.	Jim's GPA is 3.8. Thus, he graduated with honors.

Table 12.11: Showing Time or Order

Transition/ Connector	Explanation	Example
after	*Subordinating Conjunction* Use a comma after a subordinating clause that begins a sentence.	*After* she graduates, she plans to travel. She plans to travel *after* she graduates.
until	*Subordinating Conjunction* Use a comma after a subordinating clause that begins a sentence.	Until Kelly graduates from high school, she will live in San Francisco. Kelly will live in San Francisco *until* she graduates from high school.
when	*Subordinating Conjunction* Use a comma after a subordinating clause that begins a sentence.	I got an F *when* I plagiarized from the novel. *When* I plagiarized from the novel, I got an F.
finally	*Conjunctive Adverb/Transition* Use *finally* to connect two related clauses separated by a semicolon; use at the beginning of one sentence to show its relationship to the previous one.	Finally, he finished the paper after three long months.
meanwhile	*Conjunctive Adverb/Transition* Use *meanwhile* to connect two related clauses separated by a semicolon; use at the beginning of one sentence to show its relationship to the previous one.	I am studying physics; *meanwhile*, my sister is studying engineering.
next	*Conjunctive Adverb/Transition* Use *next* to connect two related clauses separated by a semicolon; use at the beginning of one sentence to show its relationship to the previous one.	*Next*, Bob will quit studying and go to the gym.
then	*Conjunctive Adverb/Transition* Use *then* to connect two related clauses separated by a semicolon; use at the beginning of one sentence to show its relationship to the previous one.	She went to the movies with her friends. *Then* they went out for a coke. I combined the cake mix with water and eggs; *then* I put it in the oven.

Table 12.12: Expressions

Transition/ Connector	Explanation	Example
not only..., but also	*Correlative Conjunction** Use *not only..., but also* to connect two equal sentence elements (like two verbs, nouns, adjectives, or phrases). The sentence elements are usually similar in length. They have the same grammatical structure.	He *not only* studies in the evening, *but* he *also* works.
both...and	*Correlative Conjunction** Use *both...and* to connect two equal sentence elements (like two verbs, nouns, adjectives, or phrases). The sentence elements are usually similar in length. They have the same grammatical structure.	*Both* my chemistry *and* computer science classes require research papers.
either...or	*Correlative Conjunction** Use *either...or* to connect two equal sentence elements (like two verbs, nouns, adjectives, or phrases). The sentence elements are usually similar in length. They have the same grammatical structure.	We can *either* take a final exam *or* write a final research paper in that class.
neither...nor	*Correlative Conjunction** Use *neither...nor* to connect two equal sentence elements (like two verbs, nouns, adjectives, or phrases). The sentence elements are usually similar in length. They have the same grammatical structure.	*Neither* the weather *nor* the accommodations were as nice as we had hoped.
whether...or	*Correlative Conjunction* Use *whether...or* to connect two equal sentence elements (like two verbs, nouns, adjectives, or phrases). The sentence elements are usually similar in length. They have the same grammatical structure.	*Whether* he works this summer *or* goes to school, he will move in August.
so...that	*Intensifier*	The teacher is *so* happy *that* the class is doing well.

Did you know?

Correlative conjunctions get their name from the fact that they work together **(co-)** and **relate** sentence elements to one another.

A WORD OF WARNING

Do not rely on transition words to provide cohesion. Most effective writers use transition words judiciously and only use them when they have an excellent reason for doing so. Effective writers realize that transition words are not interchangeable.*

Effective writers understand transition words have different meanings and connotations.*

Writers can use transition words like *nevertheless* to seem scholarly and other words like *what's more* to seem friendly. To use transition words effectively, you'll need to understand how to use them, where to put them in your sentences, and what they mean.

You'll find that instructors vary widely in their acceptance of students' use of transition words. Some instructors expect and prefer students to use a few. Others expect and prefer students to link their sentences with other cohesive devices.

The best thing you can do is to develop multiple ways of making your sentences cohere in diverse types of situations and in diverse types of writing. Pay attention to the ways authors use cohesive devices in their own writing.

Learning Transition Words

It is challenging to learn how to use transition words, and you'll need to dedicate time to learning them. You'll quickly discover their importance and, when you first learn them, you may tend to use them everywhere. **This is a mistake**. You'll also find that some transition words (such as *therefore* and *hence*) are much easier to use than others (such as *in contrast to, in comparison with,* and *contrary*). You'll generally first learn to use sentence transitions at the beginning of sentences and only later learn to use them in more sophisticated ways.

Studying the use of transition words in this book and in your assigned readings will help you learn them. Your instructor will also instruct you in their use. Relying on a good learner's dictionary like Longman's free online *Dictionary of Contemporary English* can also help you.

*interchangeable
(adjective): capable of being put or used in the same place

*connotation
(uncountable noun): a quality or an idea that a word makes you think of that is more than its basic meaning

Insider Tip

When in doubt about how to use transition words, consider leaving them out. The words that you use to link words are very important since they can serve as valuable signposts,* helping the readers understand the relationships between concepts and informing the readers where you are taking them. Using the wrong transition word can lead a reader to completely misunderstand what you are saying.

---

*signpost

(noun): something that helps you understand how something is organized, where to go, or what will follow, used especially in particular types of writing like news reports and argumentative writing

Point to Remember: You can make your writing look more sophisticated by learning to use transition words in the middle of your sentences. Below is an easy way to use them with sentences that contain modal auxiliaries.

Examples: John can, **however,** do anything he wants.

Moore's representation of altruism **might,** in fact, be flawed.

Hermit's study **could, nevertheless,** be inconsistent with the evidence.

Notice that when you use **transition words** after modal auxiliaries, you add commas before and after them.

Think Alouds. Your instructors will provide you models of writing that include targeted transitions, they'll show you how to use them, and describe how they themselves use them. This makes their thinking process overt and visible.

Conversations about Texts. You'll first read a text and then practice answering, and later asking yourselves, questions about what specific transition words mean and whether or not these transition words link ideas and sentences appropriately. You can also use *word charts* such as those below that list transition words in manageable groups related to use such as comparison and cause-effect. Keep in mind that the words are not interchangeable. Force yourself to learn one or two new ones each week, use them in your writing, and use your instructor's feedback and explanations to develop a strong command of them. Paying attention to the ways in which accomplished writers use transition words will help you build your competence using them.

A WORD OF WARNING

Unless you want to make your writing look somewhat simplistic or uncreative, stilted, and overly formulaic (very predictable and not interesting), reconsider your use of *to conclude, in sum, first, second* and *third* and do not use them without an excellent reason in argumentative writing. If in writing argumentative text, you find yourself using transition words like *further, also,* and *moreover* to list your points and not to show the relationship between them, your writing may be becoming too descriptive instead of analytical. When in doubt, leave transition words out. You'll encounter many instructors who tell you not to use them. Strengthen your writing and omit them. Think about using other ways of making your writing cohere.

Transition Words Song

(Contributor, Unknown)

Below is a song that will teach you the meanings of many transition words. Read the song, focus on the transition words, and try to figure out what they mean. Note that authors often use words creatively in songs. You should not use transition words as the author has in this song in your academic writing. The author has included them in the song just to teach you the meaning of them.

http://lcps.org/cms/lib4/VA01000195/Centricity/Domain/11987/Transition%20Words%20Song.pdf

Listen, ok,
Way before games were what we all played,
You could find me on a *Rampage* in the arcade. **First**, it started with *Pong*,
A table-tennis game, **but** it wasn't too strong.
For instance, it was only black and white.
Nonetheless, kids would play it every night.
Next came *Space Invaders*,
Where you shoot aliens with little lasers.

Kids wanted to play.
Consequently, Machines appeared all over the place,
Indeed, Atari fulfilled lots of orders,
And made 2 billion dollars in quarters.
Meanwhile, you have to know, *Pac-Man* was the captain at eating ghosts.
And then the 80's craze,
The industry experienced a golden age.

PCs and home consoles came,
You didn't need to drop quarters to play games.
Equally important, games were sick, *Legend of Zelda* in '86.
Simultaneously, *Super Mario Bros*,
On Nintendo came into a lot of our homes.
Immediately, it became a hit,
You ran through mushrooms to get big.

Beyond sales, there's a story,
These games had our imaginations soaring.

Of course, we were just in a chair,
But on the screens, we'd fly through the air.
We had a need for speed – honest,
So we rolled with a hedgehog we called *Sonic.*
Then the 90s, games were ill,
Such as *SimCity*, where we learned to build.

Similarly, the game that sold the most,
On the PC was *The Sims*, so you know.
3D chips had us *Quaking* and *Doomed*, First person shooters came with a boom.
Despite the appeal to the youth, um,
Some saw the violence as too gruesome.
Accordingly, ratings were introduced,
To make all these games easier to choose.
PlayStation had hits like *MLB*,
Specifically, *Final Fantasy.*
Truly Xbox CDs had graphics,
And the cartridges couldn't catch it.

Moreover, CDs were cheaper to make,
On the other hand, CDs were cheaper to take,
Cheaper to copy and to steal,
But in 2006 that's when things got real.
Wii finally made games appeal,
To the whole family, and they played for real.
And on mobile phones, we can all be nerds,
When we shoot down pigs with our *Angry Birds.*
In sum, in summary, to sum up, too, On the whole, in the end, to conclude,
The transition from *Pong* to today,
Has given us amazing games along the way.

Your Turn

Find the Right Transition Words

If you are having difficulty understanding the meanings of transition words, try completing the following activity. Transition words have been left out of the following paragraph. Select appropriate words from the list below, and figure out which blank they should go in. There can be more than one transition expression that fits in some blanks. Select the one that you think fits best. Notice how these particular transition words work well for informational text that gives directions. You'll need to vary your use of transition words according to the **genre** (type of writing) you compose.

How to Make a Peanut Butter and Jelly Sandwich

Word Bank: Hence   However
                    Otherwise   As a consequence
                    Alternatively After this

There are several steps to follow when making a peanut butter and jelly sandwich. The first and most important step is selecting your ingredients and gathering them together. Before you start, you will want to gather a kitchen knife, bread (usually one or two slices per sandwich), peanut butter, and jelly or jam. There are many different kinds of bread to choose from.

1. _____, you will have to do a little experimenting to select the bread you like. After you have gathered all your ingredients, spread the peanut butter on the bread. You will probably want to spread it evenly. You may want to stir it before you spread it.

2. _____ it may be lumpy.

3. _____, spread the jelly on the other piece of bread.

4. _____ you can use jam. Don't put too much on your bread or you will not be able to taste the peanut butter. After this, press the two pieces of bread together, but don't press too hard.

5. _____, you may end up making a mess and destroying your sandwich. Next, cut the sandwich diagonally. After you have done this, you are ready to enjoy your sandwich.

Source: Olson, Carol Booth, Robin Scarcella, and Tina Matuchniak. *Helping English Learners to Write.* NY: Teachers College Press, 2015.

Emily Duan, a former writing student, warns:

"When I first took writing courses, I didn't use pronouns in my writing. Instead, I tried to use a lot of synonym like I did in Chinese. Now I use pronouns in my English writing and my instructors say my sentences are connected."

Pronoun Reference

One important way to add cohesion to your writing is by using pronouns to refer to a noun that you have just mentioned. The technique is **subtle**. Readers do not notice pronoun reference unless they pay careful attention to it. Many consider it a more sophisticated way of linking sentences.

When using pronouns to replace or refer to nouns, be sure that a pronoun agrees with its antecedent noun (the noun it replaces or refers to) in number, person, case, and gender. The following are some of the most common pronoun agreement problems that student writers have.

COHESION

Because of the difficulties students have using pronoun reference, information on its use follows.

Check if a noun is singular or plural

Use singular pronouns to refer to singular nouns, and use plural pronouns to refer to plural nouns.

- The *pilot* of Air Force One is on-call; *her* phone could ring at any time.

- *Pilots* of Air Force One are on-call; *their* phones could ring at any time.

Check if a noun is definite or indefinite

Use a singular pronoun with an indefinite pronoun (see 3g).

- **Okay.** *Each* has *his* own special call number.
- **Okay.** *Each* has *her* own special call number.
- **Okay.** *Each* has *his or her* own special call number.
- **Not okay.** *Each* has *their* own special call number.

If you are unsure of which pronoun to use in this situation, it is always possible to rephrase the sentence to avoid the situation.

- **Okay.** *Each* pilot has a special call number.
- **Okay.** All *pilots* have *their* own special call number.

Check if a noun is generic

Use a singular pronoun with a generic noun, a noun that is general or unidentified by name.

- *Each pilot* has *his* own special call number.
- A *pilot* of Air Force One must have *her* plane ready at all times.

Check for compound antecedents

Use a plural pronoun to refer to antecedents that are joined with an *and*.

- *The pilots of Air Force One* and *Navy One* work at the request of *their* president.

Check for pronouns with correlative conjunctions

Use a singular pronoun to refer to antecedents that are joined with either...or/neither...nor.

- *Either* the pilot of Air Force One *or* the pilot of Navy One will take *his* plane to the disaster area.
- *Neither* the pilot of Air Force One *nor* the pilot of Navy One has *his* plane ready.

Use a plural pronoun to refer to antecedents that are joined with both...and.

- *Both* the pilot of Air Force One *and* the pilot of Navy One will take *their* planes to the disaster area.

Insider Tip

Languages have different ways of introducing and changing topics. In English, writers do not use transition words for that purpose. Generally, in English when you want to introduce a new topic, you'll introduce the topic with a noun, not a pronoun. When you want to establish the topic and let your readers know you'll be discussing that topic a while, you'll change from a noun to a pronoun (or something else—not the same noun). When you want to introduce a new topic, you'll usually switch from using pronouns to a new noun. Doing that let's your readers know that you are discussing a different topic.

Your Turn

Read the passage below with a partner and identify at least four different ways that the author, Marshall Thomas, establishes cohesion. Find ten examples of pronoun reference.

The Hidden Lives of Dogs

The dog who adopted a human mannerism is my husband's dog, who amazed us all one hot day this past summer after my husband had bought himself an ice cream cone. As my husband took the first taste, he noticed that the dog was watching. So he offered the cone, expecting the dog to gobble it. But to everyone's astonishment, the dog politely licked a little ice cream just as my husband had done. My husband then licked a little more, and again offered it to the dog, who also licked a little more. In this way, taking turns, they ate the ice cream down to the cone. Then my husband took a bite. The dog watched him. Assuming that the dog would bolt the rest of the cone, my husband passed it on for what he thought would be the last time. But drawing back his lips to expose his little incisors, the dog took the most delicate of nibbles. Twice more my husband and the dog took turns biting the cone, until only the tip remained.

Astounding? Not really. For eight years, my husband and this dog have built a relationship of trust and mutual obligation, neither making unreasonable demands on the other or patronizing the other, or trying to subordinate the other, but each doing exactly what he wants, usually in the other's company. Only in such a setting, only when both participants consider themselves equals, could this scene have taken place. Only a dog, who thought for himself, a dog who wasn't brainwashed by excessive training, a dog who depended on his own observations and imagination for guidance, would ever figure out the very human method of taking alternate bites as a form of sharing. After all, when two dogs share food, they eat simultaneously while respecting each other's feeding space, which is a little imaginary circle around the other's mouth. But the idea of taking alternate bites is totally human. Even so, the dog fathomed it, *and without ever having seen it done*. Who ate the tip of the cone? My husband ate it. The dog let him have the last turn.

Source: Thomas, Elizabeth Marshall. *The Hidden Lives of Dogs*. Boston/New York: Mariner Books, 2010. Print. xiii.

Reading Comprehension Questions

1. What are two of the most important types of cohesive devices in the English?

2. What types of cohesive devices do expert writers use?

3. Do all sentences in an essay need to be linked in some way? Why?

4. How can writers use related parts of speech to make their writing seem connected?

5. What are some subtle ways of linking sentences?

6. Why do most competent writers use cause verbs like lead to, result in, or influence instead of subordinate clauses with because to indicate causation?

7. What five verbs that are used to describe an effect? Why are these words so important in college?

8. Which transition words discussed in this chapter are the most difficult for you to use? List five. Explain why these words are so difficult. Do the meanings of the words cause you difficulty or the ways in which the words are used in a sentence?

9. What are five transition words or clause connectors that you would like to use more frequently in your writing? How can you use these particular transition words or clause connectors to improve your writing?

10. How can the use of transition words hurt your writing?

This chapter has presented you with many choices concerning cohesion. You will need to select the right cohesive devices for the particular text you are writing and then use them effectively. Like the tile setter who has to select the right tile to make a beautiful mosaic or the child who is putting a puzzle together, the words you select have to fit your text.

Revising, Editing, and Polishing Your Writing

Revising, editing, and polishing are key to your success as a writer. When you **revise**, you make changes to a piece of writing by adding parts or deleting them, reorganizing parts, or making improvements to them. When you **edit** your writing, you remove errors or parts of your writing that are not acceptable. When you **polish** your writing, you make slight changes to a piece of writing to improve it before the writing is completely finished. If you are writing a paper that an instructor will grade or a manuscript that you hope to publish, you may spend much time revising, editing, and polishing your writing. If you are writing a short list or a diary, you may spend little if any time on such processes.

Revising Your Major Writing Assignments

Your preliminary and first drafts of major papers won't be perfect and you shouldn't expect them to be. Your instructors will likely give you the opportunity to revise your papers many times, and that will help you write effective pieces.

You may feel that you have written exactly what you want to say in your first draft, and the quality of your writing is excellent. You may even be used to completing a single draft of a writing assignment in a single sitting and think that writing other drafts is unnecessary. However, the real truth is your first drafts are rarely the best. Most great writers are never able to state what they want to in just one draft. Many write preliminary or zero drafts in which they embrace the opportunity to explore their ideas. As you participate in brainstorming activities, read, and engage in class discussions, it's a good idea to write down those ideas that you are most concerned about. This will give you more ideas for writing and make it easier to ask for specific feedback. To communicate clearly and accomplish your purpose, you'll want to revise your drafts carefully, actively evaluating your writing to improve it.

Imagine if someone built an airplane with little planning and no testing. Would you feel confident being a passenger on that airplane, or would you prefer to fly in an airplane that someone has thoroughly planned and extensively tested? An airplane passenger should have a smooth, untroubled journey and so should a reader. It is your responsibility as a writer to make this happen through revising.

Ryan Hu, a former student, states:

"My first drafts were always bad, but I was determine to improve them. I spent hours and even days revising, editing, and polishing them. The mark of a champion writer is perseverance. My work always paid off."

Diane Huang, a former student, warns:

"At first I was stubborn and didn't want to revise my writing much and didn't want to take the time to change it. But that wasn't good and didn't work. Then I learned some good strategies that gave me the confidence I needed to make good revisions and saved me time."

Begin Revising by Rereading

Rereading your own writing can be challenging. You've possibly left words out that you do not notice and your sentences might make sense to you and no one else. If you are an international student, you might have even included synonyms or words that you've translated from your first language that don't work well. You might think your evidence is great, but your reader might not be able to understand how it supports the points you are making. If Chinese or Korean is your first language, you may have written sections of your paper without using pronouns, just as you might in your first language. If you are a California student, you may have used features of informal English instead of features of academic English. You may not recognize problems when rereading your own writing. So, what do you do?

Revising Major Paper Assignments

The following are tips for revising the major paper assignments that you are likely to complete in your writing courses. These papers ask you to make an argument and support it. Find the tips that work best for you.

Insider Tips

Getting started revising your paper: Below are some ideas you might try using to improve your ideas and get a picture of the changes you'll need to make:

- Leave yourself plenty of time to think about your paper and to make revisions. Schedule time to revise your paper.
- Read your paper out loud, from the beginning to the very end to see if your ideas seem logical or if your organization makes sense. Reading aloud can slow you down and that can help you pay more attention to your writing and prevent you from skimming over important parts that need to be revised or deleted.
- Ask a classmate to read your essay to you and give you opinions about the content that could be strengthened, deleted, or rearranged.
- Read your paper out loud, take a break, and read it a second time out loud. When you put aside* your writing and come back to it, you might come back to the task of revising reinvigorated* and see your paper with fresh eyes.

*to put aside

(verb phrase): to put down something you are writing, in order to do something else

*reinvigorated

(adjective): making you feel energetic or strengthened

Revising your first drafts:

To help you decide whether to delete paragraphs, add them, or move them:

- Try writing your thesis statement and topic sentences on a separate piece of paper.
- Set priorities. Revising is more effective when you are focused on one thing at a time.
- Focus on large issues that affect your paper as a whole first, rather than small issues such as commas.
- Try writing down your thesis statement and major claims on a piece of scratch paper.
- Try listing ideas, outlining, or graphing after you write your first drafts. You might also try this before you begin writing.

Jerry Leung, a former writing student, advises:

"All the time you spend revising your writing will be worth it. And if you are not that good of a writer, don't worry. You'll get better if you are humble and if you are willing to listen to instructors' suggestions and make changes. Don't be afraid to make the changes your instructors or others suggest. Yes, it will take time. So what? Take the time to do things right. Don't settle for writing that you think is good enough. You can take your writing up an entire level. You can make it more interesting and meaningful."

Strengthening Specific Aspects of your Writing

Try reading your paper in parts.

- **Introductions**: Take a close look at your introduction. Few writers are able to write a good one the first time they write. Make sure that you've given your reader enough background knowledge to understand your thesis statement and follow your line of reasoning Ask yourself these questions:
    - Do I answer the prompt?

    - Do I give my audience enough background knowledge to understand my paper?

    - Do I have a specific, arguable thesis that prepares the reader for my paper?

- **Body Paragraphs:** Take a close look at your body paragraphs. Try putting a short title on each body paragraph. Make sure all sentences address the title and have a strong topic sentence that supports your main point. Take out any sentences that digress.*

    - Try identifying one or two paragraphs that need work and strengthen them by revising the topic sentences, adding better evidence, and adding cohesive devices.

    - Try reading parts of the body you want to improve out loud. That will help you focus your attention on key sections of your writing. If you are having a hard time getting started revising your paper, this particular technique may be especially useful. Ask yourself these questions:
        - Are my paragraphs ordered logically?

        - Do all my paragraphs refer back to my thesis (or a single controlling idea)?

        - Do each of my paragraphs have a single, developed idea that is expressed in a topic sentence?

        - Do my paragraphs have examples and analyses that support the thesis statement?

- **Conclusions:** Take a close look at your conclusion. Think about the main message you want your reader to get. What message should your reader walk away with?

*to digress

(verb): to write about something that is not your main subject or point

Try reading for just one aspect of writing at a time.

- **The readers' possible reaction.** Think about the readers' possible reaction to your writing. What is the **tone?** In other words, what quality, feeling, or attitude is expressed in your writing? Is it academic or informal? Think about how you come across. Do you come across* as an authority on the subject on which you are writing or as someone who doesn't know very much about it? What is the audience's purpose for reading your paper? Have you met the audience's expectations?

- **Content.** Consider the content. Think about whether you have included everything the assignment requires. Consider whether you have given audience enough information to understand your paper.

- **Organization.** Think about your organization. Every time you write a different type of paper on a different topic with a different purpose and in a different context, you will need to vary your organization to find an effective way of conveying your message. Consider whether all your information makes sense and connects to each other. Does each paragraph have a clear topic sentence with only one controlling idea? Have you organized you paragraphs in a way that makes it easy for your readers to understand your paper?

- **Rearranging paragraphs.** Try to put them in an order that better supports your points. Try cutting up and reordering your paragraphs and main points. Delete the ones that don't directly support your points.

- **Quotations.** Try focusing on your quotations. You'll want your readers to understand how your quotations support your main points. Strengthen the connection.

- **Important points in your paper.** Try developing each point you make. Add a few details to strengthen them.

- **Quality of evidence.** Try improving the quality of your evidence and the connection of your evidence to your thesis statement. Do you show that you understand your sources and you are not simply quoting or listing other people's ideas? Do you properly give credit to ideas that are not yours?
    - Have you used the correct style when incorporating evidence in your paper?

- **Transitions.** Try adding stronger connections between sections of your paper.

*to come across

(verb phrase): If someone comes across in a particular way, they seem to have particular qualities. They might come across as being rude, compassionate, mean, or knowledgeable.

Editing and Polishing Your Writing

Editing and polishing may seem like optional parts of the writing process, but they are actually essential parts of the process. While it may seem that content is the most important aspect of your writing, the way your content appears affects how your audience judges your writing and you, the writer, overall. The consequences of forgetting a punctuation mark might not be as drastic as forgetting the decimal point in a math problem, but others will label you "careless" or "lazy" when you forget to use a period. Fortunately, there are ways to make editing and polishing easy.

One way to make the editing and polishing process more efficient is to separate it from the larger part of the revision process. This means revising for aspects like organization first, and then polishing sentences afterwards. If you try to revise for everything at the same time, you may change some words, only to re-write the entire sentence later. In addition to separating stages of the revision process, you can develop your own systematic process for polishing sentences. This may involve reading aloud, reading your paper sentence by sentence backwards, focusing on grammar points you know you typically struggle with, or printing and reading from a physical copy of your paper. Everyone has their own proofreading process that works best for them and it is a learning process to find what works best for you. You may find that in talking with others or your instructor, you will learn new proofreading strategies or get tips on what you can focus on when proofreading.

After all the long hours you put into composing your major papers and revising them, you don't want your readers left thinking about the errors in your writing. The best students often spend long hours carefully editing and polishing their writing to make sure that it is as well edited and polished as it can be before they submit their final versions to their instructors.

What if you are using language creatively and breaking the rules of conventional grammar? Talk to your instructor. The English language is evolving. You may find your instructor welcomes your innovation or wants you to place it in quotation marks.

Editing and Polishing Major Paper Assignments

What follows are general tips for editing and polishing your papers. You might find some of the suggestions helpful.

- Set your paper aside for a day or two (or at least an hour) and then return to edit or polish it. You'll be more likely to catch errors if you haven't just finished writing your paper. You'll have more distance from your writing, and you'll critique your paper more objectively.

- Read your paper out loud several times. When you read out loud, it is difficult to skip over small errors, like errors related to prepositions and noun plurals. Reading aloud helps you to identify errors related to *collocations* (words that always go together), misplaced modifiers, and problems with pronoun reference. You can also ask peer tutors in the Writing Center to read parts of the paper for you and tell you when they are confused.

- Keep a list of the main errors you need to edit for, and read the paper once for each error type. If you focus on one error at a time, you'll be more likely to identify it.

- Use all available resources—including learner dictionaries, writing specialists at the Writing Center, and your instructor. You don't have to rely on your knowledge of rules. You can look them up in grammar books, class handouts, and citation guidelines.

- If you have problems editing on the screen, print a copy. Many students find it easier to identify errors on printed copies than on a screen.

- Check verb tense consistency by marking time expressions and their appropriate verb tenses.

- Use a learner dictionary such as the *Longman English Dictionary Online* to check for correct verb forms, word forms, and count/non-count nouns.

- Use this book to check for problem expressions.

- If subject-verb agreement is a problem for you, mark the subjects and verbs and check for agreement.

- Pay attention to your instructor's feedback. Ask him/her to clarify any comments you don't understand. Be sure to make any necessary revisions.

- Use correction symbols to help you recognize your grammar mistakes. (See Table 13.1.)

- Check to make sure your pronouns have correct and clear antecedents.

- Reread the quotations you have used and make sure you have copied them correctly. It is easy to miscopy quotations.

- If you have a specific problem that recurs all the time, such as switching tenses or subject-verb agreement, read over your paper an extra time and focus only on that problem.

- Run the spellchecker before you submit your essay. Then, double-check your spelling. Spellcheckers alone are inadequate.

- Check for MLA format.

Juan Rodrigo, a former writing student, warns:

"Make fair judgments of your classmates' organization and content. Respond constructively and conscientiously in Peer Review sessions and blogs. I learned a lot by helping my classmates."

Paper Formatting Checklist

- ☐ Typed
- ☐ Double-spaced
- ☐ 12 Point, Times New Roman
- ☐ 1" Margins
- ☐ Header (header=last name + page # on top right corner, ½" from the top)
- ☐ Required length (see rubric)
- ☐ Double-spaced heading on *top left* of first page with each of the following and nothing else:
- ☐ Your Name
- ☐ Instructor's Name
- ☐ Class level/ Paper #, Draft #
- ☐ Date

Correction Symbols

Many instructors use the following correction symbols (Table 13.1) to help students edit their papers. You will find the symbols at this website: http://www.humanities.uci.edu/esl/undergrad/symbols. php.

Table 13.1: Correction Symbols

Symbol	Meaning	Example	Advice/Practice
agr	agreement	Between you and I, each one of us needs *their* own job.	http://www.humanities.uci.edu/esl/undergrad/agrlink.php
cs	comma splice	I had a question, I asked the professor.	http://www. grammar.ccc.commnet.edu/grammar/runons.htm
dm	dangling modifier	After talking to him, the information was clear.	http://www.owl.english.purdue.edu/owl/resource/597/01/ http://aliscot.com/bigdog/dangling.htm
frag	fragment	If you were a scientist.	http://www.humanities.uci.edu/esl/undergrad/sslink.php
id	idioms / set expressions	He was involved on the math projects.	http://esl.about.com/od/grammarintermediate/a/adjective_prepositions_combos.htm
mixed	mixed constructions	He decided to go to school is because he felt better.	http://www.nipissingu.ca/english/hornbook/mixcon.htm
num	number	He finished his *researches*, but now he needs more *equipments* and *times*.	http://www.humanities.uci.edu/esl/undergrad/numberex.php
prep	prepositions	His birthday is in September 12.	http://www.humanities.uci.edu/esl/undergrad/preplink.php
p	punctuation	Though odd this story is true.	http://owl.english.purdue.edu/owl/resource/566/01/
red	redundancy	This *class* seems easy, so I'm going to take this *class*.	http://grammar.about.com/od/words/a/redundancies.htm
ref	unclear pronoun reference	My essay and my keys are in my car. Will you please bring *it*?	http://www.humanities.uci.edu/esl/undergrad/agrlink.php
ro	run-on	No one knows the answer it is hard to solve each problem.	http://www.humanities.uci.edu/esl/undergrad/sslink.php
sp	spelling	*Achieving* dreams is *important*.	http://owl.english.purdue.edu/owl/resource/660/1/
s-v	subject-verb agreement	Everybody *have* traditions.	http://www.humanities.uci.edu/esl/undergrad/svlink.php
t	tense	I *will* be in class yesterday.	http://www.humanities.uci.edu/esl/undergrad/vtlink.php
vb	verb form	He is *enroll* in French, and he is *try* to *added* another class. He will *has* to spend more time *study*.	http://www.humanities.uci.edu/esl/undergrad/passivelink.php http://www.humanities.uci.edu/esl/undergrad/verbformlink.php http://www.humanities.uci.edu/esl/undergrad/verbformlink.php http://www.humanities.uci.edu/esl/undergrad/verbformlink.php

Symbol	Meaning	Example	Advice/Practice
wf	word form	We will become *independence* thinkers and writers.	http://www.sharedvisions. com/svuhome. cfm?id=455 &category=Parts http://www.humanities.uci.edu/esl/ undergrad/TypicalSuffixes5.pdf
ww	wrong word	He was *very* tired that he left.	http://iteslj.org/quizzes/0101/jb-verytooso.html
^	insert	She will be enrolled just ^ time.	http://www.humanities.uci.edu/esl/ undergrad/artlink.php
∂	delete	He fell off *(of)* his bicycle.	http://www.humanities.uci.edu/esl/ undergrad/artlink.php
¶	paragraph	Researchers have found evidence of insecticides in our ocean. One of the first studies was completed two years ago.	http://owl.english.purdue.edu/owl/ resource/606/01/ http://lrs.ed.uiuc. edu/students/fwalters/para.html
//	parallelism	Winning and *lose* is part of playing the game.	http://owl.english.purdue.edu/owl/ resource/623/01/
#	add a space	It's *infront* of the building.	http://www.oxforddictionaries.com/ us/words/oxford-dictionaries-spelling-challenge
⌒	move here	The boy revised his work who was sitting next to me.	http://www.sharedvisions.com/?sid=1
∿	transpose	She's on time usually.	http://www.sharedvisions.com/?sid=1
~	rephrase	He hasn't got a clue.	http://owl.english.purdue.edu/owl/ resource/573/01/
??	Not understand-able	It's like which that you need.	http://www.sharedvisions.com/ svuhome.cfm?id=455&category=Parts
art	article	This is *a* biggest classroom in our building.	http://www.humanities.uci.edu/esl/ undergrad/artlink.php

*Notice that the right hand column provides you with useful exercises that you can complete to improve your knowledge of grammar and other features of English.

Christopher Orlando, a former student, who had lived in the United States most of his life, explains,

"I'm really grateful for this class because I never had any detailed feedback on my writing before I got to UCI. My high school teachers just told me that my ideas were great and gave me As on my papers, but that didn't help me improve my grammar or vocab much. I'm finally making good progress, but I wouldn't be making it without my Academic English instructors marking my errors."

Quia Quizzes

If you have difficulty using grammatical features accurately or understanding the correction symbols (Table 13.1), try completing Quia quizzes. For Quia quizzes, Google "UCI Correction Symbols" and then click on the sites that read numex.php or svlink.php. You can also find Quia quizzes here: http://www.humanities.uci.edu/esl/undergrad/uciedits.php

Scroll down on the page until you see a link that says "sentence level" and click on it and take the Quia quiz that comes up. You can take as many quizzes as you like, as you will get a different quiz every time you click on the link. If you are having trouble in your writing with any grammar point, take Quia quizzes, print out the score sheets and place them in the back of your portfolio. Your instructor will be impressed by your effort and you will probably see real improvement in your writing. What Quia quizzes teach you is how to apply your knowledge of grammar to edit your writing.

How Instructors Give Feedback to You on Your Writing

In your **zero** draft, the draft that many students write before they write their first draft, you'll find that your instructors will ignore the errors you have made to encourage you to get your ideas down. In your first draft, they'll tend to focus on your content and organization. They'll hold you much more accountable for using standard written forms in your later drafts. However, even in these later drafts, you'll often find that your instructors try not to mark each and every one of your mistakes, but instead indicate your patterns of errors. Their goal is to teach you to edit your own writing.

Every type of writing calls for different types of feedback at different stages of the writing process. You'll need to work closely with your instructor to make sure that you receive the type of feedback that best helps you develop as a writer and convey your messages effectively. You'll probably find that you receive much more feedback than you did in high school. When your instructor gives you feedback, understand that it is given to help you.

Editing Logs

Many students find that keeping track of the errors they make and the ways they can correct their errors helps them to reduce the number of errors that they make in their later writing assignments. This is why editing logs, such as the one below in Table 13.2 can be helpful. Reflecting on language errors and the strategies you can use to avoid making them can be a powerful way to gain editing skills.

Table 13.2: Sample of Editing Log

Language Errors to Focus On	Symbol	Examples from My Paper	Corrected Version

A former Academic writing student commented,

"At first I thought my instructor was mad at me when she pointed out errors in my writing. Then, I realized he was actually being kind. His feedback helped me improve a lot."

Anisa Abdu, a former student, advises:

"Make it a practice to understand what the writing assignment asks you to do before you start to write. Think about what you already know about the writing assignment and what you need to learn. Find something about the assignment that interests you. Mark the due date of each draft in your calendar and let your instructor know as soon as you can if there is any aspect of the assignment you don't understand. You won't have to do so much revision if you understand the writing assignment."

Melissa Ying, a former student, argues:

"There's no sense trying to write a paper when you haven't developed the vocabulary to write it. Some of the writing assignments are challenging, but if you work on developing your vocabulary before you do them, it will save you a lot of time and you'll end up doing well on them. I used to go to the peer tutors and an international peer mentor just to discuss the topics of the writing assignment and talk about the vocabulary I might need to use before beginning the drafting process. My time with these individuals was critical to my success in completing my writing assignments."

Reading Comprehension Questions

1. What is the difference between editing writing and revising it?

2. When your instructor gives you lots of feedback, does that mean that your instructor is angry or displeased with you?

3. How can you revise your paragraphs to make sure that they support topic sentences?

4. What strategies can you use to revise your writing?

5. What can you do to improve the organization of your introduction?

6. What can you do to improve the organization of your body paragraphs?

7. What strategies can you use to edit your writing?

8. What do the following correction symbols mean?
   frag, id, prep, p, ref, s-v, t, id, art, wf, ^

9. What website can you turn to for help, if you make many verb tense errors in your writing?

10. Read the paragraph below that was written by a student. The instructor has corrected it. How will the correction symbols and instructor feedback help the student correct her writing?

Volcanoes

Volcano eruptions are powerful and destructive force. Imagine hearing a volcano erupt thousands of miles away.

          V+ ing   num

Imagine look through binoculars and see the top of ___ mountain

collapse. Imagine discovering an ancient roman city buried in
 wf
volcano ash.

volcano = noun	Don't forget to capitalize proper nouns.
volcanic = adj.	"imagine" is followed by a verb + ing.

Reading Comprehension Activities

Activity 1

Directions: Using the given correction symbols, edit the paragraph below. The errors are underlined.

Bill Gates

In 1974, Bill Gates decided to drop out <u>in</u> (prep) Harvard. With his high school friend Paul Allen, he wrote operating software for the newly emerging <u>computers personal</u>. (~) They formed Microsoft and created MS-DOS. Twelve <u>year</u> (num) <u>after</u> (ww), Microsoft dominated the personal computer market___ (cs) Gates became the nation's richest billionaire.

Source: Berkin, Carol. *Making America: A History of the United States.* Boston: Houghton Mifflin Co, 2006, p. 968.

Activity 2

Directions: Find and correct the error(s) in each sentence. Each sentence has at least one error. Errors may be in vocabulary, grammar, spelling, or punctuation. Use the correction symbols to indicate error type.

1. After years of studying and obtaining a bachelor's degree and master's degree, Mary Ellen decided to back to her country.

2. Paul is such a talented student that he is easy to understand all of his lectures.

3. Paul hardly does his homework because he believes homework is extremely important.

4. Although I want to go see the new movie, but I have to do my homework.

extremely important.

4. Although I want to go see the new movie, but I have to do my homework.

5. Most of students believe that doing homework prepares them to understand their lecture better.

6. I need to know English. Because I will start my own company.

7. The quotation mentioned earlier, it states that Fred is very homesick.

8. It is difficult to study the English language there were a lot of words and expressions to memorize.

9. One of my favorite songs is "Let It Go."

10. Some older people have trouble to hear well.

11. I love my class! It helps me to learn knowledge so that I can become even more knowledged.

12. In order to succeed in learn English, students need to be hardworking, focusing, and motivated.

13. Because of John was late to work for the fourth time, he was fired from his job.

14. Even the book is so expensive, I still want to buy it because it is so useful to my writing.

15. He is lack of financial support from his parents because his parents want to teach him to be more independence.

Your writing does not have to be perfect when the words first appear on the page. You have multiple times to rewrite your papers and make sure your message is conveyed effectively.

Using Grammar Effectively

Professors may react in various ways to your use of English grammar. Some will welcome your efforts to communicate, regardless of whether you follow the grammar rules and norms of "Standard" US-American English. Some may recognize that in this global world, many types of English are used and they may be receptive to whatever English grammar you use. If English is not your first language and professors know this, some may acknowledge the challenges you may have when communicating in English and may overlook any problems you have following English grammar rules. On the other hand, some may complain about your grammar if you do not follow the conventions of academic English.

A while back, Professor Baker forwarded to his colleague the following e-mail message from a student named Duy who wanted to work in his lab:

> How do you do? My name is Duy Nguyen. I am a student currently on the freshman level. I am going to be attend Biology 5C next year, but during the summer, I would like to continue my study on the subject. Although my major is in Social Science, I am consider to have Biology as my second major. I am currently attending Professor Campbell lecture. He suggested to me that maybe I should seek around to for research projects, since it would be much more beneficial and interesting to have actual hands on experience. He suggest that maybe I should contact you to see would it be possible for you to provide me with some information. As I have understand that you are currently conducting a research on the subject of plasma, and I would like to know more about it, that is, if I am not costing any inconvenience. Thank you very much, and have a good day.

Professor Baker did not allow Duy to work on his research project. He forwarded Duy's message to a colleague with the following comment about Duy's language use: *"Syntax, spelling, whew!"*

Besides a number of rhetorical problems, Duy's message reveals his lack of knowledge of grammatical structures—knowledge that some professors expect him to have obtained earlier. Note that Duy's use of the possessive is not consistent with the conventions of academic English. (He should have written *Professor Campbell's* in the sentence, *I am currently attending Professor Campbell lecture.*) He does not always use conditional structures that begin with the word **if** correctly. (The professor expected him to use a sentence like this one: *He suggested that I contact you to see if you could provide me with some information.*) His email demonstrates that he has not learned the grammatical restrictions governing academic English vocabulary. For instance, he does not know that the word *cause* goes with *inconvenience* in the expression *to <u>cause</u> an inconvenience* (not <u>cost</u> *an inconvenience*), and he uses the incorrect expression *on the freshman level* instead of the word *freshman*. It is apparent that Duy's grammar problems were serious enough to bother the professor. It is equally clear that Duy would benefit from learning grammar to obtain his goals at college.

The goal of writing and English language coursework is to help you acquire enough grammar knowledge so that you will succeed in undergraduate courses. You'll need to use English to communicate independently as well as collaboratively. When you are working in a profession—for instance, as an engineer, a doctor, a lawyer, a teacher, or a business professional —or you are studying in graduate school, individuals will come to you for a professional opinion. Others will expect you to be able to make independent judgments and advise them. Many will expect you to communicate these judgments and advice to them in English. You won't always have time to turn to others for support. Those who depend on you won't expect you to say, *"Wait a minute. I need to get some help from my friends."* or *"Hang on just a second and let me get a good translation of my ideas."* In graduate school, professors will expect you to think creatively and convey your thoughts to them without relying on others. When expected to communicate in English, knowing English grammar will help you.

This chapter will help you learn the conventional forms of English grammar used in academic settings. The first section outlines misconceptions about English grammar learning and describes the approach to grammar you'll take in writing courses. The next section explains the terms you'll use to describe grammatical features and reviews the basic grammar rules you'll learn. The third section provides grammar rules and tips that you can use as reference materials. It includes basic information pertinent to English sentence structure, including complex and compound-complex sentences.

Misconceptions about English Grammar Learning

This section describes six frequently misunderstood concepts about English grammar learning and discusses theoretical as well as practical evidence that refutes these common misconceptions.

Myth 1: Advanced grammar does not need to be studied or learned in class because students can acquire it naturally on their own. There is little, if any, scientific evidence for this belief. Students can acquire some types of English grammatical features by themselves, without ever attending English classes in specific situations, especially if they are good language learners, have already learned multiple languages, and have acquired enough English to understand their textbooks and interact with English speakers. However, they are generally unable to acquire the grammatical features that characterize academic language on their own. Receiving instruction on these features helps learners pay attention to them and this in turn can speed their acquisition of the features. Students who do not take English courses when required— because they hope that they will improve their English by themselves, just by reading and talking to English speakers—end up making little progress acquiring academic English.

Myth 2: Grammatical forms have no meaning. To use grammatical features purposefully and effectively, you'll need to learn their *grammatical* meaning, their *semantic* meaning, and their *situational or pragmatic* meaning. **Grammatical** refers to that which is expressed by word order or grammatical features. **Semantic** refers to the definition meaning of words. **Pragmatic** refers to the study of how words, phrases, clauses, and sentences are used with special meanings in particular situations. The word *the*, for instance has a specific grammatical meaning (it signifies nouns), semantic meaning (it means definiteness), and pragmatic or situational meaning (it refers to old information). We use *the* to refer backwards to something that we have already mentioned and refer forwards to something that we can take for granted will happen. (For instance, in the sentence that follows the word *the* refers backwards to *book*.)

Backwards: *'Outliers' is a controversial book. The book has contributed to our knowledge of the role of practice in success.*

In the next sentence, the word *the* refers to something the writer believes will happen.

Forwards: <u>The</u> *stock market will fall in the coming months.*)

We also use the article *the* to emphasize knowledge that the reader and writer share. (For example, the author assumes that the readers know the names of the individuals referred to in this sentence, *The individuals who support this view believe that…*)

Myth 3: Memorizing grammar terms and learning grammar rules do not improve writing. Knowledge of grammar rules helps you to improve your editing skills, use handbooks, and discuss your writing and the writing of others analytically. There is also some evidence that it can accelerate your development of specific features of grammar.

Myth 4: Once students take and pass a test on a specific grammar feature, they have learned this feature. Just because you can use your knowledge to pass tests does not indicate that you can use your knowledge of the grammar feature to communicate effectively in speech and writing in diverse situations. It can be very difficult to apply conscious knowledge of grammar rules to improve writing without the time and motivation to do so.

Myth 5: Once students learn to use specific grammar features correctly in their writing, they will always continue to use them correctly. Alas, language development does not proceed like that. You'll need constant exposure to the use of grammar features and practice in using them to retain their **correct** use. You should also not be surprised if you use features correctly in some situations and then incorrectly in others before finally using features mostly correctly. For instance, you may make good progress learning the literary present tense, but your mastery can vanish and your performance decline when you go to apply your knowledge in new situations that require both the use of the literary present tense and the past tense. Your backsliding* will continue until the knowledge you have learned about the literary present tense is internalized* and you learn how to use it with the past tense. The learning curve* for grammatical features is not a linear one, but is, according to second language researcher Diane Larsen-Freeman, "characterized by peaks and restructurings."

Source: Larsen-Freeman, Diane. "Teaching Grammar." *Teaching English as a Second or Foreign Language.* Ed. Marianne Celce-Murcia, Donna Brinton, and Margaret Ann Snow. 4th ed. Boston: National Geographic Learning/Cengage, 2014. 256-70. Print.

Myth 6: Not all students can learn grammar because they are too old or have the wrong learning style. No research has yet shown that college students are incapable of learning grammar—regardless of their learning style.

---

*to backslide

(verb): to start using language that you used to use, after having learned a better way of using language

*internalize

(verb): if you internalize a particular grammatical feature, it becomes a regular part of your language use

*learning curve

(noun phrase): the rate at which you develop something

Jiayuan Liu, a former writing student, explains:

"Before I came to the United States, my school had given me a certificate. It stated I had reached an advanced proficiency level in English. Even my test scores told me I was pretty good in English grammar. Once I got here I learned that my certificate and previous test scores did not indicate that I had learned all I needed to do well at UCI. I found out I had <u>a lot</u> more grammar to learn."

How You'll Approach Grammar

Consistent with more recent research on the development of English grammar, this section briefly describes how you will approach English grammar in English language and writing courses. You will learn how (1) to use grammar in diverse situations, (2) to gain good control of grammatical features, (3) to learn grammar incrementally over time, (4) to use grammar to improve your writing, and (5) to develop your conscious knowledge of grammatical features.

In your courses, you'll learn how to use grammar in diverse situations. You may have studied a lot of grammar in your elementary and secondary schools and feel that you already know a lot of it. Your previous education may even have led you to believe that you have completely mastered the grammar that you are studying in your English courses. However, this is, in all likelihood, not the case. Most students find that although they have already studied much grammar, they have difficulty using this grammar in specific contexts. You may know how to use qualifiers like *somewhat* or *most* or modal auxiliaries like *should*, but you may not know how to use them to qualify thesis statements. You may know how to form passive structures *(The play was written by Shakespeare)*, but not how to use passive structures to de-emphasize the researcher's responsibility in undertaking bad research *(Research was undertaken)*. You may not know how to use passive structures when you do not know who the agent is, when you want to deliberately hide the identity of the agent, when the agent is obvious and you can easily figure out who the agent is from the context, when the agent is redundant, and so on. Or you may not know how to avoid the passive structure. Each time you encounter a new writing assignment, you'll need to use different grammar features and use them differently than you have ever used them before. For example, you may already know about count and non-count nouns and the use of articles.

However, once you have to write a paper on *bacteria*, you may realize that you do not know if the word *bacteria* is singular or plural or you do not know if you need to use an article when referring to bacteria. You may know how to use the personal pronoun **I** in most everyday situations, but you may not know how to use it in specific types of writing, like reflective writing, or in different disciplines, for instance, to mark a claim that you think others in the discipline might disagree with (*I believe that…*), to hedge (*I suppose that…*), or to establish intimacy with readers. Your previous instructors may have been silent when it came to teaching you how you can use your knowledge of grammar in different situational contexts. They hoped you would be able to transfer your knowledge from one situation to the next. English instructors, on the other hand, know that many grammatical features need to be taught and re-taught in different contexts for you to gain deep knowledge of them. They'll teach you useful grammatical features again and again, giving you ample opportunities to use your grammatical features in writing about different topics, in different genres, and for different purposes. By the time you reach English language and writing courses, you should have enough knowledge of the ways that grammatical features are used in different contexts in order for you to continue broadening your knowledge of these features on your own.

Your instructors expect you to gain good control of grammatical features but not to master them fully. Learning particular features requires a great deal of practice, even for the most skilled learners. Your instructors realize that grammar is best acquired over time, mostly through the instruction of these features, exposure* to them, practice using them in speech and writing, and instructional feedback.

*exposure

(uncountable noun): the chance to experience something new, like language features

Because grammar is acquired incrementally over time, instructors will teach you different aspects of the same basic grammatical features in different ways in different contexts and with diverse texts and writing assignments. Each time they re-teach you grammatical features, you broaden your knowledge of the ways in which the grammatical features are used in different situations.

Much emphasis is placed on learning to use grammar to improve your writing. Your instructors know that it is much harder for you to apply grammar rules in your academic writing than it is for you to memorize rules. This is why your instructors will give you much practice in applying grammar rules to improve your writing. They'll provide you with many grammar activities and exercises, and then ask you to apply what you have learned to improve your writing. You may be tempted to copy the answers from your friends. This will not help you. You will be held accountable for using grammar accurately in your writing and required to take a series of quizzes on key grammatical features. There are many additional online websites and additional resources that will help you improve your knowledge of English grammar. Ask your instructor for additional advice.

Considerable emphasis is placed on developing your conscious knowledge of grammatical features, so that you can use this conscious knowledge to reflect on your language use, identify errors in your writing, and correct your own errors. You'll be asked to reflect on your use of grammatical features and discuss them. This will help you gain *metalinguistic ability*—the ability to talk about your language use—and that will help you develop editing skills. You'll also be given many opportunities to talk about your learning. This will help you gain *metacognitive ability*—the ability to think about your thinking and the ways for editing your writing that work for you.

Useful Grammar Site:

Purdue Online Writing Lab (https://owl. english.purdue.edu).

Using the Same Language to Describe Grammar Terms

Since you'll talk a lot about grammar in your course, it's important that your classmates and you use the same language to discuss it. You may have learned slightly different definitions of or have slightly different ways of talking about grammatical concepts than your classmates and instructor. To eliminate misunderstandings about grammar, you'll use the list of definitions of important grammar terms that is given below. There are other terms, other labels for these terms, and even other ways of defining these terms. The terms below are the ones most frequently used in grammar handbooks and ones you may have learned earlier. While it is true that you don't need to memorize grammar terms to learn grammar, you'll most likely find the terms below beneficial. They'll help you talk about grammar, discuss the ways authors use it, examine the effect of specific grammatical features on readers, analyze your own use of grammatical features in writing, edit your writing, and assess your own grammatical development.

Insider Tip

Schedule time to learn grammar. Complete the assignments in your grammar textbook. Don't wait for your instructor to assign grammar homework. Find the grammar sections in your grammar textbook that you find most helpful and start studying them on your own.

In her most recent 2015 book *Founding Grammars: How Early America's War Over Words Shaped Today's Language*, linguist Rosemarie Ostler explains that even Abraham Lincoln memorized grammar terms. She states, "Learning that a local farmer owned a copy of schoolteacher Samuel Kirkham's popular English Grammar in Familiar Lectures, he [Abraham Lincoln] walked several miles to borrow it. From another friend he borrowed a copy of the best-selling grammar book of the time, *English Grammar*. . . Typically for that time, Lincoln mastered the books by memorizing them. He would have started at the beginning, with definitions—'A noun is the name of any person, place, or thing.'"

Source: Ostler, Rosemarie. *Founding Grammars: How Early America's War over Words Shaped Today's Language.* New York City, New York: St. Martins, 2015. Print.

John Nguyen, a former writing student, advises:

"It helped me to memorize the grammar terms in the first week of the course. That saved me a lot of time later."

Hansol Hyun, a former writing student, argues:

"Memorizing the lists of indefinite pronouns, modal auxiliaries, and prepositions and studying the verb tense table were what helped me pass the grammar quizzes, master subject-verb agreement, and figure out a lot of my own grammar problems. My friends who had problems never took the time to memorize."

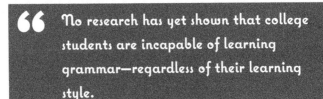

No research has yet shown that college students are incapable of learning grammar—regardless of their learning style.

Grammar Terms
Parts of Speech (Grammatical Functions of Words and Phrases)

adjective – a word that modifies or adds more information to a noun (*pretty, sad, tired, big*)

adverb – a word that modifies a verb, adjective, adverb or clause (*slowly, silently, very*)

conjunction – a word that joins words, phrases, or clauses (*and, but, or, after, when, while*)

The teacher started the class *and* we all sat down. *When* she spoke, we all listened.

determiner – a word which precedes nouns and classifies, identifies, or indicates their quantity

article (*a, an, the*) – a determiner indicates that a noun will follow

indefinite article – indicates an unspecified noun (*a, an*)

definite article – indicates a specific entity which both the reader and writer recognize (*the*)

demonstrative adjective – a word that indicates distance in place or time (*this, that, these, those*)

possessive adjective – a word that indicates the owner (*my, his ,her, your, our, their*)

noun – a word used to identify a person, place or thing

count nouns – things that can be counted and made plural (*chair/chairs, book/books, pen/pens*)

noncount nouns – things that are not countable and are always singular (*advice, water, money*)

proper noun – the name of a person or place (written with initial capital letters – *Mary, France*)

preposition – a word indicating the relationship between two things which may be spatial, temporal, grammatical, or metaphorical (*about, above, after, against, around, at, before, behind, beside, down, during, for, from, in, into, of, to, under, up, with, within*) *Example:* The pen is *on* the table. Please see me *after* class.

pronoun – a word that takes the place of a noun or noun phrase (*I, you, he, she, it, we, they, me, him, her, us, them*)

verb – a word that shows action or a state of being (*go, bring, be, study*)

    auxiliary verb – a helping verb that is added to a main verb to indicate mood, voice, or tense (*do, have, be*)

    modal – an auxiliary verb that indicates necessity, ability, possibility, permission or obligation (*can, could, will, would, shall, should, ought to, might, may, must, have to*)

    gerund – a verb with an *-ing* ending that functions as a noun (*studying, thinking, going*)

    infinitive – a verb form that is not marked for time or person (often preceded by *to* – *to go, to be, to sing*)

    intransitive verb – a verb that does not take a direct object (*sleep* – She *slept* late yesterday.)

    transitive verb – a verb that requires a direct object to complete its meaning (*tell* – Please *tell* me your story.)

    participle – a verb + *-ing* (**present participle**) or *-ed, -en, -t* (**past participle**) that can be part of a verb phrase or act as an adjective (*going, caring, seen, tired* – she is *going*; the *caring* boy; they have *seen* it; a *tired* man)

    tense – time of the action of the verb

Table 14.1: Tenses

Tense – time of the action	Example
Simple Present	He studies every day.
Simple Past	We worked last night.
Simple Future	They will leave tomorrow.
Present Progressive	She is eating right now.
Past Progressive	I was reading when you called.
Future Progressive	I will be cooking when you arrive.
Present Perfect	He has seen the movie three times.
Past Perfect	I had been to Asia before you went.
Future Perfect	We will have taken the first exam before we start then next chapter.
Present Perfect Progressive	She has been driving for two years.
Past Perfect Progressive	I had been living in New York before we moved to Florida.
Future Perfect Progressive	We will have been exercising for an hour by the time we finish.

Sentence Structure

sentence – a grammatically complete assertion that contains a subject and a verb
She came late.

clause – any group of words that has a subject and a verb
she went

dependent clause – a clause that cannot stand alone
when I lived there

independent clause – a clause that can stand alone as a simple sentence
They've decided.

relative clause – a dependent clause that usually begins with a relative pronoun (who, which, that, whose)
The boy who lives next door is my friend.

conditional sentence – a hypothetical sentence with a dependent clause beginning with if, or unless
If I want to pass, I'd better do more work.

fragment – a group of words ending with a period (.) that does not constitute a complete sentence
Before I decided to come.
Because he loves me.

phrase – a word group that acts as a single part of speech but does not have both a subject and a verb
while talking on the phone
looking unhappy
after the prom

run-on sentence – independent clauses joined with commas, inappropriate conjunctions, or no punctuation
I ate my lunch, I polished my shoes.

subject – the noun or noun phrase that names the doer of the action of the verb
She registered on time.

For additional information, go to www.humanities.uci.edu/esl/undergrad/symbols.php.

Grammar Rules and Tips

What follows is a quick review of the basic grammar rules that readers generally expect writers to follow in most situations. You might use this review if you are having difficulty with grammar, are confused or curious about the basics, or need grammar information to pass quizzes or complete assignments. Learning the basics early on in the course will help you discuss authors' use of grammar, analyze your own use of grammar, and evaluate your own development of grammatical features. Your instructors will quiz you on the information in the first weeks of your class in an effort to help you get an overall view of the basic grammar rules that are followed by most writers in most academic situations. These are rules that expert writers may consciously break for rhetorical effect in particular situations. They intentionally use grammar creatively to communicate effectively.

Nouns

Nouns are **common**—referring to general people, places, things, or ideas or **proper**—referring to named specific people, places, things or ideas.

- **Common:** professor, college, religion
- **Proper:** Dr. Striedter, Buddhism

Nouns are **definite** (specific) referring to individuals within a group of nouns or **indefinite** (general) referring to the whole category of the group.

- **Definite:** The students in Prof. Coleman's class must work hard.
- **Indefinite:** Students must work hard. (all students in general)

Nouns are **count**, also called countable, or **noncount**, also called uncountable. Only count nouns have a plural form.

- **Count:** A girl walks to the bus stop. Girls walk to the bus stop.
- **Noncount:** Advice is beneficial; Honesty can be hard to find.
- **Regular** plural nouns generally use –**s** endings, **irregular** plural forms generally do not end in –**s**.

  Regular: Singular: girl, mother   **Plural:** girl**s**, mother**s**

  Irregular: Singular: man, child   **Plural:** men, children

Determiners

- **Determiners** include:
  - **Possessive pronouns/adjectives:** my, your, his, her, its, our, their (her disease, our dog)
  - **Demonstrative pronouns/adjectives:** this, that, these, those (this girl; those girls)
  - **Quantifiers:** all, any, each, either, every, few, many, more, most, neither, several, some, etc. (each girl; some girls)
  - **Numbers:** one, two, three, four, etc. (one girl; two girls)
- Articles : a, an, and the (*an* apple, *a* book, *the* man)
- Use the articles *a* and *an* before singular count nouns whose specific identities are unknown to the reader.
- Do not use *a/an* with noncount nouns.
- Use *the* with most count nouns whose identities are known to the reader.
- Do not use *the* with plural or noncount nouns that mean all or in general.

Verbs

- Tense is appropriate to the situation and has specific functions and forms.
  - **The present tense** indicates general facts, constant states, or habitual states and it is used for the literary present to discuss movies or fiction. It generally has an –s ending for third person singular form.
  - **The past tense** indicates actions that happened at a specific point of time or during a specific period of time in the past. Regular verbs generally end in -ed. English also has many irregular past tense verbs that have different forms.
  - **The present continuous** (also called the progressive) shows actions that are in progress at the present time but not expected to remain constant or go on indefinitely. It uses *be* in the appropriate form and base verb with the -ing ending.
  - **The present perfect tense** shows an action that began in the past and continued to the present or occurred at an unspecified point in the past. It is made by using *have* in the appropriate form and the past participle of a base verb.
- The base form of a verb should follow a modal.
  She can go. They must follow.
- **The passive voice** uses an appropriate form of *be* with the past participle of the main verb.
  She was given an A.
- **Conditional verbs** are used to make conditional sentences and have specific verb form requirements based on the types of condition. There are many different ways to express "conditional" or "hypothetical" meaning in English. One of them is to use the word "if" in the clause that expresses the condition. Verb tenses and auxiliary verbs like *can/could, will/would,* and *might* are key to making sentences conditional. Conditional verbs can be used in the past, present, or future tense.

- **The factual (real) condition:** When the situation is completely likely, use present tense in both clauses. With the factual or real condition, both clause tenses match:
  If the water *cools* to 32 degrees, it freezes.
  When it *rains* enough, the grass grows.

- **The predictive (unreal but likely) condition:** This conditional deals with "unreal, but likely" situations in the present or future. We call it "unreal" because the situation we are describing hasn't happened yet and "likely" because we can easily imagine it happening. Conditionals that indicate the predictive or unreal but likely condition use the present tense in the conditional or subordinate clause and will, can, may, should, or might in the independent clause.
  If you practice regularly, you *will* improve.
  He *may* fail the class unless he does his homework diligently.

- **The speculative (unreal or impossible) condition:** This conditional deals with situations in the present and future that are both unreal and unlikely. The situation we are describing hasn't happened yet, and we really can't imagine it happening very easily. When the situation is unreal and unlikely, use the past tense in the conditional (or subordinate) clause and *would, could,* or *might* + the base form of the verb in the main (independent) clause.
  If I won the lottery, I *would* quit working.
  If I were a lion, I *would* roar.

  In the conditional or subordinate clause, you may also use the past perfect tense and could have, would have, or might have with the past participle in the independent or main clause.
  If I had gone to college earlier, I *might have* earned a Ph.D.

- Certain verbs are followed only by a **gerund**, while others are followed only by an **infinitive**, and others may be followed by either an infinitive or a gerund.

  - **Gerund only**: I appreciate *studying* at my school.

  - **Infinitive only**: I expect *to do* well at my job.

  - Sometimes you can use a verb and follow it by a gerund or an infinitive, and doing so changes the meaning of the main verb.
    I stopped *going* to the gym; I stopped *to go* to the gym.

- **Present** and **past participles** must have appropriate endings whether used as a main verb or a modifier.
  Incorrect: She is *go* (*Going* is required.)
  Incorrect: The *talent* girl (*Talented* is required.)

Agreement: Subjects and Verbs Should Agree

- Verbs should agree with the main subject, not any other word between the subject and the verb and not the noun in the prepositional phrase.
  The students who often bully Temple Grandin need to be disciplined.

- Most subjects joined with *and* are considered plural.
  Injustice and ignorance *hurt* people in society.
  Exception: using every or each before the noun causes singularity
  Each injustice and ignorance *hurts* people in society.

- For subjects joined with *or* or *nor*, the verb should agree with the part of the subject nearest the verb.
  Jia **or** <u>her peers</u> *need to work diligently*; Her peers **or** <u>Jia</u> *needs to work diligently*.

- Most **indefinite pronouns** are considered singular: *anybody, anyone, anything, each, either, everybody, everyone, everything, neither, nobody, no one, nothing, somebody, someone, something*

- **Collective nouns** (*jury, staff, faculty, crowd, class, family*) are generally considered singular unless the meaning is clearly pointing to plural.
  Singular: *The family is very strict with the rules.*
  Plural: *The family are fighting among themselves.*

- The verb agrees with the subject even if the subject follows the verb.
  There is much prejudice in the world today.
  There are prejudice, injustice, and unfairness in the world today. (See Rule 3.)

- Gerund phrases are singular. *Treating children strictly is what many Chinese parents do.*

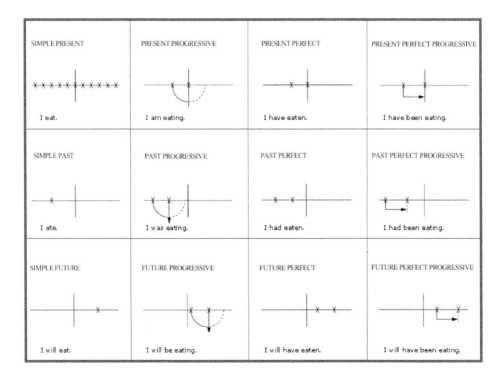

SIMPLE PRESENT	PRESENT PROGRESSIVE	PRESENT PERFECT	PRESENT PERFECT PROGRESSIVE
I eat.	I am eating.	I have eaten.	I have been eating.
SIMPLE PAST	PAST PROGRESSIVE	PAST PERFECT	PAST PERFECT PROGRESSIVE
I ate.	I was eating.	I had eaten.	I had been eating.
SIMPLE FUTURE	FUTURE PROGRESSIVE	FUTURE PERFECT	FUTURE PERFECT PROGRESSIVE
I will eat.	I will be eating.	I will have eaten.	I will have been eating.

List of English Irregular Verbs

This is a list of commonly occurring English irregular verbs, with their past simple and past participle forms.

Verb (infinitive)	Past simple form	Past participle	Verb (infinitive)	Past simple form	Past participle	Verb (infinitive)	Past simple form	Past participle
arise	arose	arisen	grow	grew	grown	shrink	shrank	shrunk
awake	awoke	awoken	have	had	had	shut	shut	shut
bear	bore	borne	hear	heard	heard	sing	sang	sung
beat	beat	beaten	hide	hid	hidden	sink	sank	sunk
become	became	become	hit	hit	hit	sit	sat	sat
begin	began	begun	hold	held	held	sleep	slept	slept
bend	bent	bent	hurt	hurt	hurt	slay	slew	slain
bet	bet	bet	keep	kept	kept	slide	slid	slid
bid	bid	bid	kneel	knelt	knelt	sling	slung	slung
bind	bound	bound	know	knew	known	slit	slit	slit
bite	bit	bitten	lay	laid	laid	smell	smelled	smelled
bleed	bled	bled	lead	led	led	smite	smote	smitten
blow	blew	blown	lean	leaned	leaned	speak	spoke	spoken
break	broke	broken	leap	leaped	leaped	spell	spelled	spelled
breed	bred	bred	learn	learned	learned	spend	spent	spent
bring	brought	brought	leave	left	left	spill	spilled	spilled
build	built	built	lend	lent	lent	spin	spun	spun
burn	burned	burned	let	let	let	spit	spat	spat
burst	burst	burst	lie	lay	lain	split	split	split
buy	bought	bought	light	lighted	lighted	spoil	spoiled	spoiled
cast	cast	cast	lose	lost	lost	spread	spread	spread
catch	caught	caught	make	made	made	spring	sprang	sprung
choose	chose	chosen	mean	meant	meant	stand	stood	stood
cling	clung	clung	meet	met	met	steal	stole	stolen
come	came	come	misspell	misspelled	misspelled	stick	stuck	stuck
cost	cost	cost	mistake	mistook	mistaken	sting	stung	stung
creep	crept	crept	mow	mowed	mown	stink	stank	stunk
cut	cut	cut	overcome	overcame	overcome	stride	strode	stridden
deal	dealt	dealt	overdo	overdid	overdone	strike	struck	struck
dig	dug	dug	overtake	overtook	overtaken	strive	strove	striven
dive	dove	dived	overthrow	overthrew	overthrown	swear	swore	sworn
do	did	done	pay	paid	paid	sweep	swept	swept
draw	drew	drawn	plead	plead	plead	swell	swelled	swollen
dream	dreamed	dreamed	prove	proved	proved/proven	swim	swam	swum
drink	drank	drunk	put	put	put	swing	swung	swung
drive	drove	driven	quit	quit	quit	take	took	taken
eat	ate	eaten	read	read	read	teach	taught	taught
fall	fell	fallen	rid	rid	rid	tear	tore	torn
feed	fed	fed	ride	rode	ridden	tell	told	told
feel	felt	felt	ring	rang	rung	think	thought	thought
fight	fought	fought	rise	rose	risen	thrive	thrived/throve	thrived
find	found	found	run	ran	run	throw	threw	thrown
fit	fit	fit	see	saw	seen	thrust	thrust	thrust
flee	fled	fled	say	said	said	tread	trod	trodden
fly	flew	flown	see	saw	seen	understand	understood	understood
forbid	forbade	forbidden	seek	sought	sought	uphold	upheld	upheld
forget	forgot	forgotten	sell	sold	sold	upset	upset	upset
forgo	forewent	foregone	send	sent	sent	wake	woke	woken
forgive	forgave	forgiven	set	set	set	wear	wore	worn
forsake	forsook	forsaken	sew	sewed	sewn/sewed	weep	wept	wept
foretell	foretold	foretold	shake	shook	shaken	win	won	won
freeze	froze	frozen	shear	sheared	sheared/shorn	wind	wound	wound
get	got	gotten	shed	shed	shed	withdraw	withdrew	withdrawn
give	gave	given	shine	shone	shone	withhold	withheld	withheld
go	went	gone	shoot	shot	shot	withstand	withstood	withstood
grind	ground	ground	show	showed	shown	write	wrote	written

Adapted with permission from Cain, Joyce S. *Grammar for Writing 1*. White Plains, New Jersey: Pearson ELT, 2012. p. 128.

Gerund and Infinitive Verb Form Reference Charts

Some verbs are followed by gerunds, some by infinitives, and some by either infinitives or gerunds. You can use the charts below to help you decide which to use, a gerund or an infinitive.

A **gerund** is a noun made from a verb. To make a gerund, you add **-ing** to the verb. **Examples**: *going, coming, thinking, writing*

An **infinitive** is the basic form of the verb + **"to."**

Examples: *to buy, to fish, to run, to watch, to tell*

How to Read the Charts

0 = The first verb is not followed by a noun or pronoun.

√ = The first verb is followed by a noun or pronoun.

* = A noun or pronoun may or may not follow the verb.

The second verb form appears in the form indicated.

First Verb	+ Noun/ Pronoun	Second Verb Form	Example
ADMIT	0	V + ING	She admits taking the pen.
ADVISE	√	TO + V	I advise you to take the class.
AFFORD	0	TO + V	Minh can't afford to go.
AGREE	0	TO + V	We agreed to see him.
ALLOW	√	TO + V	John allowed me to come.
ARRANGE	0	TO + V	They arranged to be here.
ASK	*	TO + V	We asked to see him. We asked him to be here.
ATTEMPT	0	TO + V	Jose attempted to ski.
AVOID	0	V + ING	They avoided answering him.
BE (AM, IS, ARE, BEEN, BEING)	0	V + ING = CONTINUOUS V + ED/EN/T = PASSIVE	She is playing tennis. The poem is written in French.
BEGIN	0	V + ING TO + V	We began reading at noon. We began to read at noon.
CAN	0	BASE V	She can live with me.

√ = mandatory; 0 = not allowed; * = optional

First Verb	+ Noun/ Pronoun	Second Verb Form	Example
CAUSE	√	TO + V	I caused him to fall.
CHOOSE	*	TO + V	We chose to live here. We chose him to be on the team.
CONTINUE	0	V + ING TO + V	Please continue reading. Please continue to read.
CONVINCE	√	TO + V	Sal convinced me to stay.
COULD	0	BASE V	She could try harder.
DECIDE	0	TO + V	Han decided to leave early.
DEMAND		TO + V THAT + someone + BASE V	He demanded to see me. He demanded that I leave.
DESERVE	0	TO + V	Maria deserves to win.
DO / DOES DID	0	BASE V	They didn't see me there. Do you live in the dorm?
ENJOY	0	V + ING	She enjoys swimming.
EXPECT	*	TO + V	I expect to arrive at 9. I expect him to arrive at 9.
FEEL	0	V + ED/EN/T	The baby feels tired.
FINISH	0	V + ING	Please finish writing now.
FORCE	√	TO + V	Don't force Sarah to stay.
FORGET	0	TO + V	She often forgets to buy milk.
GET	0	V + ED/EN/T	We got married in NY.
HAD BETTER	0	BASE V	You had better be on time.
HAVE / HAS / HAD	0	V + ED/EN/T = perfect tense	She has broken the date. They have tried to fix it.
HATE	0	V + ING TO + V	Dong hates speaking English. Dong hates to speak English.
HEAR	√	BASE V	We heard him leave.
HELP	√	BASE V	They helped her pass the class.
HOPE	0	TO + V	I hope to be here next year.
IMAGINE	0	V + ING	I can't imagine living in Africa.
INSIST		THAT + SOMEONE + BASE V	They insist that he leave.

√ = mandatory; 0 = not allowed; * = optional

First Verb	+ Noun/ Pronoun	Second Verb Form	Example
IMAGINE	0	V + ING	I can't imagine living in Africa.
INSIST		THAT + SOMEONE + BASE V	They insist that he leave.
INSPIRE	√	TO + V	He inspired me to do it.
INTEND	0	TO + V	We intend to graduate in 4 years.
INVITE	√	TO + V	Bob invited Joe to go out.
KEEP	0	V + ING	Please keep trying!
LEARN	0	TO + V	I learned to drive on the freeway.
LET	√	BASE V	They let us take their car.
LIKE	* 0	TO + V V + ING	We like to play. We like him to play. We like reading mystery novels.
MAKE	√	BASE V	They made him study more.
MAY	0	BASE V	We may see you later.
MIGHT	0	BASE V	She might go home today.
MIND	0	V + ING	I don't mind waiting for you.
MISS	0	V + ING	We miss celebrating New Year's.
MUST	0	BASE V	You must see a doctor.
NEED	0	TO + V	Sam needs to study more.
OFFER	0	TO + V	She offered to drive me home.
ORDER	√	TO + V	I order you to pay her back.
OUGHT	0	TO + V	You ought to pass this class.
PERSUADE	√	TO + V	We persuaded him to take off.
PLAN	0	TO + V	Diego plans to visit Guatemala.
PRETEND	0	TO + V	Don't pretend to know it.
PRACTICE	0	V + ING	She practices typing in the lab.
PREFER	0	TO + V V + ING	I prefer to live on campus. I prefer living on campus.
PROMISE	0	TO + V	They promised to write us.
RECOMMEND	0	V + ING THAT + SOMEONE + BASE V	I recommend reading more. I recommend that he read more.
REFUSE	0	TO + V	They refused to see me.
REMIND	√	TO + V	We reminded him to practice.

√ = mandatory; 0 = not allowed; * = optional

First Verb	+ Noun/ Pronoun	Second Verb Form	Example
SEE	√	BASE V	They saw my mother leave.
SEEM	0	TO + V	Ariel seems to be happier now.
SHOULD	0	BASE V	You should try it.
START	0	TO + V V + ING	We started to dance. We started dancing.
STOP	0	TO + V V + ING	He stopped to take her picture. She said, stop taking my picture.
SUGGEST	0	V + ING THAT + SOMEONE + BASE V	I suggest listening carefully. I suggest that you listen carefully.
TEACH	√	TO + V	Chu taught me to speak Chinese.
TELL	√	TO + V	We told him to take the bus.
TRY	0	TO + V	They tried to be here on time.
USED TO	0	BASE V	We used to live in Mexico.
WANT	*	TO + V	Tia wanted to leave. Tia wanted him to leave.
WARN	√	TO + V	I warned Frank to get help.
WATCH	√	BASE V	We watched the flower grow.
WILL	0	BASE V	They will take that class.
WOULD	0	BASE V	They wouldn't do that.
WOULD LIKE	*	TO + V	I would like to go to bed now. I would like you to go to bed now.

√ = mandatory; 0 = not allowed; * = optional

Source: Joyce S. Cain, Eye on Editing. Pearson Education ESL; 1st edition (Chapter 10) (August 8, 2001) ISBN-10: 0201621320.

Count and Noncount Nouns and Determiners

When a noun is singular and countable, you must use a determiner. When talking in general, use a plural count noun without an article. Use "the" with a noncount noun only if the noun is specific.

NONCOUNT NOUN no S on noun	SINGULAR COUNT NOUN no S on noun	PLURAL COUNT NOUN +S on noun (or irregular)
√		√
the	the	the
	a/an	
this/that	this/that	these/those
the other	the other	the other
	another	other
any other	any other	any other
any	any	any
no	no	no
some		some
little		few
a little		a few
much		many
a lot of		a lot of
a great deal of		several
most		most
most of the		most of the
all		all
	each	
	every	
		a couple of
		both
	one	two, twenty, fifty
		a variety of
		various

Noncount nouns:

She gave me the money.

They had a little time.

Don't give me any advice.

All work should be done.

Some furniture is cheap.

We do not have much milk

Singular count nouns:

The other book is mine.

Each lie is bad.

Every banana is rotten.

She'll give me a chance.

Every chair is broken.

We have one glass of milk.

Plural count nouns:

A few men are needed.

All people should be here.

The other students left.

Some cars are expensive.

Most chairs have four legs.

We have five glasses of milk.

Prepositions

A preposition connects a noun or a pronoun to another word in a sentence and indicates a relationship, often of place, time, cause, purpose, direction, or means.

Prepositions are usually one word but can also be two or more words. The most frequently used one-word prepositions are *at, by, for, from, in, of, on, to,* and *with.* Some prepositions with more than one word are *according to, along with, away from,* and *in front of.* Other prepositions you may be familiar with are *above, across, after, against, along, among, before, behind, below, beside, between, into, over, through, up,* and *without.*

- **Prepositions of time**

month / year	Aidan arrived in Yorktown *in* June. He arrived *in* 1999.
day / date	He began classes *on* Monday. He began class *on* June 5.
specific time	The classes started *at* 9:00 am.
general time	The classes ended *in* the evening / afternoon / morning.
approximate	I'll be home *about* 2:00.
	Let's meet *around* 5:00.
	He said he'd call *between* 9 and 10 o'clock.
duration	My family lived in Guam *for* six years.
	I have thought of you often *through* the past years.

- **Prepositions of place**

city / country	Fred lived in Toronto for three years. He lived in Canada for five years.
street	He worked on Battery Street.
address	He lives at 16 Queen Lane.
motion	He goes to the park for lunch. (walk to, run to, drive to, ride to, race to, fly to)
	They walked toward me.

- **Prepositions of position**

  The book is on the desk.

  The lecture notes are in my notebook.

  Let's meet at the library.

  The dog is sitting beside its owner.

  My house is between the library and the bridge.

- **Prepositions of reason**

    They will do the job *for* minimum wage.

    He was pleased *by* her kind words.

    We talked *about* the news.

- **Prepositions of manner**

    He can understand their accent *by* listening carefully.

    She is good *at* speaking foreign languages.

    They finished the test *with* ease.

- **Prepositions of comparison**

    We are so close that he is *like* my brother.

- **Prepositions of possession**

    Dino is a good friend *of* mine.

Adjectives + Prepositions

The list below contains some of the common adjective + preposition combinations. Check your dictionary for any adjective + preposition combinations that are not on this list.

A	accustomed to afraid of amazed at/by angry at anxious about ashamed of aware of awful at	F	familiar with fond of friendly to full of famous for	P	pleased about proud of		
				R	ready for responsible for		
		G	glad aboout good at guilty of	S	sad about safe from satisfied with sick of similar to slow at sorry for/about suitable for superior to surprised about/at/by		
B	bad at bored with/by						
		H	happy about homesick for				
C	capable of careful of concerned about content with curious about	I	inferior to interested in				
		J	jealous of	T	tired of terrible at		
D	dependent on different from	K	known for				
		N	nervous about	U	upset with		
E	eager for envious of excited about	O	opposed to	W	worried about		

Adapted from Cain, Joyce. *Grammar for Writing 1: An Editing Guide to Writing.* 2nd edition. White Plains, NJ: Pearson, 2012. 132. With permission.

Verbs + Prepositions

This next list contains common verb + preposition combinations. Check your dictionary for any verb + preposition combinations that you cannot find on this list.

A accuse of
adapt to
admit to
advise against
agree with (something)
apologize for
apply for (something)
apply to (someplace)
approve of hope
argue about (something)
argue with (someone)
arrive in/at

B believe in
belong to
blame for

C care about/for
choose between
combine with
come from
compare to/with
complain about (something)
complain to (someone)
concentrate on
consist of
contribute to
cooperate with
count on

D deal with
decide on
depend on
disapprove of
dream about/of

E escape from
excel at
excuse for/from

F feel like
fight for
forget about
forgive for

G glance at
gossip about
graduate from

H happen to
hear about (something/
someone)
hear from (someone)
hide from
homesick for

I insist on
interfere with
introduce (someone) to
someone)
invite (someone) to
something

K know about

L listen to
look at
look forward to
learn from
live on

M matter to

O object to

P participate in
pay for
plan on
prepare for
prevent from
protect from
prohibit (someone) from

R recover from
rely on
rescue from
respond to
read about

S search for
speak about
speak to/with
stare at
stop from
subscribe to
substitute for
succeed in

T take advantage of
take care of
talk about
talk to/with
thank (someone) for
think about

V vote for

W wait for
worry about

Adapted from Cain, Joyce. *Grammar for Writing 1: An Editing Guide to Writing.* 2nd edition. White Plains, NJ: Pearson, 2012. 132. With permission.

Practical Grammar Tips:

Students often have difficulty using certain words and expressions correctly. This could be because of the grammar rules that govern their use. If you have difficulty, referring to the word list below might help you.

- **ADVICE (noncount noun) / ADVISE (verb)**
  I gave him some good <u>advice</u>. I <u>advised</u> him not to drop the class.
  NOT – advices; advice someone; give advise

- **AFFECT (verb) / EFFECT (count noun)**
  The lack of sleep didn't <u>affect</u> him, but the <u>effect</u> of the alcohol was obvious.
  NOT – They didn't effect me; I saw the affects

- **AFRAID (adjective) / TO BE AFRAID + TO/ OF (verb phrase)**
  She <u>was afraid to</u> see him. They <u>are afraid of</u> failing the class.
  NOT – she afraid ; they are afraided

- **AGREE ON + st / WITH + so**
  We <u>agreed</u> on all the answers. She <u>agrees with</u> her father.
  NOT – she is agrees

- **ALL OF A SUDDEN**
  The rain fell <u>all of a sudden</u>. <u>All of a sudden</u> the lights went out.
  NOT – all of the sudden

- **AS A RESULT**
  We passed the test. <u>As a result</u>, we can go on to 39A.
  NOT – as the result

- **BECAUSE (+ clause) / BECAUSE OF (+ noun)**
  <u>Because</u> we had a test, we couldn't go.
  <u>Because of</u> the test, we couldn't go.
  NOT – because of we had the test

- **BELIEF (count noun) / BELIEVE (verb)|**
  We have strong <u>beliefs</u>. We <u>believe</u> in truth and justice.
  NOT – strong believes; we belief

- **BESIDE (next to) / BESIDES (in addition to)**
  He sat <u>beside</u> me. <u>Besides</u> studying together, we also worked in the same lab.
  NOT – sit besides me; beside studying together

- **BETTER / HAD BETTER**
  You <u>had better</u> see a doctor. You<u>'d better</u> see a doctor.
  NOT – you better

- **CARE ABOUT (to be interested in) / CARE FOR (to take care of)**
  I don't <u>care about</u> my grades. I have to <u>care for</u> my grandmother.
  NOT – I have to care about her.

- **CONCERN / TO BE CONCERNED ABOUT**
  Those problems <u>concern</u> me. I <u>am concerned</u> about those problems.
  NOT – I concerned about

- **DAY AFTER DAY**
  We practice <u>day after day</u> to improve our skills.
  NOT – days after days

- **DESPITE**
  <u>Despite</u> her effort, she couldn't lose weight.
  NOT – despite of her effort

- **DIFFERENT FROM/THAN (NOT to)**
  I am different <u>from</u> my parents. I am different <u>than</u> my parents. (Most instructors prefer different **from**.)
  NOT – different to

- **EACH / EVERY + singular noun**
  <u>Each</u> student has a handbook. <u>Every</u> mother loves her children.
  NOT – each students; every mothers

- **EMPHASIZE / PUT EMPHASIS ON**
  The instructor <u>emphasized</u> grammar. She <u>put a lot of emphasis on</u> verbs.
  NOT – emphasize on grammar

- **EVEN (intensifier)**
  He doesn't even know his father.
  NOT – he even doesn't

- **EVEN THOUGH / ALTHOUGH**
  <u>Even though</u> I like the teacher, the class is boring.
  NOT – even I like; although I like her, but

- **EXIST**
  Those problems <u>exist</u> everywhere.
  NOT – are exist

- **FACE / BE FACED WITH**
  We <u>face</u> new issues every day. We <u>are faced with</u> new issues every day.
  NOT – we face with; we are face new issues

- **HARD**
  She <u>finds it hard to solve</u> these problems. She <u>has a hard time solving</u> these problems.
  NOT – she is hard to solve these problems

- **HOPE**
  I <u>hoped</u> you would come. I <u>hope</u> you can come. I <u>hope</u> you will come.
  NOT – I hope I would; I hope I could

- **IN OTHER WORDS**
  It's broken. <u>In other words</u>, it doesn't work.
  NOT – in another word; in the other word

- **IN SPITE OF**
  <u>In spite of</u> her diet, she couldn't lose weight.
  NOT – in spite her diet

- **IN THE FIRST PLACE**
  <u>In the first place</u>, you shouldn't be here.
  NOT – in a first place

- **KNOW / MEET**
  I <u>met</u> him in high school. I <u>have known</u> him since then.
  Use MEET not KNOW when talking about first getting to know someone.

- **MATTER - IT DOESN'T MATTER IF**
  <u>It doesn't matter if</u> you come later. <u>It doesn't matter if</u> they are late.
  NOT – It doesn't matter they come late.

- **MOST / MOST OF THE**
  <u>Most children</u> obey their parents. <u>Most of the</u> children obey their parents.
  NOT – most of children

- **NOWADAYS**
  <u>Nowadays</u>, most people have computers.
  NOT – now a days or nowdays

- **ON CAMPUS**
  We want to live <u>on campus</u>.
  NOT – at campus; in campus

- **ONE OF THE + PLURAL NOUN**
  <u>One of the books</u> on the shelf is in French. <u>One of the men</u> has a new car.
  NOT – one of the book; one of the man; one of the men have

- **RATHER - WOULD RATHER**
  He <u>would rather</u> be in China. He<u>'d rather</u> be in China.
  NOT – he rather

- **SEEM**
  It <u>seems</u> unfair; it <u>doesn't seem</u> fair.
  NOT – it isn't seem

- **SUCCEED (v) / SUCCESS (n) / SUCCESSFUL (adj)**
  We <u>succeed</u> because we value <u>success</u> and we want to be <u>successful</u>.
  NOT – we success; we want to be success

- **THAN (conjunction with comparatives) / THEN (adverb - at that time)**
  She is taller now <u>than</u> I was <u>then</u>.
  NOT – He is taller then I. Than I left.

- <u>**THE</u> UNITED STATES**
  We live in <u>the United States</u> now.
  NOT – in United States

- **WISH (for things that are not real/true) - HOPE (for things that are possible)**
  I <u>wish</u> I could swim faster. She <u>wishes</u> she had a pet. She <u>hopes</u> she gets one soon.
  NOT – wish I will; wish I can; she wishes she has

- **YEAR-OLD / YEARS OLD**
  He is a <u>ten-year-old</u> boy. He is <u>ten years old</u>.
  NOT – ten years old boy; is ten year old

Advanced Syntactic Structures

The following language features (Table 14.2) are commonly used to help writers craft sentences for rhetorical effects, often in narratives and novels.

Table 14.2: Language Features

Language Feature	Explanation	Examples
Participles	Verbs that end in **–ing** or **–ed** and that act as adjectives	*Hissing, coiling,* and *slithering,* the snake prepared to attack. The sound of its tail, *raised and rattling,* sent shivers through me. I stepped back carefully, *terrified.* *Hissing its forked tongue* and *coiling its cold body,* the snake prepared to attack. The sound of its tail, *raised above its head* and *rattling dangerously,* sent shivers through me. I stepped back carefully, *holding my breath.*
Absolute Phrases	Nouns followed by participles	*Hands shaking, feet trembling,* the mountain climber edged along the cliff. He stopped to catch his breath for a moment, *chest heaving* and *eyes closed.* He inched forward again, *teeth clenched* and *muscles tense,* and tried not to look down. *Feet trembling on the snow-covered rocks,* the mountain climber edged along the cliff.
Adjectives out of order	Adjectives that follow rather than come before the nouns that they describe	Normal placement of adjectives: The *old, withered, pale* **lady** had just one tooth. Sentence with adjectives out of order: The *old* **lady**, *withered and pale,* had just one tooth.

Commas: Use a comma to set off participles, absolutes, and adjectives out of order from the rest of the sentence:

- *Crouching low in the tall grass,* the lion stalked its prey. (participial phrase)
- The young lion, *sleek and muscled,* locked its eyes on the gazelle. (adjectives out of order)

The Complex Sentence: In addition to learning the grammar rules that pertain to vocabulary, you will also need to learn advanced sentence structures, including how to use subordination and modification to create complex sentences.

A complex sentence consists of a simple sentence (also known as an independent clause) plus one or more dependent clauses.

Dependent clauses, like independent clauses, contain a subject and predicate; however, whereas independent clauses can stand alone, dependent clauses are dependent or subordinate to an independent clause and must be attached to that independent clause to form a complete sentence. You can track most dependent clauses back to their independent counterparts, as in the set of sentences following.

Independent clause: Each letter in our alphabet is a sign.

Independent clause: Each letter in our alphabet gives us information about our language's history and sound system.

Complex sentence: **Because each letter in our alphabet is a sign** (Dependent Clause), it gives us information about our language's history and sound system (Independent Clause).

Note that the dependent clause above includes the subordinator "because" at the beginning of the clause. A dependent clause usually begins with a subordinator—also called a subordinating conjunction—or a relative pronoun. A subordinator or relative pronoun gives information about the relationship between the independent and dependent clause.

Common subordinators	Relative pronouns
Cause:because, since, as if, why	that
	what
Concession: although, even though, certainly, though	whatever
Condition: if, unless, how, rather than, where, whether	which
	whichever
Effect: so that, in order that	who
Place: where	whoever
Sequence: after, before, while, until	whom
	whomever
Time: when, as, until, once	whose

Dependent Clause: Dependent clauses can be nominal (used like nouns), adjectival (used like adjectives), or adverbial (used like adverbs). This means that dependent clauses can be used as subjects, objects, or modifiers. Although it is sometimes difficult to distinguish which type of dependent clause is being used, it is a good idea to learn the different clause types because your choice of punctuation depends on how a clause is being used.

Noun (or Nominal) Clauses: Dependent noun clauses can function as subjects, direct objects, subject complements, objects of prepositions, or appositives. Since these types of clauses are dependent or subordinate, they are always attached to an independent clause or a critical part of an independent clause. Noun clauses usually begin with a relative pronoun or with one of these subordinators: when, where, how, why or whether. There are two types of noun clauses: nominal relative clauses and appositive clauses.

Nominal Relative Clauses: Nominal (noun) relative clauses take the place of a subject, direct object, or an object of a preposition. A good way to see whether you are using a nominal (noun) relative clause is to see if you can substitute a pronoun (it, she, he) for the clause in question.

- In place of a subject: *What sounds a letter makes* is complicated. (Dependent Clause/ Nominal Relative Clause)
- In place of a direct object: For new language learners, it is sometimes difficult to know

which letter represents a particular sound. (Dependent Clause/ Nominal Relative Clause)
- In place of a subject complement: This alphabet disconnection is *why many linguists suggest changing our alphabet.* (Dependent Clause/Nominal Relative Clause)
- In place of an object of the preposition: Many linguists theorize about *when the alphabet will become more transparent.* (Dependent Clause/Nominal Relative Clause)

Appositive Clauses: Appositive clauses follow nouns that are general or abstract in nature, such as a theory, reason, fact, or story. The appositive clause begins with a "that" and provides more information about the abstract noun.
- The alphabet disconnection theory *that letters do not clearly match sounds* is widely known by linguists. (Dependent Clause/Appositive Clause)

It is important to be able to distinguish these dependent clauses as noun clauses because neither one of these dependent noun clauses requires a comma. Putting a comma around these clauses to highlight them or separate them in some way from the independent clause is a comma error.

Adjective (or Adjectival) Clauses: Adjective clauses, another type of dependent or subordinate clause, modify noun phrases, which can be made up of either nouns or pronouns. There are two types of adjective clauses: the comparative clause and the relative clause.

Comparative Clauses: Comparative clauses compare two noun phrases and use the phrase as XXX as to make the comparison, where XXX is filled in with an adjective. The clause to the left of the as XXX as phrase is the beginning of the independent clause, and the clause to the right of the as XXX as phrase is the dependent clause.
- That sign is *as uninformative as the one I saw at the zoo last week.* (Dependent Clause)
- She is *as tall as the sign is.* (Dependent Clause)

Relative Clauses: Relative clauses, the most common type of dependent clause, are used to modify or give more information about the noun phrase to the clause's left. These clauses usually begin with a relative pronoun, such as that, which, who, whom, or whose.
- Highway signs *that are funny* often defeat the purpose of their warning. (Relative Clause)
- The student *who is signing for the deaf audience* is obviously still learning American Sign Language. (Relative Clause)
- The highway workers *whose job it was to paint the new sign* forgot the paint. (Relative Clause)

Relative pronouns can sometimes be dropped if they can be understood to be part of the relative clause.
- The signs *[that] the highway workers need to paint* (Relative Clause) are the ones *[that] taggers have covered with graffiti* (Relative Clause).

Relative clauses can be essential or necessary for the full meaning of the sentence to be understood, or they can be non-essential. An essential relative clause is described as a restrictive relative clause. Restrictive relative clauses never take commas around the clause.
- Highway signs *that are covered in mud* can cause accidents. (Restrictive Relative Clause)

In the sentence above, ALL highway signs do not cause accidents; only highway signs that are covered in mud can cause them. Thus, the relative clause is essential to understand the meaning of the full sentence.

- The architect *who designed the building* has a plaque with his name on it near the front. (Restrictive Relative Clause)

Likewise, in the sentence above, it is only the architect who designed the building who has a plaque, not just any architect. Therefore, this relative clause is also essential to the sentence.

A relative clause that is not essential to understand the full meaning of the sentence is described as a non-restrictive relative clause. Nonrestrictive relative clauses always take commas around the clause.

- The signs along Route 66, *which are often stolen*, classify it as a national monument. (Non-Restrictive Relative Clause)

In the sentence above, the relative clause is not essential for us to understand the meaning of the main sentence. In the relative clause, we get extra or nonessential information. With or without the relative clause, we still understand that the signs along Route 66 label it as a national monument.

- The architect, **who wore a seersucker suit to the ceremony**, was awarded a plaque. (Non-Restrictive Relative Clause)

Likewise, in the above sentence, the relative clause is not essential. Whether he wore a seersucker or wool suit is not important; the architect would still have been awarded the plaque either way.

Adverb (or adverbial) Clauses: Adverbial clauses begin with a subordinator (sometimes called a subordinating conjunction) and usually give information about cause/reason, concession, condition, effect, place, sequence, and time. The clauses do this by answering the questions when? where? why? how? how frequently? and in what manner? Adverbial clauses are always dependent or subordinate to the main or independent clause.

Common subordinators
Cause: because, since, as if, why
Concession: although, even though, certainly, though
Condition: if, unless, how, rather than, where, whether
Effect: so that, in order that
Place: where
Sequence: after, before, while, until
Time: when, as, until, once

- *Because she was caught with the freeway sign in her car*, she was arrested for theft. (Adverbial (Dependent) Clause)

Notice that the adverbial clause above gives the reason why the woman was arrested, thus giving information about cause.

Adverbial clauses can function like adverbs, moving to various points in a sentence. When an adverbial clause is at the beginning of the sentence, use a comma to separate it off from the main or independent clause.

- *Because the highway trooper watched him closely*, the driver followed the detour sign. (Adverbial Clause)

When an adverbial clause appears in the middle of a sentence, you should also set it off by placing commas around the adverbial clause.

- The driver, *because the highway trooper watched him closely*, followed the detour sign. (Adverbial Clause)

However, when an adverbial clause appears at the end of a sentence, it usually does not take a comma.

- The driver followed the detour sign *because the highway trooper watched him closely*. (Adverbial Clause)

Common Sentence Errors with the Complex Sentence

Check for fragments: Dependent clauses do not express a complete thought, and they need to be attached to an independent clause to be grammatically complete. Because dependent clauses are clauses, they contain a subject and a full verb, a fact that sometimes leads a writer to use a dependent clause as a complete sentence. When dependent clauses are presented as a full sentence, they are fragments.

Fragment: *Because the highway trooper watched him closely.* (Dependent Clause)

OK: The driver took the detour *because the highway trooper watched him closely.* (Dependent Clause)

Fragment: *When she saw the tornado.* (Dependent Clause)

OK: *When she saw the tornado*, she took it as a sign to take cover. (Dependent Clause)

Check for unnecessary commas: A noun clause can replace a subject, direct object, subject complement, or object of a preposition. When using a noun clause to replace these items, avoid placing an unnecessary comma between the noun clause and the rest of the sentence.

Extra comma: *What I like about Saturdays*, is seeing all the yard sale signs in my neighborhood. (Dependent Noun Clause)

OK: *What I like about Saturdays* is seeing all the yard sale signs in my neighborhood. (Dependent Noun Clause)

Check for restrictive or non-restrictive punctuation: Be sure to use the correct punctuation for relative clauses. When they provide essential information, they are restrictive and should not have commas. When relative clauses provide non-essential or extra information, they are non-restrictive and should always be separated from the rest of the sentence with commas.

Extra commas: The protester, *who had the derogatory sign*, was removed from the lecture. (Restrictive Relative Clause)

OK: The protester *who had the derogatory sign* was removed from the lecture. (Restrictive Relative Clause)

In the above example, the relative clause gives necessary information— the reason the protester was removed from the lecture. Therefore, the relative clause is restrictive and does not take commas.

Missing commas: M. Night Shyamalan who directed Sixth Sense and Signs has not won an Academy Award. (Non-Restrictive Relative Clause)

OK: M. Night Shyamalan, *who directed Sixth Sense and Signs*, has not won an Academy Award. (Non-Restrictive Relative Clause)

In the example above, the information that Shyamalan directed the movies Sixth Sense and Signs is not essential to the main point that he has not won an Academy Award. Thus, the relative clause is non-restrictive and needs to have commas surrounding it.

Check for adverbial clause punctuation: When including an adverbial clause in your writing, be sure to use the appropriate punctuation. If the clause appears at the beginning of the sentence, use a comma between it and the independent clause. If the adverbial clause appears in the middle of the sentence, surround the clause with commas. And, finally, if the adverbial clause appears at the end of the sentence, do not separate the dependent adverbial clause and the independent clause.

Missing comma: **As I left the movie** I saw a sign advertising next week's feature. (Dependent Clause)

OK: **As I left the movie**, I saw a sign advertising next week's feature. (Dependent Clause)

Extra comma: I saw a sign advertising next week's feature, **as I left the movie**. (Dependent Clause)

OK: I saw a sign advertising next week's feature **as I left the movie**. (Dependent Clause)

The Compound-Complex Sentence

This section introduces what is a compound-complex sentence, in an effort to provide the readers with more information about sentence structures. Unlike the aforementioned complex sentence, a compound-complex sentence is made up of two or more simple sentences or independent clauses (this is the compound part) and one or more subordinate or dependent clauses (this is the complex part).

While she waited for a sign from the employees (Dependent Clause), *other shoppers sneaked into the toy store* (Independent Clause), and *they were the ones fortunate enough to find the most popular toy for Christmas* (Independent Clause).

When you punctuate a compound-complex sentence, you use the rules for both compound and complex sentences. For instance, in the above sentence, the dependent adverbial clause appears at the beginning of the sentence; thus, it needs a comma between it and the independent clause. In addition, the combination of a comma and coordinating conjunction is used to join together the two independent clauses.

Common sentence errors with the compound-complex sentence: Pay attention to the common sentence errors for both compound and complex sentences, and you will be successful in punctuating a compound-complex sentence.

- Check for run-on or fused sentences
  Run-on/fused sentence: Students who use both American Sign Language and Signed English understand that some of the signs are the same **(and)** this makes it easier for them to learn both.

  OK: Students who use both American Sign Language and Signed English understand that some of the signs are the same, and this makes it easier for them to learn both.

- Check for comma splices
  Comma splice: Students who use both American Sign Language and Signed English understand that some of the signs are the same **(,)** this makes it easier for them to learn both.

  OK: Students who use both American Sign Language and Signed English understand that some of the signs are the same, and this makes it easier for them to learn both.

- Check for fragments
  Fragment: Students who use both American Sign Language and Signed English understand that some of the signs.

  OK: Students who use both American Sign Language and Signed English understand that some of the signs are the same, and this makes it easier for them to learn both.

Reading Comprehension Questions

1. Can students acquire grammar naturally by themselves? Do they have to study grammar books to learn grammar? Why?

2. Does it help to memorize grammar rules? Why?

3. Is it true that adults are not capable of improving their grammar? Why?

4. Why is it helpful to learn the definitions of grammar terms?

5. What is the difference between a common noun and a proper noun?

6. What are collective nouns?

7. Which irregular verbs (infinitive form, present simple form and past participles) do you rarely use? (Refer to the List of Irregular Verbs on page 217.)

8. What are five adjective + preposition combinations that you frequently use in your writing?

9. What are three words or expressions that you have difficulty using correctly? (Refer to the list of Problem Words and Expressions beginning on page 226.)

10. What is a relative clause and how is it used?

Punctuation, Capitalization, and Spelling

This guide to basic punctuation, capitalization, and spelling rules in the English language will help you edit your writing.

Punctuation

Why is punctuation important? Correct punctuation can be critically important if you want to make yourself understood correctly. When you speak, you can make yourself understood through your stress on different words or syllables, intonation, rhythm, and pauses as well as with eye, face, hand, and body signals. But when you write, you often end up relying on the language itself and punctuation. Poor punctuation can result in communicating a meaning that is different from the one that you intended, or it can result in ambiguity, so that people aren't sure what you are saying.

The following section contains instruction on using a period, comma, colon, semicolon, question mark, and exclamation point. Each type of punctuation is followed by an explanation and example sentences.

Marsha Kim, a former writing student, cautions:

"I had a lot of problem learning to use periods and commas until I learned what a sentence is and how to avoid writing run-on sentences that didn't end where they should. It helped me avoid sentence fragments when I read my sentences aloud and figured out what my subjects and verbs were."

Li Xiu Ying, a former student, advises:

"My use of punctuation improved when I started paying attention to the ways authors used punctuation marks."

Period

Use a period to end a complete sentence. A sentence is a group of words containing a subject and verb.

Examples:

- He went to Detroit last week. They are going to visit.

If the last item in the sentence is an abbreviation that ends in a period, do not follow it with another period.

- This is John Doe, Ph.D. He is the vice president of Apple Inc.

Comma

The comma can separate the grammatical components of a sentence. There are also mechanical and stylistic uses of the comma. There are a number of different uses for a comma in English.

1. To separate a list of items

This is one of the most common uses of a comma. Notice that a comma is included before the conjunction "and" which comes before the final element of a list.

Examples:

- I like reading, listening to music, taking long walks, and visiting with my friends.
- They would like books, magazines, and other learning materials for their library.

2. To separate long phrases and dependent clauses from the rest of the sentence

Examples:

- In order to earn a degree at college, you will need to complete all required courses.
- Although he wanted to come, he wasn't able to attend the event.

3. To separate two independent clauses that are connected by a conjunction such as "but"

Examples:

- They wanted to purchase a new car, but their financial situation would not allow it.

- I'd really enjoy seeing a movie with you this afternoon, and I'd like to go out afterwards for dinner.

4. To introduce a direct quotation

Example:

- The boy said, "My father is often away during the week on business trips." His uncle replied, "If he is not home this weekend, I can take you to the baseball game."

5. To separate appositives (a noun, or noun phrase) or non-defining relative clauses

Examples:

- Bill Gates, among the wealthiest people in the world, comes from Seattle.
- My cousin Charles, who is a fantastic tennis player, is in great shape.

6. To separate two adjectives when the adjectives are interchangeable

Examples:

- He is a strong, healthy man. (He is a healthy, strong man.)
- We stayed at a large, expensive summer resort.

7. To set off words and expressions (like nevertheless, after all, by the way, on the other hand, and however) that interrupt the sentence flow

Examples:

- He was, however, very nervous about the conflict.
- Although Jake did not succeed as an undergraduate student, he did, nevertheless, go on to succeed in graduate school.

8. To set off i.e., e.g., and for instance when these words and terms are followed by a series of items

Examples:

- You may be required to bring many items, e.g., sleeping bags, pans, and warm clothing.
- Thomas Edison's ideas led to multiple inventions, i.e., the phonograph, the automatic telegraph, the dictaphone, and a reliable and inexpensive electric light bulb.

Question Mark

The question mark is used at the end of a question.

Examples:

- Where do you live?
- How long have they been studying?

Exclamation Mark

The exclamation mark is used at the end of a sentence to emphasize a statement and express strong feelings. It turns a statement into an exclamation (a shout). Exclamation marks are common in informal writing, but should be avoided in most kinds of academic writing.

Examples:

- (Informal English): That ride was fantastic!
- I can't believe he is going to marry her!

Semicolon

Below are common uses for a semicolon:

1 To separate two independent clauses if one or both of the clauses are short and the ideas expressed are usually very similar or related

Examples:

- He loves studying; he can't study enough.
- What a difficult situation; it must make you nervous.

2. To separate two independent clauses linked by a transitional expression (e.g., accordingly, consequently, for example, nevertheless, thus)

Examples:

- Heavy snow continues to fall at the airport; as a result, all flights have been canceled.
- Inflation makes it difficult to keep track of prices; thus a quart of milk might cost $8 in the morning and $18 in the afternoon.

3. To clearly separate lists that contain internal commas

Examples:

- I went on a vacation and went hiking, which I love; read a lot, which I needed to do; and slept late, which I hadn't done for quite a while.
- The new store has groceries on the lower level; luggage, kitchen items, and electronics on the ground floor; men's and women's clothing on the second floor; and books, music, and stationery on the third floor.

Colon

1. When two or more sentences follow a colon, capitalize the first word following the colon.

Example:

- He made three points: First, the company was losing over a million dollars each month. Second, the stock price was lower than it had ever been. Third, no banks were willing to loan the company any more money.

2. To provide a list of items

Examples:

- He had many reasons for joining the club: to get in shape, to make new friends, to lose some weight, and to get out of the house.

- The bookstore specializes in these three subjects: art, architecture, and graphic design.

3. To emphasize a phrase or a single word

Examples:

- After three weeks of deliberation, the jury finally reached a verdict: guilty.

- In business and personal correspondence

4. To indicate a level of formality in business and personal correspondence.

Examples:

- Dear Ms. Smith:
- cc: Tom Smith
- Attention: Accounts Payable
- PS: Don't forget your swimsuit.

Insider Tip

Punctuation can cause challenges for the most advanced learners of English. Be aware of the types of punctuation errors you tend to make. Edit these errors in your writing.

"There is an underlying rhythm to all text. Sentences crashing fall like the waves of the sea, and work unconsciously on the reader. Punctuation is the music of language. As a conductor can influence the experience of the song by manipulating its rhythm, so can punctuation influence the reading experience, bring out the best (or worst) in a text. By controlling the speed of a text, punctuation dictates how it should be read. A delicate world of punctuation lives just beneath the surface of your work, like a world of microorganisms living in a pond. They are missed by the naked eye, but if you use a microscope you will find they exist, and that the pond is, in fact, teeming with life. "

Source: Lukeman, Noah. *A Dash of Style: The Art and Mastery of Punctuation.* New York, W.W. Norton & Company, 2006. Print. 14.

Insider Tip

You can find many examples of the rules for using capital letters being broken by advertisers, by graffiti artists, and by Internet users. In writing academic papers, most professors prefer you use the formal rules for capitalization presented in this chapter.

Capitalization

Why is capitalization important? In this era of texting, more and more students are ignoring capitalization. Yet, capitalization plays a critical role in conveying meaning and can mark you as an educated person who pays attention to detail. If you don't capitalize when expected, your professors might think you are uneducated or sloppy. This is probably not what you want your professors to think. Also, it is easier to read text that has both lowercase and capital letters. Capital letters indicate when a new sentence begins and provide essential information that readers should pay attention to, like names and dates.

Indicate the First Word

1. **Indicate the first word in a sentence.** Capitalization is used for the first word in every sentence.

    - Traffic signs are sometimes difficult to understand.

2. **Indicate the first word in a quotation.** Capitalization is also used to indicate the first word in a quotation.

    - My brother told the police officer, "But the sign was covered by a tree branch."

3. **Indicate the first word inside parentheses.** Capitalization is used when a full sentence is placed within parentheses. If the parenthetical statement is inserted into another sentence, do not capitalize.

    - My brother told the officer that the sign was covered by a tree branch. (However, it wasn't.)

    - My brother told the officer (from our father's precinct) that the sign was covered by a tree branch.

    - My brother told the officer (the officer was from our father's precinct) that the sign was covered by a tree branch.

4. **Indicate the first word in a sentence following a colon.** Capitalization after a colon is optional; however, capitalize the first word after a colon if you want to emphasize the sentence.

    - My brother has had several tickets: he has been caught driving with a broken headlight, driving too fast in a school zone, and not stopping for a pedestrian in the crosswalk.

    - The police officer voided the ticket: He was from our father's precinct.

Eric Sanchez, a former writing student, states:

"I learned to write in Spanish first and then English later. Capitalization sometimes was a problem for me because in Spanish nationalities are not capitalized as they are in English.

Indicate Proper Nouns and Proper Adjectives

Capitalization is used to indicate proper nouns and proper adjectives.

1. **Indicate proper nouns.** Proper nouns name specific people, places, things, or ideas.

   - People: Abigail Breslin, Joaquin Phoenix, Aunt Joan, Uncle Ralph, Senator Jones, Reverend Smith, Dr. Black, Chief Johnson, Professor White

   - Places: Europe, Australia, Alaska, Washington, D.C., the South, the Northeast, the Mississippi River, the Grand Canyon, New York City, United States

   - Organizations, governmental institutions, and academic institutions: Federal Bureau of Investigation, Department of Labor, the United Nations, Long Beach City College, Harvard University

   - Abbreviations of titles and organizations: AAA, FBI, MD, MLA, PhD, UN, UCLA

   - Monuments and buildings: the Washington Monument, the Willis Tower, the Taj Mahal, the Eiffel Tower

   - Languages: Chinese, English, Arabic, Swahili, Spanish, French, Japanese, Russian, Mandarin, American Sign Language

   - Races: American Indian, Alaskan Native, Pacific Islander, African American, Black, White, Asian

   - Nationalities: Spanish, Ethiopian, Arabic, Chinese, South African, Greek, American

   - Religions and religious terms: Buddhism, Islam, Christianity, Judaism, Shinto, Protestant, Catholic, Baptist, Buddha, Mohammed, God, Jesus, Moses, Talmud, Bible, Koran, Allah, Jehovah, Genesis

   - Course titles: English 101, Biology 1001, French 300, Eng- lish Composition 101, Modern War Ethics, An Introduction to Computer History

   - Days and months: January, March, May, Sunday, Tuesday, Thursday

2. **Indicate proper adjectives.** Capitalization is also used for proper adjectives, which are usually derived from proper nouns and can be found inside a proper noun phrase.

   - Chinese food, English language, Spanish eyes

Indicate Titles and Subtitles

Capitalization is used for titles of books, stories, plays, poems, songs, articles, films, newspapers, magazines, works of art, musical compositions, and photographs. Always capitalize the first word in the title, no matter the type of word. Also, if using MLA (Modern Language Association) style, capitalize all other words in the title or subtitle except for articles (a, an, the), conjunctions (for, and, nor, but, or, yet, so), and short prepositions (in, on, for, to). If using another style, such as from the APA (American Psychological Association), be sure to check specific guidelines.

- Books: *The World According to Garp*
- Books with subtitles: *Chinese Astrology: Exploring the Eastern Zodiac*
- Short stories: "Everyday Use"
- Plays: *Hamlet*
- Poems: "Casey at Bat"
- Songs: "Rudolph, the Red-Nosed Reindeer"
- Articles: "Fifty Ways to Avoid the Flu"
- Films: *Moulin Rouge*
- Newspapers: *The New York Times*
- Magazines and journals: *Vogue, English Journal*
- Works of art: Starry Night
- Musical compositions: Romeo et Juliette Photographs: The Kiss Vessels: Spruce Goose, Queen Mary

Indicate acronyms

Acronyms are made up of the first letter of each word in a phrase. For instance, FBI is the acronym for "Federal Bureau of Investigation." Acronyms are usually capitalized except for those that have become regular words such as scuba, laser, and radar.

- Acronyms : CBS, CEO, CIA, FAQ, SAT, USA, WGN

Wei Mu, a former writing student, states:

"I never learned how to print capital letters very well. I had to practice using capitals."

"We have a language that is full of ambiguities; we have a way of expressing ourselves that is often complex and elusive, poetic and modulated; all our thoughts can be rendered with absolute clarity if we bother to put the right dots and squiggles between the words in the right places. Proper punctuation is both the sign and the cause of clear thinking. If it goes, the degree of intellectual impoverishment we face is unimaginable."

Source: Truss, Lynne. Eats, Shoots & Leaves: *The Zero Tolerance Approach to Punctuation.* New York: Gotham Books, 2003. Print.

Spelling

Only in the last few hundred years or so have we had exact spellings in the English language. Before then, spellings often varied widely. Once we had published dictionaries, we had specific spellings. Having rules for spelling words and fixed spellings is said to facilitate communication, making it easier for others to understand our writing. With dictionaries and standard spellings, we don't waste mental energy figuring out how words are spelled. Unfortunately, others might judge us negatively if we spell incorrectly. When we spell words incorrectly, others can think we're poorly educated or careless.

> "Precisely because technology can get tripped up — distinguishing between, say, *your* and *you're* or those thorny twins *its* and *it's* — "spelling is as important as it's ever been."
>
> J. Richard Gentry, an expert in reading and spelling education and the author of Spel is a Four-Letter Word.

Some Basic Spelling Rules

You might find the following basic spelling rules helpful. Note there are some exceptions to the rules, but the rules hold for most words.

- When combining the vowels "i" and "e," follow this simple rhyme: "i" before "e," except after "c."
- When combining most other vowels, consider how the vowel will be pronounced with this rhyme: Two vowels walk together and they play a game. The first one speaks and says its name. (When two vowels go walking, the first one does the talking. For example, in the case of *speak*, the word is pronounced with a long "e" /spik/ or /spēk/.
- "E" at the end of a word is silent, but causes the stressed vowel to be a long vowel (say its name). For example, *sequence* has three vowels. The first "e" is stressed and so therefore, the silent "e" on the end causes the first "e" to be a long "e" /sikwəns/ or /'sēkwəns/.
- "Q" is never used without a "u" after it: quick, quantify, quality.
- The letter "s" is almost always doubled when it comes after a short vowel: loss, miss, less.
- The letter "v" is always followed by an "e" at the end of the word, no matter which vowel sound is preceding it: have, give, elective.

For a more comprehensive list, visit: http://tpri.org/news/documents/English%20Language%20Spelling%20Pattern%20Tool.pdf

Reading Comprehension Questions

1. What do each of the punctuation marks below mean and when would you use them?

   period (.)   semicolon (;)

   comma (,)   colon (:)

2. What is the difference between a comma and a semicolon?

3. Do writers generally use exclamation marks in formal business letters or in informal email messages? Why?

4. When two complete sentences are closely related in meaning and you want to link them, what punctuation mark would you use?

5. Punctuation indicates how sentences should be read. They also determine how long readers should pause between parts of sentences and between sentences when they are reading aloud. Which results in a longer pause, a comma, a semicolon, or a period?

6. What are some examples of five categories of proper nouns that should be capitalized?

7. What is an acronym and why do writers use them?

8. What do readers think when writers misspell words?

9. What strategies can you use to improve your spelling?

10. What words should you capitalize in the titles of the papers you write?

> " The way we present ourselves in writing influences others' judgments of our abilities. When we punctuate incorrectly, fail to capitalize letters, or spell words inaccurately, others can think we're poorly educated and shouldn't be taken seriously. Some readers might question whether our thinking and reasoning are as inaccurate as our knowledge of punctuation, capitalization, and spelling conventions. "

Different Kinds of English: British and US-American English

Paul Spencer and Jerry Lee

Global English

With the emergence of English as a global language, English often blends with other languages, resulting in new and original forms. Today, there are many unique varieties of English. Some kinds are used in predominantly English speaking countries such as Australian English or Jamaican English and others are used in countries where English is not the primary language. For example, Indian English is used in India and Chinese English is used in China. Research by linguists has shown that these Englishes are used with precision and consistency by their speakers and therefore should not be viewed as "incorrect" forms of English. For instance, a Korean speaker of English may say, "I have five furnitures," using a noncount noun as a count noun, whereas a speaker of US-American English would likely say, "I have five pieces of furniture." Neither form is inherently more correct than the other.

However, different people will have different attitudes and beliefs regarding different Englishes. In fact, many professors will insist that you write according to the standards of a particular variety of English such as US-American English. Regardless of what is taught and expected in a particular class, the most important thing to remember is that no variety of English is "better" or "more correct" than another. Even if your professor encourages you to write in a particular variety of English, it does not necessarily mean that you must treat it as the *only* English you should learn. In fact, research shows that proficiency in only one form of English is limiting for communicating in a globalized society. It is therefore important to be aware of how different Englishes can have different features and how the use of these features varies as a function of context. The following section describes the differences between US-American and British English to help illustrate how diverse the English language can be.

Rosina Lippi-Green, an American author, states:

"What is surprising, even deeply disturbing, is the way that many individuals who consider themselves democratic, even-handed, rational, and free of prejudice, hold on tenaciously to a standard language ideology which attempts to justify restriction of individuality and rejection of the Other."

US-American English and British English

Up to now whether you have learned British or US-American English has probably depended on the countries you have studied in. Many of you have studied British English but are now studying in the United States. Don't worry. It is acceptable to use either British English or American English in most academic writing and both varieties are generally understood by most English speakers.

Differences in Vocabulary and Spelling

Differences in vocabulary between British and US-American Englishes are common and can sometimes lead to confusion. Thankfully, these differences do not have a significant effect on most academic writing. They affect discussions of specific topics, like food, transportation, or sports. One well-known example is the word "football." In British English, the word refers to soccer, which is the term used in the US to refer to a game played with a round ball. In the US "football" refers to an entirely different sport. While some misunderstandings do occur (certain body parts can share the same word but with very different meanings), thanks to plenty of cross-cultural influence from movies, television and music, both kinds of vocabulary can be well understood throughout the English speaking world even if usage occasionally differs. Additionally, the spelling of certain words may also be slightly different, but neither form should be viewed as better than the other. "Colour" and "favourite" in British English are "color" and "favorite" in US-American English. British forms of "centre," "travelling," and "realise" are "center, "traveling," and "realize" in US-American English.

Differences in Grammar

In terms of grammar, there are slight differences between British English and US-American English. A good example is with subject-verb agreement for collective nouns. Words like "team," "family," or "group" tend to take the singular verb form in US-American English, whereas British English favors the plural form. Examples are "My family is/are very important to me" or "Los Angeles is/are the best team in the league." Both forms are acceptable in academic writing but you may have to remind your professor of this if they are not familiar with British English. Past participles of verbs can also take on different forms too, for example "gotten" is more common in the United States, while "got" is more widely used in British English.

Summary of Some Differences between British and US-American Englishes

	British English	**US-American English**
spelling	colour, centre, travelling, organise	color, center, traveling, organize
vocabulary	petrol, holiday, courgette, Maths, Autumn, rubbish, runners	gas, vacation, zucchini, Math, Fall, trash, sneakers
grammar	The group are working hard.	The group is working hard.
	It has got dark.	It has gotten dark.

When writing for American readers, here are two additional considerations:

The modal "shall" is used in British English but has become less common in American English in recent years in the United States. Americans can perceive it as formal or stuffy.

The British tend to use the word "one" more frequently than Americans do in many types of writing. Although "one" is frequently used in American textbooks, using "one" as a pronoun in such sentences as "It is good to voice one's opinion" can come across as overly formal to Americans, at least in some kinds of writing. It can also at times lead to problems with pronoun agreement. Using "they" or "individuals" is

Key Point:

Different people will have different attitudes and beliefs regarding different kinds of English.

a possible alternative to using "one." One final thing to keep in mind regarding punctuation is that British English refers to the mark that ends a sentence as a "full stop," while this is a "period" in American English. Quotation marks in American English are sometimes referred to as "inverted commas" in Britain where they are more often 'single' as opposed to "double" marks.

Concluding Thoughts

It is important to repeat the point that no variety of English should be viewed as more superior to another variety. Unfortunately, some people may view British English as the most "original" and "authentic" English. Also, unfortunately, some people may believe that US-American English is more correct than other forms of English, such as Philippine English. However, the reality is, even British and US-American Englishes are not used consistently, as there is much variation even within each variety. Further, these Englishes are not even the most commonly used varieties in the world, as speakers in countries like India and China far outnumber users of English in Britain and the US. Therefore, you should avoid viewing English as a single "language," being open to learning about the conventions of different Englishes around the world, while remembering that no single variety is better than the others.

Reading Comprehension Questions

1. What is global English?

2. Are some varieties of English better than other varieties? Is Chinese English less correct than US-American English?

3. Which variety of English have you learned? Why have you learned that variety and not another variety?

4. Why is it acceptable to use both British English and US-American English in most US universities?

5. Is US-American English the only English you should learn? Why?

6. Based on what you have read, why do you think different varieties of English develop?

7. People often judge others on the basis of their speech. Sometimes they believe that people who speak slowly are dumb or people who speak quickly and interrupt one another are smart. Sometimes they think people who speak softly are weak. Why do you think people judge others on the basis of their use of language?

8. What are two key differences between the grammar of British English and the grammar US-American English?

9. How do you think many US-Americans instructor view the repeated use of "shall" in writing?

10. Which of the words that follow use British spelling? colour, favorite, centre, theatre, realize, favourite

CHAPTER SEVENTEEN

SECTION VI: Reading

Reading in University Contexts

With major contributions from Brenna Shepherd, Robin Stewart, and Victorya Nam

A dvanced readers, university-level readers, recognize that reading is purposeful. The sooner you learn how to purposefully and thoughtfully complete your academic reading assignments, the sooner you'll start to expand your vocabulary, read critically, and become a better student and writer. Students who read for their classes are more likely to understand the content covered in lectures and more likely to do well on tests and papers. They are also more likely to engage with* their coursework, expand their understanding of the English language, and improve their ability to use this language not only in their reading but also in their speech and writing.

*to engage with
(verb phrase): to become involved with something in order to understand it

Before coming to college, you were expected to read texts for specific purposes. Maybe your teacher wanted you to summarize something. Maybe you had to read a textbook for class or take a reading comprehension test. University reading is similar to high school reading in that you are still reading for specific purposes. However, those purposes have changed.

This chapter will help you (1) understand the types of texts you may have to read and their purposes, (2) learn how and why you read these texts* critically, and (3) introduce you to ways to improve your reading, which can help you succeed in all your classes.

*text
(countable noun): any written or spoken material, including books, poems, and lectures

Types of Texts

Students are expected to know how to read, analyze, and learn from a variety of texts. The main kinds of texts you'll read in your lower-division classes are textbooks that are generally meant to introduce you to a field of study, such as philosophy, psychology, or organic chemistry. They'll provide you with an overview of the concepts and theories that are important in a given field of study.

Upper-division classes may require you to do research in order to write lengthy papers or compile reports. When researching, you'll need to be able to critically read and analyze academic articles. These articles are published in scholarly journals related to specific topics and fields of study (e.g., *Science, Journal of Research in Reading*). When approaching these types of texts, it's important to read with a critical eye in order to obtain the important information to do well in your classes. Academic articles have specific organizational patterns and features that vary depending on the discipline. In social science, for example, one common type of article includes an abstract, a short paragraph explaining the entirety of the article; an introduction, which explains the thesis of the research and the reason it is relevant to the field of study; a literature review which summarizes prior studies related to the same topic; a methodology section and a findings section, which explain the method and results of the research; a discussion section, which explains how the research findings are relevant to the field of study and suggests further areas of research related to the topic that need to be more thoroughly investigated; and a conclusion, which sums up what the author wants the readers to understand from the paper and possibly provides some direct conclusions or "take-aways," the insights the author hopes the readers will walk away with. Becoming familiar with the organizational structures and features of articles can help you easily identify important information and can benefit you when you write research papers for your upper-division classes.

Types of Structures

A primary goal of this chapter is to help you understand the types of readings that you are likely to encounter in college courses accurately, so that you can respond to them appropriately, meaningfully, and critically. You'll often read informational texts. These texts focus on explanations of issues, themes, and ideas and have specific text structures. **Text structures** refer to the ways that authors organize information in text. The following chart shows some basic text structures for informational writing, including the signal words associated with types of informational writing, a graphic organizer that

describes the underlying structure, and a sample paragraph. You may want to spend some time learning these structures if you are unfamiliar with them, as they can help you predict and make sense of expository texts. Recognizing the underlying structures of discipline-specific texts can help you focus your attention on key concepts and relationships, anticipate what's to come, and monitor your comprehension as you read.

A WORD OF CAUTION:

Most informational texts that you come across at the university include a combination of the text structures below as well as other text structures, and vary in their use of them.

Description

Definition: The author describes a topic by listing characteristics, features, and examples.

Signal words: characteristics are/features are/for example

Graphic Organizer	Sample Passage
	While regular ocean waves and tsunamis share a few similarities, they also have some obvious differences. Both are made of energy transfer and can be described by their wavelength, speed, frequency, period, amplitude (height), and energy. In addition, shoaling, increasing in height when entering shallow water, is common to both regular waves and tsunamis. However, regular waves and tsunamis have several important differences. Whereas regular waves are caused primarily by wind, tsunamis are most often the result of undersea earthquakes. Normal ocean waves are a surface feature and the water beneath the surface is barely affected. In contrast, tsunamis propagate through the entire depth of the ocean. While regular waves cannot go further than a mile, tsunamis can traverse the entire earth. Of course, the obvious difference between the two types of waves is their size. Regular waves have a wavelength of a few meters at best. On the other hand, tsunamis can have wavelengths of over a hundred miles and are capable of causing untold damage.

Sequence

Definition: The author lists items or events in numerical or chronological order.

Signal words: first, second, third / next / then / finally

Graphic Organizer	Sample Passage
1. _____ 2. _____ 3. _____ 4. _____ 5. _____	A tsunami typically goes through four stages. The first phase, "Initiation," occurs with the event that triggers the beginning of a tsunami, usually an undersea earthquake. The next stage is the "Split." Within several minutes of the earthquake, the initial tsunami is split into one that travels out to the deep ocean (distant tsunami) and another that travels toward the nearby coast (local tsunami). After the tsunami splits, the third stage, "Amplification," occurs. As the local tsunami approaches the shore, its amplitude (height) increases. At the same time, the wavelength decreases. When the deep ocean, distant tsunami approaches land, amplification and shortening of the wave also will occur, just as with the local tsunami. The final stage of a tsunami is the "Runup." It occurs when a peak in the tsunami wave travels from the near-shore region onto shore. Most tsunamis do not result in giant waves, but instead come in much like very strong and fast-moving tides.

Comparison

Definition: The author explains how two or more things are alike and/or how they are different.

Signal words: Different / in contrast / alike / the same as / on the other hand

Graphic Organizer	Sample Passage
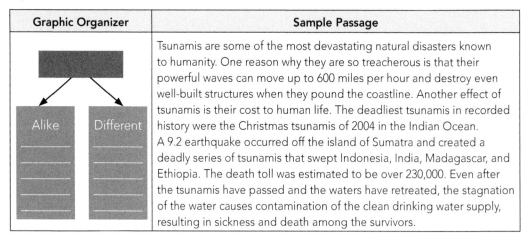	Tsunamis are some of the most devastating natural disasters known to humanity. One reason why they are so treacherous is that their powerful waves can move up to 600 miles per hour and destroy even well-built structures when they pound the coastline. Another effect of tsunamis is their cost to human life. The deadliest tsunamis in recorded history were the Christmas tsunamis of 2004 in the Indian Ocean. A 9.2 earthquake occurred off the island of Sumatra and created a deadly series of tsunamis that swept Indonesia, India, Madagascar, and Ethiopia. The death toll was estimated to be over 230,000. Even after the tsunamis have passed and the waters have retreated, the stagnation of the water causes contamination of the clean drinking water supply, resulting in sickness and death among the survivors.

Cause and Effect

Definition: The author lists one or more causes and the resulting effect or effects.

Signal words: reasons why/if…then/as a result/therefore/because

Graphic Organizer	Sample Passage
Cause → Effect 1, Effect 2, Effect 3	Tsunamis are some of the most devastating natural disasters known to humanity. One reason why they are so treacherous is that their powerful waves can move up to 600 miles per hour and destroy even well-built structures when they pound the coastline. Another effect of tsunamis is their cost to human life. The deadliest tsunamis in recorded history were the Christmas tsunamis of 2004 in the Indian Ocean. A 9.2 earthquake occurred off the island of Sumatra and created a deadly series of tsunamis that swept Indonesia, India, Madagascar, and Ethiopia. The death toll was estimated to be over 230,000. Even after the tsunamis have passed and the waters have retreated, the stagnation of the water causes contamination of the clean drinking water supply, resulting in sickness and death among the survivors.

Problem and Solution

Definition: The author states a problem and lists one or more solutions for the problem. A variation of this pattern is the question-and-answer format in which the author poses a question and then answers it.

Signal words: problem is/dilemma is/puzzle is/solved/question…/ answer

Graphic Organizer	Sample Passage
Problem → **Solution**	Throughout history, tsunamis have been among the worst natural disasters. They are capable of causing untold damage and taking countless lives. In fact, in the Indian Ocean tsunami of 2004, over 230,000 people lost their lives. Unfortunately, since there is no way to eliminate tsunamis, we must look for ways to minimize their impact. One solution is to plan ahead with emergency measures and evacuation plans and routes. In addition, we need to conduct more research to improve the present early warning devices. Also, communities need to build more secure structures, preferably on higher ground. A final solution would be to construct sea walls and barrier reefs in vulnerable areas.

Source: Adapted from Tompkins, Gail. *Literacy for the 21st Century: A Balanced Approach.* Upper Saddle River, NJ: Pearson, 2013. Reprinted with permission.

If you struggle with understanding your textbook or have difficulty locating information in your textbook quickly, it could be because you are not recognizing the organizational structure of what you are reading, and you are unaware of the signals that alert you to particular text structures. The more you are familiar with the particular organizational structures and features that authors use, the better inferences you can make regarding the content of the reading. The faster you can figure out the meaning of the content, the more time you'll have to read it critically.

What Critical Reading Means

In order to understand what it means to critically read, you first have to understand what it means to be critical. When you are critical, it means you are judging whether the text is reliable, unbiased, and useable, e.g., for your own research. It doesn't mean you are criticizing or expressing disapproval of your readings. Critical reading is a more active way of reading than simply reading to get a grasp of the ideas in a text. It is a deeper and more complex engagement with a text and involves analyzing,* interpreting,* and evaluating.* When you read critically, you use your critical thinking skills to question both the text and your own reading of it.

Different disciplines have distinctive modes of critical reading (e.g., scientific, philosophical, literary) and different types of texts call for different types of critical reading. In English language and writing courses, critical reading entails questioning what you read. Your instructors will ask you to go beyond understanding the ideas in articles, chapters, and books. You'll also analyze, interpret, and evaluate them. This will take effort on your part. You can't just skip over words or guess what the author is saying when you read critically. You have to go beyond the literal meaning of words to find their significance and their unstated meanings.

The Process for Reading Critically

To read critically, you concentrate on what you are reading, focusing on the language and rhetorical features that are used as well as their meaning and effect. As you gain advanced reading abilities, you'll consider many elements of your reading, for instance, what it means and why it means what it means. You'll also consider how your reading communicates, why it was written, and even who the readers of the text were supposed to be. You'll end up doing a lot of detective work to answer those types of questions. To help you begin to read critically, your instructors may suggest that you interact with the text in different ways: for instance, highlighting important points and examples, taking notes, testing answers to your questions, brainstorming, outlining, describing aspects of the text or argument, reflecting on your own reading and thinking, and raising objections to the ideas or evidence presented. When they ask you to read chapters that appear in popular nonfiction, they'll ask you to analyze, interpret, and evaluate your reading and critique the arguments presented.

Essential Words for Critical Reading

*analyzing

(gerund): carefully examining reading to understand it better and see what the text is made up of

*interpreting

(gerund): explaining the underlying meaning of a text, including the intention behind the text and the author's effort to portray something in a particular way in a specific social and historical context

*evaluating

(gerund): judging how good, useful, or successful a text is

Analysis asks: What are the patterns of the text? When examining these patterns, your critical thinking skills will be engaged in analyzing the points and claims the author makes:

- What is the thesis or basic argument?

- What are the supporting points? How do they relate to each other? How do they relate to the thesis statement?

- What examples are used as evidence for the supporting points? How do they relate to the points they support? To each other? To the thesis statement?

- What techniques of persuasion are used (e.g., appeals to emotion, reason, or authority)?

Interpretation asks: What do the patterns of the argument mean? You'll need to be aware of the cultural and historical context, the context of the author's life, the context of debates within the discipline at that time, and the intellectual context of debates within the discipline today.

- What debates were the author and the text engaging with at that time?

- What kinds of reasoning (e.g., historical, psychological, political, philosophical, scientific) are employed?

- How might your own reading of the text be biased? For instance, are you imposing 21st century ideas or values on the text? If so, is this problematic?

Evaluation asks: How well does the text do what it does? What is its value? Evaluation is making judgments about the intellectual, aesthetic, moral, or practical value of a text. When you are considering the intellectual value of a text, you raise questions such as these:

- How does the information or ideas in the text contribute to what is known about the topics discussed? Are the main conclusions original?

- Does the evidence and reasoning adequately support the thesis statement, claims, or theory presented?

- Are the sources reliable?

- Is the argument logically consistent? Convincing?

- If the author uses data to support claims, are experiments, questionnaires, or statistical sections designed and executed in accordance with accepted standards? (Keep in mind that these standards vary as a function of discipline.)

- If the writer has proposed or discussed a theory, what are the strengths and weaknesses of the theory? How would others who have competing theories criticize this text? How could the author reply?

- Overall, is the approach in this text better than competing approaches? In other words, what are its comparative strengths and weaknesses? In reading critically you need to keep competing approaches in mind.

Samira Dimitri, a former writing student, cautions:

"In high school I usually accepted every word in every book I read. I had to learn to read in a whole different way once I got to college."

The Differences Between Reading and Critical Reading

The following chart summarizes some of the differences between reading to obtain a basic understanding of content and reading for critical analysis. It provides one perspective of critical reading.

	Reading for Basic Understanding of Content	Reading for Critical Analysis
The Purpose	Getting a basic grasp of the text	Forming judgments about how a text works
The Activity	Understanding key ideas	Analyzing, interpreting, and evaluating
The Focus	Figuring out what a text says	Figuring out what a text does and means
The Questions Readers Ask	What is the text saying? What information can I get out of the text?	How does the text work? If arguments are being made, how are they presented? What kinds of reasoning and evidence are used? What are the underlying assumptions?
The Reader's Acceptance of the Author's Ideas	Taking for granted that the author's assumptions are right	Questioning the author and the author's assumptions
The Reader's Response	Restating the main ideas of the text or summarizing them	Analyzing, interpreting and evaluating the ideas and language used in the text

Ways to Improve Your Ability to Read Critically

Below are several strategies that you can try to improve your ability to read critically.

1. Using Before, During, and After Strategies

Before/After/During Strategies can help you process challenging text, building your comprehension and fluency as well as your ability to analyze, interpret, and evaluate text.

Before Reading

- **Self-Reflect:** Think about the experiences, assumptions, knowledge, and perspectives that you bring to the text. What biases might you have? **Biases** are your opinions about whether people, groups, or ideas are good or bad. They influence how you interpret text. Are you able to keep an open mind and consider others' points of view or question the author's?

- **Prepare to Read:** Find out as much as you can about the topic of the reading before you read. (See below.) If you are not familiar with the topic, you might check out a Youtube video or do some research to develop a working knowledge of the topic. That will help you develop background knowledge and language to understand your reading.

During Reading

- **Read to Understand:**
  - *Examine the text and context.* Who is the author? Who is the publisher? Where and when was it written? What kind of text is it? Make predictions about the content.

  - *Skim the text.* Preview and refine predictions. **Skimming** means you read something very quickly to get the main ideas of the reading. Look at the headings, subheadings, guiding questions, visuals, illustrations, anecdotes, and appendices.

  - *Read and reread.* Read aloud to slow yourself down and focus on key parts or specific language. Listen to audio-recordings of your readings in addition to reading the texts themselves. Sometimes audio recordings even contain author commentary.

  - *Note areas of confusion and resolve them.* Figure out the meanings of unfamiliar words or terms, for instance, by looking them up in dictionaries or glossaries, or by asking others for help. Go over difficult passages to clarify them.

- **Write as You Read:** Annotate the text. Take notes directly on your copy of the text. Make sure to write down the main ideas of specific paragraphs and the overarching, key ideas of the text. (See the section on annotation below.) When you come across unfamiliar words, you'll need to find out what they mean. You can turn to dictionaries or glossaries, and you'll most likely find them very helpful. Words may have multiple meanings, and the meanings change depending on the context in which the words are used. Trying to learn the meaning of a new word by guessing from contextual clues is a useful skill to develop but not much help if you do not understand many of the words in the text. Contextual clues may appear in the same sentence where the word is used or in the preceding or following sentences.

After Reading

- **Evaluate the quality of the text, review important points in the text, and consider how you might use the information in the future.** Ask yourself such questions as these:

  - What is the meaning of what I have read?

  - Why did the author end the paragraph (or chapter, or book) in this way?

  - What was the author's purpose in writing this?

  - Does the writer try to get the reader to care about the subject, cause, or problem? How? By appeals to emotion? Statistics or other facts? Anecdotes? Detailed descriptions? Something else?

  - Is the writer knowledgeable? Why or why not?

  - What biases or values are conveyed by the writing?

  - What do the language, tone, and approach of the text tell the reader about the writer?

  - What kind of evidence is presented to support the author's argument, views, or points? Is it fact or opinion? What is the source of the information—does it come from an informed authority in the field?

  - What is the author's main argument, view, or point?

  - What is the tone of the text? Is the author objective? Does the author try to convince the reader to have a certain opinion? If so, what viewpoint does the author try to convince the reader of? What reasons does the author provide for choosing this viewpoint?

2. Annotating Your Reading

Another way that you can be a critical reader is by learning to annotate. You may already understand that taking notes in your classes can help you achieve higher grades. What you may not know, however, is that not all notes are equally effective. One type of note taking, called passive note taking, is inconsistent at helping students learn and retain knowledge. **Passive note taking** involves little thought. Students passively write down what the instructor says or they copy headings, complete sentences, or phrases from textbooks. They highlight or underline portions of the text, but they don't really think about what it is that they are underlining, which may cause them to underline sections that are not important or to miss important information. What happens when you take notes quickly in a passive way, is that little of the knowledge you have learned from your reading sticks. Rather than copying others' words and not organizing your notes in a way that makes sense to you, consider annotating instead. Not only will it help you read critically, but it will also help you improve your writing. When annotating in English, you can look at the language of the text to search for important vocabulary to write your notes. This will help you remember what you have read as well as help you remember the vocabulary you will need to complete your writing assignments and do well on tests.

There are many ways to annotate. Your success in annotating will depend on your ability to choose ways that work for you and use them effectively and flexibly. According to Simpson and Nist (1990), annotation can involve the following:

Simpson, Michele L. and Sherrie L. Nist. "Textbook Annotation: An Effective and Efficient Study Strategy for College Students." *Journal of Reading,* 34.2 (1990): 122-129.

- *Writing brief summaries of texts in the margins or on note cards.* This requires you to think about what you have just read and reflect on the most important parts. Summarization is a large part of college writing—both to learn and remember information and to show your instructors what you have learned. Practicing this skill can potentially help you throughout your time at college.

T-Chart Graphic Organizer

Advantages	Disadvantages

- *Listing ideas (cause-and-effect or characteristics, for example).* One good way to make a list is to organize it by categories. For example, if you need to learn the differences between characteristics of plant cells and animal cells, you could make a T-chart. Draw a line down the middle of your page and a horizontal line across the top. At the top, write on the left side, The Characteristics of Plant Cells and on the right side, write, Animal Cells. Then, list all the characteristics of plant and animal cells in the vertical columns. You have just organized your ideas and this will help you learn and retain information.

- *Noting examples in the margins.* Instead of simply underlining or highlighting main ideas, you can write yourself a little note as well. For example, if you are reading a novel that you will later need to write a paper about, as you read, you can make notes like, "Possible example," or "Good quotation," so that when you write your paper later, you will be able to more easily remember why you underlined something.

- *Putting information into graphic form.* Many students learn best through pictures or graphics. If you need to learn the process of how a star is formed, it might be best to organize that information in picture form. That way, you'll make a connection between a process and a picture. Even if the process is in pictorial form in your book, physically drawing it can help you understand it and remember it.

- *Making possible test questions.* This technique may be especially important if your purpose for reading a text is because you will take an exam based on the book. In order to do this, you will have to think like a professor and consider main ideas and relevant details. Then, write a list of test questions. When you study for your test, you'll already have an idea of what to study.

- *Noting areas of confusion.* As you read, you may be surprised or confused by a word, a grammatical construction, or a concept. If you make note of those areas that you are uncertain of, you can ask your professor or teaching assistant for help.

- *Underlining or highlighting selectively.* Underlining or highlighting can be a useful part of annotation when used correctly. The key idea is to be selective – only underline or highlight for a purpose.

3. Using Cognitive Strategies

You can also use cognitive strategies to gain the ability to read critically. **Cognitive** means knowing or thinking, and **strategies** are specific tools or tactics that people use to solve problems. The following list can help you annotate your reading. You can copy and complete the Cognitive Strategies Sentence Starters directly on your reading or on Post-it notes as you read.

Cognitive Strategies Sentence Starters

Planning and Goal Setting
- My purpose is…
- My top priority is…
- To accomplish my goal, I plan to…

Tapping Prior Knowledge
- I already know that…
- This reminds me of…
- This relates to…

Asking Questions
- I wonder why…
- What if…
- How come…

Predicting
- I'll bet that…
- I think…
- If…, then…

Visualizing
- I can picture…
- In my mind I see…
- If this were a movie…

Making Connections
- This reminds me of…
- I experienced this once when…
- I can relate to this because…

Summarizing
- The basic gist is…
- The key information is…
- In a nutshell, this says that…

Adopting an Alignment
- The character/point I most identify with is…
- I really got into the text when…
- I can relate to this author because…

Forming Interpretations
- What this means to me is…
- I think this represents…
- The idea I'm getting is…

Monitoring
- I got lost here because…
- I need to reread the part in which…
- I know I'm on the right track because…

Clarifying
- To understand better, I need to know more about…
- Something that is still not clear is…
- I'm guessing that this means, but I need to…

Revising Meaning
- At first I thought, but now I…
- My latest thought about this is…
- I'm getting a different picture here because…

Analyzing the Author's Craft
- A golden line for me is…
- This word/phrase stands out for me because…
- I like how the author uses to show…

Reflecting and Relating
- So, the big idea is…
- A conclusion I'm drawing is…
- This is relevant to my life because…

Evaluating
- I like/don't like this part because…
- This part could be more effective if…
- The most important message is…

Analyzing Rhetoric
- The author's attitude towards the subject that she writes about is because…
- The author appeals to the readers' interests by…
- The author makes the presentation of ideas seem logical because…

Source: Olson, Carol Booth. *The Reading/Writing Connection: Strategies for Teaching and Learning in the Secondary Classroom.* Boston: Allyn and Bacon, 2003. 8. Reprinted with permission.

Yang Hao, a former writing student, advises:

"Use sentence starters when annotating your reading. They will help you become interested in your reading."

4. Joining a Reading Group

Joining a reading group with students who are taking the same course with you can also lead to improvements in your ability to read critically. Reading groups can help you not only to improve your understanding of the material but can help you to get to know your classmates. You can ask for help to better understand certain concepts you are struggling with or simply check on the pronunciation of certain words. Try to engage in social and academic activities with your group members as opportunities arise. This will be helpful not only to expand your knowledge of the English language but also to enhance your awareness of university life.

Reading in Your Free Time for Pleasure

An important way to improve your ability to read is to select the readings that you are interested in and read them in your free time for enjoyment purposes. You can end up significantly increasing your knowledge of the ways writers use language in specific contexts by becoming hooked* on reading. Reading widely and frequently is important in gaining confidence and competence as readers. It will help you gain the reading proficiency required to analyze and evaluate reading critically.

*hooked

(adjective): enjoying something so much that you are unable to stop doing it

Alice Yang, a former writing student, discusses the effect of pleasure reading:

"Once I started reading what I was interested in, my English vocabulary improved a lot. What's more, even my grammar improved."

Expanding Your Vocabulary

Most of us would agree that vocabulary knowledge is necessary for reading. But vocabulary can be challenging to learn, since word meanings are often arbitrary* and can vary depending on the situational contexts in which they occur. Why do we call a *horse* a *horse* and not a *lion*? How come we can say *unknown, unlucky*, and *unpleasant*, but we can't say *unright*? While learning new words can be challenging, there are proven strategies that can increase your knowledge of vocabulary.

*arbitrary

(adjective): decided or arranged without any reason or plan

The first step to becoming a life-long learner of vocabulary is to start noticing all the new words around you. Research shows that you often need to be exposed to specific words repeatedly before you add them to your personal vocabulary. Knowing a word does not simply mean that you can spell it, define it, and pronounce it. That's just the beginning. In order to truly know a word, you also need to be able to **use** it correctly in every way that that word is used.

Collocations

Collocations play a critical role in English vocabulary. Collocations refer to words and their associated words that combine together in a typical and expected way. Consider, for example, the phrase *on the other hand*. This is an example of a collocation because Americans use these four words in this exact way. They would never write *on the other hands*. Phrasal verbs are also examples of collocations. Phrasal verbs are usually two-word phrases that consist of a verb and a preposition or particle. Adding a preposition or particle after the verb often gives the verb a new meaning.

What's the difference between *run into* and *run away*? Why is it *to pay attention to* and never *to pay attention on*? Learning how words are used together in sentences can dramatically improve not only your reading capability, but also your ability to write more fluently.

You'll come across many collocations in your textbooks that add precise, detailed information. Which of the following two collocations is more likely to be used in an academic context?

- *This is a good book and contains a lot of interesting details*, or
- *This is a fascinating book and contains a wealth of historical detail.*

The second is more likely in an academic context, as it contains more precise information than the first.

How do you learn collocations? The first step is to become aware of collocations. Notice **the words that always go together** when reading. Pay attention to key words and the words that **"go"** with them, and underline collocations. On any given page, you are likely to come across numerous collocations. Practice using the collocations that you are learning from your reading. Quizzes and exercises that provide you with additional practice learning collocations are easily accessible on the web.

Discipline-Specific Vocabulary

As you read your textbooks, you'll discover discipline-specific words that you do not recognize. Most disciplines have their own special words and phrases that have specific meanings within the field. These are technical words that may be new to you like *mitochondria* in biology. You'll need to learn the discipline-specific vocabulary of each discipline you study and attain specific tools to develop and analyze it—learning the grammar and patterns of the vocabulary and its uses. This is because university textbooks often make reference to extensive discipline-specific vocabulary. **Key terms** that are often found in a list called a **glossary** at the back of your textbook will help you learn this vocabulary. By studying the glossary, you can quickly become aware of which words will be important in your class. The main vocabulary words introduced in those texts are often called **key words** and are considered very important to that field of study. In addition to key words, introductory textbooks also present main ideas. These are often easy to identify because they may have boldface headings or be otherwise highlighted. Your instructor will probably expect you to know and be able to use or explain these concepts on tests, reports, or papers. You may find it helpful to create flashcards or take notes related to these concepts and key words.

Many fields of study also have words that you may have learned before, but these words are used in new or particular ways in specific disciplines and may have special definitions within a discipline that differ from the definitions that are commonly known. For example, in Earth sciences the word *filling* refers to increasing atmospheric pressure at the center of a depression; however, you may know the word to mean a *dental filling*. In addition, words such as *retrieval, response,* and even *behavior* when used in psychology have much more technical meanings than their meanings in everyday use.

You'll need to learn how to use both types of words—discipline-specific words and commonly occurring words that have discipline-specific definitions—as you are learning about, discussing, and writing about that field of study.

Academic Words

Researchers have compiled a list of words, called the Academic Word List, which are the basic academic vocabulary required for accessing a majority of texts you will encounter in your classes at university. This list includes 570 word families. A word family is similar to a word, except that it also includes all the derivations of a word. For instance, for the word *single* (adjective), has a related word form, singularity (noun), and the word *comprehend* (verb) also has a noun, **comprehension**. Exercises for *learning* the words on the Academic Word List are readily available online, so go search for them and start learning. You will find the complete list easily on the web.

Jung Hye Young, a former writing student, cautions:

"I thought I knew most the words on the Academic Word List. They were familiar to me and didn't seem very academic. When my instructor asked if I ever used them in my writing, I had to admit that I didn't. I didn't know how to use them and the truth was I didn't know even their meanings very well. I skimmed over them quickly when reading. So I started paying more attention to them when I read and practiced using them. Once I learned the words on the Academic Word List well, my reading improved a lot."

Fan Cheng, a former writing student, advises:

"Reading my textbooks carefully in English helped me participate in class and do well on tests."

Using Dictionaries

As an English language learner, your translation dictionary may have become your best friend. However, that relationship may not be very healthy—or helpful for that matter. Translation dictionaries most commonly give the definitions of words in isolation. The problem with this is that words are not used in isolation. Words function within sentences to make meaning. There are a variety of dictionaries that you can use more effectively, and each one has its own purpose and specialty.

Learner Dictionaries

Not all dictionaries are created for the same audience. Many dictionaries are created for speakers of a particular variety of English, such as the *Oxford English Dictionary*, which mainly emphasizes British English. Some are meant for native English speakers, like the well-known Merriam-Webster dictionary, which can provide readers with complicated definitions of words. Learner dictionaries are created for language learners, which means that they can provide you with a plethora of advantages (if you don't know the word *plethora*, look it up now in your learner dictionary). Here are some of the advantages of using a learner dictionary:

Simple definitions. It's hard to use a dictionary to look up an unknown word when many other words in that definition are also unknown. Learner dictionaries typically use the most common English vocabulary to explain words.

Grammatical information pertaining to the use of words in sentences. Most English dictionaries do not give grammatical information about words or indicate the ways that words are used in sentences. For example, they don't tell whether a noun is countable or not. However, the best learner dictionaries give considerable information about words and the grammatical rules that govern their use. Now you never need to guess whether you can write *advices* in your essay. (You can't, by the way. *Advice* is noncount). Learner dictionaries also give you sample sentences.

Collocations and idioms. Although most dictionaries will give you an example sentence using the word you've looked up, most will not provide you with idioms. Learner dictionaries not only often explain common idioms, but they also provide phrasal verbs (verbs used with prepositions) and other word combinations (collocations) that are commonly used in English.

Reading Comprehension Questions

1. What are the different types of ways that writers organize informational writing?

2. What does critical reading involve? Which is more important analyzing reading, interpreting reading, or evaluating reading? Why?

3. What are three major differences between reading for basic understanding and reading for critical analysis?

4. What does skimming mean? When is it useful to skim?

5. What is the difference between active note taking and passive note taking?

6. List four different ways of annotating. Which way do you prefer and why?

7. Which of the cognitive strategies sentence starters listed in this chapter would you be most likely to use? Why?

8. What are three different ways to increase your vocabulary?

9. What is discipline-specific vocabulary and why is it used?

10. What is the purpose of learner dictionaries and why do many students find them useful?

> Advanced readers, university-level readers, recognize that reading is purposeful. The sooner you learn how to engage with texts in English, the sooner you will start to expand your vocabulary, read critically, and become a better student and writer.

Oral Interaction and Presentations

Karen Lenz, Hansol Lee, and Cathy Vimuttinan

Interacting with your classmates and instructor will help you develop, clarify, and refine* your views on course topics and is particularly helpful when completing writing assignments. You'll find it plays a key role in your development of speaking and writing. This chapter explains why interaction is important, why it can be challenging, when you'll interact in writing classes, what you'll need to learn to interact successfully, and which strategies might help you interact. The last part of the chapter provides tips and resources for improving your general oral language abilities and techniques for asking and answering questions.

*refine

(transitive verb): to improve something by gradually making slight changes to it

Michelle Qi, a former student, warned:

"When I first came to college from China, I didn't want to say something stupid and make a fool of myself. I avoided talk in class. This was big mistake. Unfortunately, learning a language almost guarantee saying something stupid. That really is okay. You just have to know: It's okay. Even great language learners feel stupid at time. Just talk and soon you'll be participate in class confidently and competently."

Bowen Wu, a current student, states:

"Hi everyone, this is Bowen. I am an international student from China. I hope that I can share some experiences learning English with you. There are big differences between different languages. My English was always not understood when my first time came to America as an international student. Later, I realized that it was wrong to follow Chinese thinking habits when speaking English. Because of that, I started to talk with my professors and American classmates more so that I was able to have more chance to practice. By practicing speaking, I have made great progress in English because I have learned to think in English."

The Importance of Oral Language Development

*input

(noun): language content that is understandable to language learners. Understanding spoken or written language input is one of the important mechanisms that result in increasing learners' language skills. Language learners often ignore incomprehensible language input. Most researchers report this does not lead to language development.

*language production

(noun phrase): a process of producing spoken or written language by translating an abstract concept in your mind into a grammatically correct linguistic form, and then articulating the form to deliver the concept

*corrective feedback

(noun phrase): formal or informal feedback you receive from your peers or instructors on your language performance or use, particularly for future improvement

reservoir

(noun): a large amount of something that is available and has not been used

Students need to understand the importance of oral interaction in academic writing courses. Being able to orally produce the language can provide a foundation for your further general language development. Language teachers and researchers have long supported the idea that oral language plays a significant role in helping language learners internalize language. Humans talk before they learn how to write and, given this, they have much more experience speaking than writing. The language that you hear serves as input* or data that you can internalize and use for further language development. It provides you with models that you can emulate and incorporate into speech. In addition, when you communicate orally, you encourage others to provide you with more models for language development. Later these models might become a part of your language development. Your own language production*, that is, your own use of speech, sometimes called output, helps you clarify concepts and come to your own understanding of language. It also helps you slow down to attend to the features of language and pay attention to your language use. Furthermore, oral interaction provides you with opportunities to develop new cultural experiences and discover new language resources and strategies. In addition, your peers and instructors give you corrective feedback* that provides you with opportunities to refine your English and strengthen your command of the language. Sometimes you may have difficulty understanding what others are saying or experience difficulties communicating. However, these moments are indeed invaluable turning points. They lead you to find better ways to communicate. This process allows you to ask for what was said to be clarified, rephrased, or confirmed to achieve a clear understanding of unfamiliar language features. This is one of the most important aspects of language learning. The relationship among listening, speaking, reading, and writing is complex and can mutually support one another. Development of any one of them can contribute to your general reservoir* of second-language knowledge.

Challenges of Interacting

Despite the benefits, participating in class might be challenging for you, especially if you are not used to speaking up in front of your classmates or stating your opinion and defending it. If you are an international student, you might find that the classroom culture in the US is different from that of your home country and you may not have much experience speaking up in class in front of your peers. Your expectations about what constitutes appropriate oral communication can affect your willingness to participate in class. Your instructor, your peers, and you bring years of life experience and cultural knowledge to the classroom. You might find that your expectations regarding instructor relationships and behavior might be very different from those of your instructor or even those of some of your classmates. You may expect your instructor to behave in a more formal way and may be puzzled if he or she uses an informal instructional style, for example, encouraging students to interact informally in groups or to move freely around the room. You may also want your instructor to maintain tightly ordered classroom activity in which students follow a set of rules. You may prefer that your instructor provides you with extensive correction of grammatical forms or pronunciation throughout the lesson rather than at specified points in the lesson or not at all. Your instructor's failure to conform to your expectations may give you the impression that your instructor is inadequately prepared for class. This is not the case. Your instructor is just following US-American norms and conventions*.

convention*

(countable noun): a behavior that is expected and preferred

Like you, your instructors bring to the classroom their own expectations regarding appropriate instructor and student behavior. Most US-American instructors expect students to be self-reliant and comfortable in expressing and defending personal opinions. They will constantly encourage you to take part in class discussions. They will intentionally ask you to answer questions and to share your opinions about assigned readings. They'll encourage you to challenge your classmates politely, communicating your message and attitude—not only through words but also gestures, facial expressions, and tone of voice. Your instructor will give you participation points for your oral participation, with the intent of helping you build the habit of expressing yourself orally, so that you will feel comfortable speaking in your courses.

> If you are a student who has been educated in the United States, you may feel comfortable communicating in class, but still need to improve your ability to convey your ideas academically. You may still be developing academic and discipline-specific words and learning to distinguish the difference between everyday, informal expressions used in basic communication with friends and more academic expressions.

Insider Tip

Different perspectives provide you with opportunities to enhance and develop patience and understanding and see your topic from the perspectives of others. Considering others' views helps you to refine your own.

When You'll Speak in a Writing Class

Your writing class is the place where you can work through confusing portions of your writing and brainstorm possible approaches and ways to support your claims and opinions. Participating orally in class will not only earn you points for participation, but also help you develop essential skills and resources for university-level writing, engaging critically with a topic. During the lesson, your instructor will ask you to communicate orally in a variety of situations:

- Activities Involving Choral Repetition
- Communicative Language Exercises
- Peer Review
- Collaborative Activities
- Discussions
- Oral Presentations

Each of these situations is discussed in the following pages.

Activities Involving Choral Repetition

Although used infrequently, on occasion your instructor will ask you to repeat what she or he just said. Choral repetition is when your instructor models language and your classmates and you repeat it together at the same time, usually with the same rhythm. Although repetition when learning English can be boring, it can also be valuable even for advanced language learners. Many studies on language acquisition show that very high numbers of repetition can be necessary for a word or grammatical feature to become truly owned and a part of your long-term memory. When you listen to words and sentences and repeat them chorally, you can learn the sound patterns of the language. So, when your instructor asks you to repeat an academic word or recite an entire sentence orally, don't be ashamed. You might even want to speak up loudly. Recite words and sentences as many times as you can. You will need to pay attention to the words and sentences and use these words and sentences in actual communication to learn them.

Edwin Ocampo, one former student, advises:

"Your English language and writing courses will provide you with a safe place to discuss your ideas, defend them, and compare them to your classmates' ideas."

How much repetition is necessary to learn a new word or grammatical feature? The answer probably varies widely, depending on the word or grammatical feature, the learner, the context in which the word is learned, the learner's use of the word or grammatical feature in subsequent real-life communication, and the learner's motivation to learn the word or grammatical feature. See below for some general guidelines:

Amount of Times You Need to Repeat Language Orally to Learn It

- If you are an **excellent** language learner who is highly motivated
  – You need at least 5 repetitions

- If you are an **average** language learner who has average motivation
  – You need at least 12 repetitions.

- If you are a **poor** language learner who is poorly motivated
  – You need at least 30 repetitions.

A WORD OF WARNING:

Be careful not to become reliant on using memorized words, phrases, and sentences to communicate. They can prevent you from communicating meaningfully.

Communicative Language Exercises

You will need to do more than repeat language to learn it. You will need to use it communicatively. This is why your instructor will often pair you with other students and ask you to interact in a meaningful, communicative task. One such type of task involves partner work that enables students to hold conversations at the same time. Speaking in pairs may seem odd to you at first, especially if you have never experienced it before. After all, you may not know your partner and feel awkward speaking English with someone you do not know well. Also, your partner might know less English than you do and speak your home language. It might be far easier and more natural for the two of you to converse in that language and not English. However, consider partner work an opportunity for you to get to know others in the class and practice using academic English. Because your partner may lack proficiency in academic English and may not provide the best model of academic English language use, you will find it useful to use your textbook and other class materials as well as sentence frames such as the ones below to support your language development during partner work. The frames consist of sentences with key content words and expressions within the sentence omitted. The following partner activity involves sentence frames and is one that your instructor might

Key Point:

Regardless of the type of language learner you are, you will benefit from repeatedly being exposed to language, paying attention to its features, repeating it in class, and using it when communicating meaningfully.

assign. In the activity, your partner and you compare the claims you have each made in your essays.

Partner A: Ask your partner to make comparisons.

1. How are _____ and _____ alike?

2. What other similarities do _____ and _____ have?

3. What is the most significant similarity between _____ and _____?

4. Is there anything else that makes _____ and _____ similar?

Partner B: Answer your partner's questions, using the sentence frames below.

1. Both _____ and _____ are alike because _____.

2. Like _____, _____ has _____.

3. The most significant similarity between _____ and _____ is _____.

4. _____ and _____ are/have _____.

A WORD OF CAUTION

Sentence frames can result in formulaic or unnatural sounding speech if you do not adapt them to your needs. You should use them as a starting point to practice language until conversing becomes natural and intuitive to you. Incorporating chunks of language and modeling your speech after a pattern is one way to practice new forms of language. However, you should not rely on sentence frames alone to communicate. You will need to use them flexibly.

Peer Review

You will also participate in a number of peer review activities in your class. After you have written your drafts, your instructors will ask you to participate in a peer review in which you offer your classmates constructive feedback on their writing. If you are an international student, you may have never done a peer review in your home country and you may feel embarrassed about showing your writing to other students or discussing your own opinions in English when you can discuss them better in your first language. You may feel that other students may look down on you if you have made grammatical mistakes in your writing. However, you will quickly learn that all students, even those who have lived in the United States all their lives, also make grammatical mistakes. You will also discover that in certain contexts, you might be able to explain certain grammatical rules much more effectively than some of your classmates can. The more you talk to your classmates in a small group setting in English, the more confident you will become in sharing your views with the entire class, and the more your oral English will develop. More importantly, by learning how your classmates think and write about the same writing prompt, you will learn to look at your own writing from a different perspective.

Collaborative Activities

Your instructor will also ask you to collaborate on group projects and assignments. You may be asked to conduct research that supports your paper assignment, make a group poster presentation, or make a group PowerPoint presentation. Each individual is expected to participate equally. Collaborating with classmates provides you practice expressing your thoughts in English (for example, summarizing or paraphrasing the key ideas of an article or chapter you have just read). You can also ask for help to better understand certain concepts you are struggling with or simply check your pronunciation of certain words. Your group members and you can even take turns rehearsing upcoming class presentations.

Minjun Lee, a writing student, warns:

"When I first was required to do group work, I didn't like it and let my classmates do all the work. I wish I had contributed to the group. My instructor lowered my participation score. More importantly, I lost a valuable language learning experience."

Discussions

Instructors will also ask you to participate in discussions. Often the discussions pertain to course readings. You can refer to your notes and drafts of your papers when you participate in these class discussions. When you write down what you want to say, you may feel more confident, or at least less nervous, when you participate in them. You can also use *sentence starters* such as those shown in the following table. As the expression implies, sentence starters start the sentences and prompt you to complete them.

These sentence starters in Table 18.1 can help you manage and participate in discussions.

Table 18.1: Sentence Starters

Language Function	Explanation	Sentence Stems
To compare and contrast	Showing how two things are alike and different	"X and Y are similar because…" "X and Y are different from each other because …"
To explain	Giving examples	"This is an example of …" "This is important because …"
To analyze	Discussing the parts of a larger idea	"The parts of this include …"
To hypothesize	Making a prediction based on what is known	"I can predict that …" "I believe that … because …"
To evaluate	Judging something	"I agree with this/John because …" "I disagree because …" "I recommend that …" "A better solution would be …" "The factors that are most important are…"
To add to others' ideas	Adding additional information or ideas	"I would add that…" "I want to expand on your point about…"
To request clarification	Requesting that others clarify their remarks	"What do you mean by…?" "Can you tell me more about …?"
To elaborate and/or clarify	Elaborating and clarifying what has been said	"I think ___ means that…" "In other words…"
To paraphrase and summarize	Paraphrasing and summarizing what has already been said	"We can say that…" "The main points we have been discussing are…" "To summarize the main points of this discussion, I believe we have said…"

Source: Adapted from Fisher, Douglas, Nancy Frey, and Carol Rothenberg. *Content-Area Conversations: How to Plan Discussion-Based Lessons for Diverse Groups of Students*. Alexandria, VA: Association for Supervision and Curriculum Development, 2010. http://www.ascd.org/publications/books/108035/chapters/Procedures_for_Classroom_Talk.aspx

Insider Tip

The more you participate in in-class discussions about your writing topics, the easier it will be for you to write about them.

Oral Presentations

Most writing courses require students to make one or more oral presentations related to their writing assignments. When you begin to prepare for your presentations, Young-Kyung Min suggests that you ask certain questions, detailed at www.bothell.washington.edu/wacc/for-students/eslhandbook/speaking.

Making Oral PowerPoint Presentations in Writing Courses

When your instructor asks you to present information to the class orally and use PowerPoint slides for visual support, it is important to remember that presenting is *not* the same thing as reading or reciting. When you present, you should explain ideas and talk to your audience. Do not recite something you memorized or read information from note cards or slides.

Your PowerPoint slides can include the following:

- Questions that get your audience thinking about your topic
- Short statements that explain your main points
- Charts, graphs, or photographs that help your audience understand your main points

Armando Dilayan, a former writing student, advises:

"It's not a bad thing if you don't get all your words out perfectly. No one will expect you to. Take a deep breath, get your ideas together and keep trying. If you need to, rely on your notes, simplify what you're trying to say, or ask your classmates or instructor for help."

When Preparing for an Oral PowerPoint Presentation, Follow These Steps:

1. **Review the assignment details.** Read the assignment prompt carefully and determine what it is that you need to present to the class and how much time you will have to present it. You might also think about the materials you are asked to use in conducting research, whether or not you can work with a partner, and whether or not your instructor has given you additional requirements pertaining to what should or should not be included in your PowerPoint slides.

2. **Clarify your purpose.** Look carefully at the part of the assignment prompt that states the main purpose of the presentation. For example, is it your job to define a concept, describe a person or place, explain an idea or process, make an argument, or explain your opinion?

3. **Research your topic and organize your ideas.** If your instructor has asked you to use outside sources to do research, use reliable sources that will help you achieve your purpose. Remember that you have a time limit, so determine which information is the most important to share. Then, organize your ideas and determine which information you should include in your introduction, body, and conclusion.

4. **Brainstorm ways to present your information.** Think about the types of presentations you have seen and enjoyed in the past. What made those presentations engaging, interesting, and memorable? Make a list of what you can do to help your audience understand and remember the information you share.

5. **Create your PowerPoint slides.** Your PowerPoint presentation should have a clear introduction, body, and conclusion. Your slides should be simple and easy to read, with a good mixture of both text and visuals. When choosing visuals, don't just think about finding a visual that relates to your topic; instead, think about finding a visual that helps you explain one of your main points or that helps your audience understand and seriously consider one of your main points. Finally, keep your time limit in mind when creating a PowerPoint presentation. Do not create so many slides that you have to rush through them in order to finish within your time limit.

6. **Practice your presentation.** Practice your presentation in front of a mirror, a friend, or a camera. Set a timer to see if you need to add or delete any details. Make sure you are able to explain your main ideas without having to read or memorize too much information.

Rationale for Making an Oral Presentation in a Writing Course

Writing for an audience and speaking to an audience may seem like different skills, but they both require you to consider who your audience is, why your message is important for your audience, and how you will best convey information to your audience. Both writing and speaking require you to organize your ideas and state information clearly. Therefore, giving an oral PowerPoint presentation is not only a good way to share and learn information, but it also is a good way to practice skills that will help you in your writing.

Oral Presentation Dos and Don'ts

Dos

- **Do** explain your information in a way that is interesting for your audience.
- **Do** plan your presentation and review your purpose.
- **Do** look around the room at your audience.
- **Do** move around and use gestures.
- **Do** breathe, smile, relax, and speak slowly and clearly.
- **Do** create simple PowerPoint slides.
- **Do** use fonts, sizes, and colors that are easy to read.
- **Do** use visuals that are easy to read and help your audience understand your main points.
- **Do** edit your PowerPoint slides for grammar.
- **Do** practice your presentation in front of a friend or record a video for self-evaluation.

Insider Tip

Consider the image you are projecting. Project* yourself with appropriate authority and enthusiasm and do not appear aggressive, argumentative, arrogant, bored, or apprehensive.

*to project yourself

(verb phrase): to try to make other people have a particular idea about you

Don'ts

- **Don't** read or memorize and recite your information.
- **Don't** try to cover too much information in a short amount of time.
- **Don't** look at the screen for long periods of time.
- **Don't** stand still or be stiff.
- **Don't** rush through your presentation or apologize for making mistakes.
- **Don't** put too much text on your PowerPoint slides.
- **Don't** use small fonts or colors that are hard to read.
- **Don't** use visuals that are complicated and hard to read.
- **Don't** use a PowerPoint with lots of grammar mistakes.
- **Don't** resent without practicing first.

*to project your voice

(verb phrase): to speak clearly and loudly

Presentation Evaluation

You may be asked to use a rubric like the one below to evaluate a classmate or yourself. Because it is difficult to think about all of these categories at once, your instructor may ask you to focus on one category at a time, or you may be asked to evaluate a video of a presentation so that you can pause it and take notes.

	Yes, definitely	Yes, mostly	No, not really	No, not at all
Your name:_____ Presenter's name: _____				
Structure				
Presentation had a clear introduction.				
Presentation had clear main points that were appropriate, given the purpose of the presentation.				
Presentation had clear transitions between main points.				
Presentation demonstrated a good choice of supporting details.				
Presentation had a clear conclusion.				
Audience Considerations				
Presenter used appropriate terminology and other language and explained words and expressions that classmates might not understand.				
Presentation was engaging and interesting.				
Delivery				
Presenter made eye contact with members of the class and did not look at the screen or notes too much.				
Presenter spoke with appropriate speed, volume, and articulation.				
Presenter was prepared and had a good understanding of content.				
PowerPoint				
Headings were clear and easy to understand.				
Slides gave important information but did not give too much information or contain confusing visuals.				
List at least two things the presenter did well:				
List at least two things the presenter could do to improve:				

Notes from presentation:

_____

_____

_____

Key Points:

- *If you are asked to make a presentation on a topic in another class, watch English-language YouTube videos about the topic in the specific discipline area of your class. That will help you to understand how speakers in these disciplines deliver their presentations. Pay close attention to the language (vocabulary, grammar, and organization), gestures and other body language and visual aids used.*

- *Locate online resources such as English-language dictionaries and YouTube videos that can help you improve your pronunciation.*

- *Ask trusted classmates with a strong command of English in your classes and/ or discipline to give you feedback on your oral presentations before they are due.*

Insider Tip

If you think that you do not have a good understanding of the topic of your presentation, you should do additional in-depth research about the topic and talk with your instructor, librarians, classmates, or Writing Center peer tutors.

Tips for Developing General Oral Language Proficiency

While you'll want to develop specific oral language skills for communicating in your writing courses, you'll also want to gain greater general oral language proficiency. Below are tips for improving speaking and writing outside of your writing courses.

Campus Events and Workshops

You can utilize campus events and resources to enhance your oral communication skills. If you are an international student, your active participation in these events can help not only improve your speaking abilities but also help you better understand US university life and culture.

Answering Questions and Asking Them

Knowing how to ask and answer questions is useful in academic settings. In this section, you'll learn techniques for answering your instructor's questions and asking questions in class.

Techniques for Answering Your Instructor's Questions

Nearly all your instructors will call on you to answer probing questions in front of your classmates. This can be unnerving. However, just remember that your instructor will not respond to your answers in a critical way and no one in the class expects you to respond perfectly. All your classmates are language learners. Everyone, including classmates who were born in the United States, is still in the process of acquiring academic English.

Also remember that your instructor asks questions for good reasons, including:

Insider Tip

Listening to others can greatly improve your auditory skills. You might try listening to YouTube talks related to your paper and reading assignments and audio recordings of your readings when opportunities arise.

- Developing your interest in the lesson and motivating you to become actively involved in it
- Evaluating your preparation and checking on your completion of assignments
- Nurturing critical thinking skills
- Helping you develop an inquiring attitude
- Reviewing and summarizing previous lessons
- Fostering insights by revealing new relationships between ideas
- Assessing your achievement of instructional goals and objectives
- Stimulating you to pursue knowledge on your own
- Modeling effective questioning techniques

Strategies for Answering Challenging Questions

You can always admit that you do not know the right answer. You can also ask your instructor to restate a question if it's not clear to you, or if you need more time to gather your thoughts or repeat the question back to the instructor to buy more time. You can also anticipate the questions your instructor might ask and prepare in advance by previewing class materials before class whenever possible. See a list of typical questions your instructor might ask you on the next page. In addition, you can take notes and practice reading your notes out loud.

Below are typical questions that your instructor might ask you.

1. **To assess learning**

   What is the most important idea that was generated in today's discussion?

   Can you explain this concept in your own words?

   Can you summarize the author's main point?

2. **To ask you to clarify a vague comment**

   Could you elaborate on that point?

   Can you explain what you mean?

3. **To prompt you to explore attitudes, values, or feelings (when appropriate)**

   What are the values or beliefs that inform this argument?

   What is your initial reaction to this argument?

4. **To prompt you to see a concept from another perspective**

   How do you think that others with whom you may disagree view this issue?

   How does that concept apply to this new problem?

5. **To ask you to refine a statement or idea**

   When does that claim or principle apply? Always? Only under certain conditions?

   Would you say, then, that you disagree with the author?

6. **To prompt you to support your assertions and interpretations**

   How do you know that?

   Which part of the text leads you to that conclusion?

7. **To direct you to respond to one another**

   What do you think about the idea just presented by your classmate?

   Do you agree or do you see the issue differently? Explain.

   Can you think of another way to explain the phenomenon that the author describes?

8. **To prompt you to investigate a thought process**

   What assumptions informed the development of the author's view?

   What assumptions do researchers share pertaining to the claim or view?

9. **To ask you to predict possible outcomes**

   What might happen if this phenomenon did not exist and was outlawed?

   What would be the result if a different set of evidence were used to support this claim?

   Would you get a different perspective?

10. **To prompt you to connect and organize your information**

    How does this article shed light on the concept we studied last week?

    Can you develop a graph or table that organizes this information in a helpful way?

11. **To ask you to apply a principle or consider the consequences of a claim**

    How does this principle or claim apply to the following situation?

    Who can suggest how we might use this principle or claim to solve a societal problem?

    Under what conditions is this principle or claim invalid?

12. **To ask you to illustrate a concept with an example**

    Can you think of an example of this phenomenon, drawn from your experience or reading?

    Can you point us to a specific part of the text that led you to that conclusion?

    Can you identify a person that exemplifies that idea?

Wang Xiu Ying, a former student, gives you this advice:

"Don't remain silent in class. It won't help you. At first I was so shy, I sat in back of class and hope the instructor would not call on me. I realized other students were talking and they did not speak as well as me, so I moved to the front of the class. I guess what my instructor would ask the class and I wrote possible answers to possible questions in my dorm. Then, I read answers aloud in class. By end of the course, I did not have prepare to answer my instructor questions. Just do the assign readings and take notes on them in English. That's good enough."

Techniques for Asking Questions

You also need to be able to ask questions of your classmates during peer reviews and other types of collaborative group work. **Question prompts** require you to use specific question types to, for example, clarify a term, justify and defend your thinking, compare and contrast visual representations, interpret evidence, explain solutions to problems, and argue claims. Question prompts can help you learn the type of probing questions that you should be asking your instructor and classmates. You can use them until you feel comfortable asking questions in academic settings on your own. Here are some examples:

Question Prompts

- What explanation do you have for _____?
- How is _____ connected to _____?
- What are the authors implying when they state _____?
- What is the primary evidence _____ uses to support the claim that _____?
- What can you infer from _____?
- What ideas validate the claim that_____?
- How would you explain _____?
- What can you point out about _____?
- What is the problem with/weaknesses of _____'s thinking/argument/claim?
- Why do you think _____?

You can complete the question prompts with appropriate content words related to your assignments and make it a goal to use at least one during a class.

A WORD OF CAUTION

Question prompts such as those above can result in **formulaic* speech** and overly tidy conversations.

You should not rely on question prompts to communicate. You will need to use the ones that best meet your communicative needs and change them, using them flexibly.

*formulaic speech

(noun phrase) predictable, often boring language that is used in the same way

Reading Comprehension Questions

1. What is a challenge that might prevent you from participating in class and what can you do to overcome this challenge?

2. Do your instructors expect you to defend your opinions in class? Why?

3. In what specific situations will your instructors expect you to interact orally in writing classes?

4. How much repetition do you need to learn a new word or grammatical feature? About how many times do you have to repeat a new expression out loud to remember it?

5. What is peer review and how can it help you improve your English speaking ability?

6. Which of the Sentence Starters on page 278 do you find the most useful in participating in discussions? Why?

7. Having read the section on preparing PowerPoint presentations, what advice would you give to a friend who is giving a PowerPoint presentation in his class tomorrow?

8. What are six characteristics of an effective PowerPoint presentation?

9. What are five questions that one of your instructors might ask you in class?

10. Which five of the Question Prompts on page 286 do you find most useful? Why?

❝ Being able to orally produce English can provide a foundation for your further general language development. Language teachers have long supported the idea that oral language plays a significant role in helping language learners internalize language. ❞

Index

A

absolute phrase 228
abstract 22, 76, 128–129, 168, 252
  science reports 128–129
academic language 8–10, 13–14, 83
academic word List 267
academic words 5, 18, 80, 103, 267
acronyms 242
action verbs 74, 103, 106. *See also* strong verbs
adjective
  possessive 204, 211, 214
adjective clause 230
adjectives 104
  general and specific 104
adjectives out of order 228
adjectives + prepositions chart 224
adverb 211, 231
adverbial clause 231–233
affective constraints 12
agreement 215-216, 247
allusion 117
analysis 41, 46–47
analysis (in reading) 256–258
anecdote 38–39
annotating your reading 261–262
answering instructor questions
  284–287
antagonist 121
antonym 167
appeals 116–117
appendices 128
appositive clause 230
arguments 51, 60
  importance 14
  tips and techniques, importance 32–33, 60
article 168
  definite 211
  indefinite 211
asking questions 286
  techniques for asking questions 286
  typical instructor questions 285
audience considerations 55–59
audience of summary writing 29
author biographies 120
authorial intention 118, 122
authority (authoritative) 31, 51
authority (ethos) 116–117
autobiographies 120
auxiliary verb 211, 214

B

backsliding 206
biographical background 119

block format 85
brainstorming 34, 187, 256
British English 246–248
  differences between British and US-American English in vocabulary and spelling 247
  in grammar 247
  summary table of differences 247
business letter 83, 85–86
business letter in block format 85. *See also* block format

C

capitalization 240–242
causal analysis 20
cause verbs 170
challenges of Interacting 272–273
characterization 101, 121
characters 101–102, 106, 117, 121
charting/graphing 34
choral repetition 274
chronological sequence 121
circumlocution 156
citation
  analyzing a citation 155
claims 31, 34, 46
classification 19, 30
clause
  appositive clause 229–230
  comparative clause 230
  nominal relative 229
  non-restrictive relative clause 231, 233
  relative 232
  relative clause 212, 229–231, 233
clause connectors 166, 169, 171–172
climax 102, 121
clustering 34
cognitive
  types of and sentence starters 263
cognitive constraints 6
cognitive strategies
  explanation of 263
cohesion 45, 165–169, 171, 182
cohesion and narratives 103
cohesion in narratives 103, 109
cohesive devices 165–167, 169, 177
collocation 193, 265–266, 268
colon 239
comma 236–237
commentary 128, 132–133, 143–144
commentary following quotes 144
communicative constraints 10
comparison and contrast 278
complex sentence 204, 228–229, 232– 233
compound antecedent 183
compound sentence 204, 233

comprehension 259, 267
conclusions 49–50
    science reports 128–129
conclusion to narrative 102–103
conditional sentence 212, 214
conditional verb 214
conflict 117, 121–122
conjunction 171–176, 211, 229, 231, 233
conjunctive adverb 172–175
connotation 177
content-specific 103
context 1– 4, 9, 11, 16
    historical and cultural 120
conversational style 108
conversations about text 178
coordinating conjunction 171–174
correction symbols 194–195
corrective feedback 272
correlative conjunction 176, 183
countable noun 211
count and noncount with determiners chart 222
count noun. *See also* countable noun
cover letter 86–87
critical reading 256–259
    analysis 258
    description 256
    difference between basic understanding of content and
        close reading 258
    evaluation 257
    explanation 256
    explanation of 256–257
    interpretation 257
    ways to improve critical reading ability 259–260

D

data commentary and reports
    discussion 127
    equipment and apparatus 128
    header 128
    methods 128
    objective 128
    references 128
    results 128
    titles 129
definite article 211
definitions
    extended 18
    formal 18
demonstrative adjective 168, 211
denouement 102
dependent clause 212, 228–230, 232–233
description 20, 253
determiner 211, 214, 222
dialogue 104, 109
diction 60
dictionaries 243, 267–268

digress (digression) 190
discipline-specific vocabulary 266–267
discussions 277–278
draft 32–33, 35–36, 41

E

editing 192–193
editing log 198
elegies 120
emailing instructors 93–97
email messages
    structure, audience, language, tone 97–98
emotions (pathos) 116–117
entries 65, 73
ethos 2, 116–117
exclamation mark 238

F

falling action 102
feedback 187, 193, 197
figurative language 103, 116, 123
fixed expressions 35, 146, 169
flashback 122
flash-forward 122
formal language 60, 83–84
format, MLA 105, 140, 151, 158–159, 162
formatting checklist 194
fragment 212, 232
future perfect progressive 212
future tense 212, 214

G

genre 29, 33, 40, 50–51
genre and summary 25
gerund 211, 215, 218
gerund and infinitive reference charts 218–221
Global English 245
glossary 266
grammar
    conscious knowledge of grammar features 206
    conscious knowledge of grammatical features 207, 209
    grammar terms 206, 209
grammar tips
    problem words and expressions list 226–227
grammatical 204–208
graphic organizer 252–255
greetings 84

H

hero 121
heroine 121
hook 38–40, 103, 119
hyperbole 103

I

identity 2, 4
idiom 84, 108–109, 195, 268
illustration 20
imagery 103, 119
images 116
indefinite article 211
indentation 85
indents 158–159
independent clause 212, 215, 228, 232
inference 118
infinitive 211, 215, 218
informal language 48, 84, 95, 108
informational writing 3, 17, 117, 252
intensifier 176
intransitive verb 211
introductions
    language of introductions 129–130
irony
    verbal irony, dramatic irony, situational irony 124
irregular verbs list 217

J

journal writing - mini reflections 64–65

L

learner dictionaries 268
learning curve 206
listing 34, 45
literary text 117–120, 122–123
literature 117–118
logos (reason) 117

M

margins 158–159
mention 147
metacognitive 63
metalinguistic abilities 63–64
metaphor 123, 169
misconceptions about grammar. *See also* myths about
    grammar
misconceptions about grammar features 205–206
MLA format 105, 140, 151, 158–159, 162
modal 207, 211, 214
moral 118, 120–121
myths about grammar 205–206

N

narrative 101–103
narrative essay 101, 109
narrator 123
noncount noun. *See* uncountable noun
note taking 261
noun
    collective 216
        common 213
        count 211
        count and noncount 222–223
        noun clause 229
        proper 211, 213

O

oral presentations 279–281

P

page numbers
    format issues 141, 151–152
paragraph 41, 43–46
paragraph order 45
    chronological, cause and effect, clarification, compare/
        contrast 45
parallelism 196
parallel structure 103, 169
paraphrase
    paraphrasing the words in your source 151
    techniques for paraphrasing 156
paraphrasing
    steps for paraphrasing 156
participle 214, 228
    past participles 211, 234
    present participle 211
passive voice 103, 134, 214
past perfect 212, 215
past perfect progressive 212
past tense 103, 131, 206, 214–215
pathos 3, 116–117
peer review 276–277
peer review of summary 28
period 236
persona 2
personification 103
phrase 205, 211–212, 215–216, 228, 230
pleasure reading 264
plot 101–102, 104
portfolio 80
portfolio cover letter 72–73, 75
possessive adjective 211
PowerPoint presentations 279–280
pragmatic 8, 205
predicate 150, 228
preliminary draft 35, 187
preposition 211, 223
    prepositions of comparison 224
    prepositions of manner 224
    prepositions of place 223
    prepositions of position 223
    prepositions of possession 224
    prepositions of reason of reason of reason 224
    prepositions of time 223
prepositional phrases
    correct and incorrect uses in introducing texts 150

present perfect 212, 214
present perfect progressive 212
present progressive 212
present tense 206, 214–215
prewriting 33–34, 37
process analysis 20
progressive
　　future progressive 212
　　past progressive 106, 212
　　present progressive 212
pronoun reference 166, 182, 193
pronouns 103, 166–168, 182–183
proper adjectives 241
proper nouns 241
protagonist 116–117, 121
punctuating quotations with page numbers 152
punctuation 235–239

Q

quantifier 214
question mark 151, 238
Quia quizzes 197
quotation 31, 38–40
quotations
　　adding or deleting information when quoting 142
　　adding or deleting information when quoting; ellipsis 152
　　direct/indirect quotation 157
　　ellipsis 152
　　integrating quotations into your writing 141
　　quotations within quotations 153
　　steps for integrating quotations into text 143

R

reading comprehension 259
reading strategies
　　before reading, during reading , after reading 259–260
reason 116–117
reflections linguistic and rhetorical considerations 64
reflective writing 72–73, 75–76
　　purpose 63
　　tone 80
relative clause 229–230
repetition 167
reporting verbs - science reports 144–145, 163
resolution 102. *See also* denouement
resume 88–90
revising 187–190, 192
revision 192–193
rhetor 2
rhetoric 2, 13, 48, 115–116
rhetorical analysis 115–120, 123–124
rhetorical analysis structure
　　hook, introduction, body paragraphs, conclusion 119
rhetorical situation 2, 13, 116
rising action 102

S

sample summary 27
sarcasm 124
semicolon 238
sensory words 107
sentence frame 19, 116–117, 121, 124
Sentence frames used in introducing titles and authors' names 149
setting 101, 106, 116–117, 122
showing, not telling 104
signal phrase 25, 28, 141, 143
signals of time – narratives 105
simple future 212. *See also* future
simple past 212. *See also* past tense
simple present 212. *See also* present tense
slang 31, 84, 95, 103, 108
sonnet 120
source
　　analysis of source 139
　　criteria for choosing source 140
　　evaluation of source 139
　　explanation of source 139
　　synthesis of source 139
spelling 243
　　basic spelling rules 243
stance 13, 60
strategies for developing oral language proficiency 283
strong verbs 73–74, 1-3, 106. *See also* action verbs
style 56, 58
subject 212, 215–216, 228–232
subject-verb agreement 5, 193
subordinating conjunction 171–175
subordinators list 229
summaries
　　checklist 28
　　do's and do nots 22
symbolism 103
synonyms 5, 61, 103, 156, 166–167

T

TAG (title, author, genre) 40, 149
technical words 5, 19, 266
template 7, 13, 50
tense 97, 103, 106, 119, 131, 193, 195
text 3–4
　　structures 252–255
texts
　　definition of 251–252
　　types of 251–252
theme 76, 116, 118, 122, 252
thesis statement 12, 14, 102, 106, 119
think aloud 178
time order signals - narratives 105
titles 242
　　format issues 141
tone 48, 51, 58, 73, 80, 97, 115, 123, 124

tone of summary writing 29
transition 165–166, 169–180
transitive verb 211

U

uncountable noun 213
US-American English 246
    differences between US-American English and British
      English in vocabulary and spelling 246
    differences in grammar 247
    summary table of differences 247

V

vague words 61–62
validity 31
verb
    auxiliary 211, 214
    future perfect progressive 212
    future progressive 212
    gerund 211, 215, 218
    infinitive 211, 215
    Infinitive 218
    intransitive 211
    irregular 214, 217
    irregular verb list 217
    modal 211
    past perfect 212, 215
    past perfect progressive 212
    past tense 103, 206, 214–215
    present 214–215
    present perfect 212
    present perfect progressive 212

present tense 103, 106
progressive 214
simple future 212
simple past 212
simple present 18, 212
transitive 211
verbs + prepositions chart 225
vivid adjectives 104
vivid nouns 104
vocabulary
    word meanings 261, 267
vocabulary of reflections 73
voice 32, 46

W

word choice 60–61, 64
word form 157, 168, 196, 267
words
    academic words 5, 18, 29, 51, 80, 97, 103, 267
    content-specific 103
working draft 35–36
    Draft 1 35
    Draft 2 36
    Draft 3 36
    Draft 4 36
    Final Draft 36
works cited page 120, 162
writing process 32–37
wrong word 196

Z

zero draft 35, 187, 197. *See also* preliminary draft